THE MOST BEAUTIFUL GIRL IN THE WORLD

THE MOST BEAUTIFUL GIRL IN THE WORLD

BEAUTY PAGEANTS AND NATIONAL IDENTITY

SARAH BANET-WEISER

UNIVERSITY OF CALIFORNIA PRESS
BERKELEY LOS ANGELES LONDON

University of California Press
Berkeley and Los Angeles, California

University of California Press, Ltd.
London, England

© 1999 Sarah Banet-Weiser

Library of Congress Cataloging-in-Publication Data

Banet-Weiser, Sarah
    The most beautiful girl in the world : beauty pageants and
national identity / Sarah Banet-Weiser.
        p. cm.
    Includes bibliographical references.
    ISBN 0-520-21789-6 (alk. paper).—ISBN 0-520-21791-8 (pbk. :
alk. paper)
    1. Miss America Pageant, Atlantic City, N.J.   2. Beauty contests—
United States.   3. National characteristics.   4. Racism in popular
culture.   5. Miss Universe Pageant.   I. Title.
HQ1220.U5B36   1999
791.6'2—dc21   99-19922
                                                                    CIP

Manufactured in the United States of America

08 07 06 05 04 03 02 01 00 99   10 9 8 7 6 5 4 3 2 1

The paper used in this publication meets the minimum requirements of
ANSI/NISO Z39.48-1992 (R 1997) (Permanence of Paper). ∞

for
Bill, Sam, and Luke

CONTENTS

List of Illustrations   *ix*

Acknowledgments   *xi*

Introduction   1

1. "A Certain Class of Girl": Respectability
   and the Structure of the Miss America
   Pageant   31

2. Anatomy of a Beauty Pageant: The
   Swimsuit Competition   58

3. "If You Were a Color, What Color Would
   You Be?": The Interview and Talent
   Competitions in the Miss America Pageant   87

4. Bodies of Difference: Race, Nation, and
   the Troubled Reign of Vanessa Williams   123

5. The Representational Politics of Whiteness
   and the National Body: Bess Myerson, Miss
   America 1945, and Heather Whitestone,
   Miss America 1995   153

6. International Spectacles, National Borders:
   Miss Universe and the "Family of Nations"   181

   Conclusion   205

Notes   *211*

Bibliography   *241*

Index   *265*

ILLUSTRATIONS

Following page 122

1. The contestants make their entrance on stage at the Miss America pageant in September 1997
2. Miss Hawaii 1997, Erika Kauffman, poses in the swimsuit competition
3. Miss America 1996, Shawntel Smith, addresses the New Jersey State Senate on her "issue platform," a school-to-work program
4. Miss North Carolina 1997, Michelle Warren, performs at the preliminary talent competition
5. Miss Florida 1997, Christy Neuman, performs her rhythmic dance, "Robin Hood: Prince of Thieves"
6. Miss South Carolina 1994, Kimberly Aiken, in the evening wear competition
7. Vanessa Williams after winning the Miss America pageant in September 1983
8. Bess Myerson in the traditional pose after winning the Miss America title in 1945
9. Miss America 1995, Heather Whitestone, signs "I love you" after winning the title
10. Former Miss America Tara Dawn Holland crowns Katherine Shinde Miss America 1998

ACKNOWLEDGMENTS

This book emerged from my dissertation, and many people and institutions contributed to it in various ways. It is with real pleasure that I take this chance to name and thank them.

Colleagues and friends at the University of California, San Diego and the University of Southern California provided invaluable support and guidance. My deepest thanks go to Val Hartouni, who is an important influence, a crucial advisor, and a committed friend. Her confidence in me and her sustained, thoughtful attention to my writing made this project possible. Marita Sturken gave needed, enduring support to this work, and offered sustaining encouragement in both my professional and personal life. George Lipsitz is a remarkable, seemingly limitless resource, and his vast knowledge helped me to situate this project in a broader context. I am grateful to many other colleagues for their support, including Vince Rafael, Michael Schudson, Stephanie McCurry, Liisa Malkki, Karen

Bowdre, Susan Davis, Robert Horwitz, Herb Schiller, and Mike Cole, who suggested beauty pageants in the first place. I owe thanks to Robyn Wiegman for her helpful advice on the entire manuscript, but especially chapter 5. Deciding on a title for this book was quite difficult; I am especially grateful to my colleague Bill Dutton for his suggestion.

I was both fortunate and highly privileged to have been given time away from my heavy teaching schedule to work on this project. A residential fellowship at the University of California Humanities Research Institute provided time to think and write as well as a stimulating intellectual environment. While I was at the institute, George Sanchez read large sections of the manuscript and pushed me to think about race and the nation in complicated ways. Jay Mechling read the entire manuscript and made astute comments and suggestions. Deborah Massey, Katherine Kinney, Barbara Curiel, Chris Newfield, Dan Rosenberg, and Steve Mailloux all provided important conversations and support. My research group, "Media and the Nation," offered a significant context in which to try out ideas. I am grateful to all the members of my group, but especially to Vanessa Schwartz and Susan Larsen for their suggestions, friendship, and sheer presence, and to the late Roland Marchand, who read my manuscript and was a constant source of historical reference, an indefatigable colleague, and a valued friend.

This book was made possible by the help of many good friends. To them, I offer my deepest thanks: Doug Thomas, Judith Gregory, Rivki Ribak, Joy Hayes, Lora Taub, Sara Waterman, Tony Frietas, Kathleen Mansour, Tina Lenzen, and Chris Littleton. Ann Chisholm read sections of the manuscript, and, through her own fascinating work on the subject of bodies, has inspired me to think about bodies in new and interesting ways. Allison Schapker read the entire manuscript and offered helpful criticisms and comments. Her willingness to see the lighter side of academia is an invaluable gift.

I am deeply grateful to my family, all of whom were patient, loving, and committed throughout this process. My mother, Anne Banet, was a consistent supporter and a true inspiration. My father, Tony Banet, instilled within me a love for the written word and nurtured my intellectual curiosity. My siblings, Suzannah, Genney, Angela, Matt, and Joey, provided encouragement, advice, and love.

I also thank the many beauty pageant contestants, producers, and directors whose conviction and remarkable self-awareness reminded me that women's stories must be taken seriously. Naomi Schneider at the University of California Press was encouraging and patient and saw this project through since the beginning with skill and enthusiasm. Sue Heinemann and Carolyn Hill guided this project through the final stages; their helpful comments and sharp editing have surely made this a clearer book.

My sons, Samuel and Lucas, provided me with joy, love, and much needed perspective; they kept me from taking myself too seriously and reminded me of what matters most. Finally, I thank Bill Weiser for all our years of wonderful conversation, his generosity and integrity, and his kindness and love. This book is dedicated to them.

INTRODUCTION

In the 1990s it is tempting to claim that the heyday of the beauty pageant is over. Fran Lebowitz has argued that the Miss America pageant "is so old-fashioned it's actually quaint, like hoop-rolling, something from the turn of the century."[1] Although the television audience still numbers in the hundreds of millions, many people think that the beauty pageant is passé, archaic, or simply overdone. Yet in November 1996, at the Miss World pageant, held in Bangalore, India, there were highly publicized protests on both feminist and nationalist grounds, leading Peter Jennings to declare that pageants "had a nation in an uproar."[2] Throughout the 1990s, pageants held in places as diverse as Italy and war-torn Sarajevo explicitly used the stage and the contestants' bodies as forums for public debate on who constitutes a "proper" representative of national identity.[3] And in the United States a bitter and emotional debate over the fate of "America's children" was forged around the rape and murder of six-year-old Jon-

Benet Ramsey, a debate that focused on whether her active participation in children's beauty pageants was a crucial factor in her horrific death.

Clearly, any claim that pageants are over and done with seems a bit premature. Beauty pageants in the United States, especially the Miss America pageant, offer a glimpse at the constantly changing and always complicated stories about the nation itself: Who counts as part of the nation? What does it mean to be a specifically feminine representative of a nation? How are social concerns—such as racism, multiculturalism, and "family values"—mediated in and through women's bodies on a public stage? And what are the social and cultural conditions through which particular kinds of representation can occur?

The 1990s, like every other decade in U.S. history, have been formative in terms of both national and individual identities. Late-twentieth-century commodity culture is a context in which questions and concerns about "identity" emerge front and center, with a relentless momentum. We need only to look at such contentious political debates of the 1990s as those on the future of affirmative action, sexual harassment in the military, and the Welfare Reform Act to understand that controversial questions about identity and "difference" become more volatile on the national stage. In contemporary popular culture, unruly celebrities and riotous popular events force our attention and our fascination (if by nothing other than their sheer ubiquitous presence) over debates concerning "appropriate" boundaries of contemporary racial, gendered, and sexual identities. And even as specific configurations of such mass-mediated debates concerning identity shift over time, public contests over the political and cultural stakes of identity are ongoing and continually manifested in and through the mass media.[4]

The beauty pageant is one site in which the meanings ascribed to individual and cultural identities are continually negotiated and often vehemently contested. The very title of the Miss America pageant insists on this kind of negotiation: there is the illusion of self-evidence in the pageants' claim on national feminine identity, because "Miss America" encompasses both gendered and nationalist representation. But the nationalism that is simultaneously invented and reflected within the beauty pageant incorporates more than the winner's grandiose title. The beauty pageant in fact represents a complicated arrangement of claims and embodies a variety of nationalist expressions: it is a civic ritual, a place where a particular public can "tell stories to themselves about themselves,"[5] and it is a mass-mediated spectacle, firmly embedded within commodity culture, in a historical moment where almost all forms of social participation and social meaning are determined by a continuous interplay between representation and consumption. It is also a highly visible performance of gender, where the disciplinary practices that construct women as feminine are palpable, on display, and positioned as unproblematically desirable. And, it is a profoundly political arena, in the sense that the presentation and reinvention of femininity that takes place on the beauty pageant stage produces political subjects.

This book is about, among other things, the Miss America pageant. As Frank Deford once said, the Miss America pageant is "maligned by one segment of America, adored by another, [and] misunderstood by about all of it."[6] This book attends to the ways in which the pageant has been both maligned and misunderstood, and attempts to account for the various reasons it continues to be adored. It explores the ways feminist ideologies remain convinced that the pageant does irreparable damage to women, as well as examines conservative ideologies and their relentless conviction that beauty pageants are a productive means through which young women learn self-esteem and confidence. As a way to pry open both these seemingly closed and convinced positions, this book offers testimony from beauty pageant contestants and explores the answers they give about pageants, gender, race, and the nation. In so doing, it develops a different story about beauty pageants and argues that, above all else, one thing is certain: the Miss America pageant does not mean one thing to one audience. It is not merely about pageantry, or kitschy culture, or the objectification of women, or overt racism, or reactionary nationalism. It is about all these things and more.

BEAUTY PAGEANTS AS POPULAR CULTURE

This book argues that the beauty pageant defies a singular definition. Scholars, however, often simplify or even overlook its complicated production and articulation. The liability of conducting research on beauty pageants has been called to my attention in many different forms; academic reactions to my work fall into two or three equally troubled camps. One of these reactions, perhaps the most damaging one, categorizes my work as "fun," as something that does not contribute to a body of scholarly work on gender representation but instead merely reflects the common notion that popular cultural forms like pageants and other entertainment—and people's responses to them—are uniform, simple, and uncontradictory. The dearth of scholarship on beauty pageants reflects this notion; these events are often and easily dismissed as frivolous, meaningless, or carnivalesque and therefore unworthy of serious and sustained intellectual scrutiny—or, at the other end of the spectrum, pageants and other forms of mass commodified culture are seen as simply reiterating and reproducing dominant ideology. In general, beauty pageants are grouped with popular cultural forms that are regarded as either too "low" to merit serious investigation or so obvious and opaque that vigorous interrogation would be both uninteresting and unnecessary.[7]

In categorizing work on popular culture and gender as "fun" and thus unscholarly and unprovoked by intellectual curiosity, many people assume that I became interested and involved in this project because I had once been a participant in a beauty pageant (sour grapes, perhaps?). Clearly, my work (as most other scholarly work) is at least in part autobiographical, insofar as this book explores the cultural production of femininity and I am a gendered female in contemporary U.S. commodity culture. Yet this is not what the assumption presumes: rather, it assumes that because of my gender, and because of my focus on what is usually regarded as an especially opaque form of popular culture, the only intellectual curiosity that could possibly be generated would be the result of my own personal investment as a participant in a beauty pageant. This is a dangerous dismissal, because it immediately and apparently unselfconsciously defines particular cultural sites as worthy of intellectual attention and others—like the pageant—as, well, junk. In the introduction to her book, *The Queen of America Goes to Washington City,* Lauren Berlant recounts a similar tale about the cultural sites she finds interesting (which include the popular press, television sitcoms, and The Contract with America). A colleague explained that he "hated her archive"—a comment that Berlant saw as revealing "the professional juncture at which [she] and others in cultural studies stand at the present moment: because humanists traditionally get value by being intimate with the classics (literary and theoretical), those who think through popular materials and waste thought on objects that were not made for it threaten to degrade the value of intellectual life in general and the value of the humanities in particular."[8] The beauty pageant is usually regarded as an example of such "popular material," in which "what you see is what you get."

What we *do* see in the Miss America pageant, however, is often complex and contradictory. Sorting out what exactly the beauty pageant means as a national phenomenon requires an investigation that recognizes the distinct yet interrelated elements that comprise not only the actual event itself, but also the vast and varied infrastructure that supports, sustains, and simultaneously reinvents it. Popular cultural forms such as the beauty pageant have been both celebrated and vilified as sites for scholarly inquiry in the last decade; though many have challenged an understanding of U.S. popular culture as merely a vehicle for the cultural industry, the legacy of the Frankfurt School has nonetheless proved to be remarkably resilient.[9]

The classic Frankfurt School position is that popular culture is a monolithic, and thus simplistic, kind of national formation. Of those studies that have successfully challenged this position, the more interesting have also situated popular culture within the context of commodity culture— indeed, *as* a commodity—but have gone beyond this to examine the narratives that produce the cultural form as well as the individuals who are involved in its production. In other words, many recent studies of popular culture have rejected an analysis of popular culture as merely an uncomplicated echo of dominant ideology and insisted on reading popular culture as "competing for dominance in a multiplicity of discourses."[10] Recent theorists of popular culture have pointed out the importance of examining various forms of popular culture as complicated and often illuminatory statements about social institutions and formations.[11]

Among other things, what these and other scholars of popular culture have insisted upon is that popular culture is a complicated terrain, not always easily assimilable to dominant ideology and practice. Rather, popular culture exists as a space that can be simultaneously conventional and unpredictable, liberatory and reactionary, personal yet anonymous, and grounded in materiality while also being a realm where fantasy is played out. By reappraising and reconsidering those subjects or sites within popular culture that have been historically characterized as "just entertainment" or "low culture," we can better situate civic rituals such as beauty pageants within a set of political, cultural, and economic practices that provide both the logic and the legitimation for their existence. Because of their emphasis on public spectacle and display, their gestures toward monarchy and medieval pageantry, and their relentless articulations of dominant norms of femininity, beauty pageants are clearly situated as a particular kind of cultural practice and, as such, call for a deeper intellectual attention.

Indeed, the title of the most famous of all beauty pageants, Miss America, is often the most overlooked artifact of the entire spectacle. This title has always insisted that we not separate the question of America from the notion of womanhood; it quite clearly calls up a relationship between discourses of nation and discourses of femininity, ultimately formulating the equation, "woman = nation." Because there is no official state nationalist program in the United States, in order to chart the shifting meanings and emphases of specifically "American" nationalism, it makes sense to look to civic rituals, secular ceremonies, festivals, and beauty pageants.[12] Many studies address the various ways in which national identity for Americans is configured in specifically masculine terms: scholarly work on pinups (which focus on the men to whom these photographs were sent rather than the women who posed for them), studies of wartime constructions of masculinity, and academic investigations of a national masculinity articulated through the mass media have all theorized national identity as fundamentally masculine. Indeed, Benedict Anderson's classic formulation of imagined communities has functioned as an important opening for exploring male national identity.[13] The question of where women are located on a national scene is vital yet relatively unaddressed. The Miss America pageant clearly states its nationalist claim, but because scholarship on the pageant has focused on its egregious treatment of women *as* women, this claim has been all but completely overlooked.

Beauty pageants construct a specific imagined community, even while a particular vision of community occasions and informs their construction. Pageants create a national field of shared symbols and practices that define both ethnicity and femininity in terms of national identity. Following Anderson, I see nationalism as a specifically cultural artifact; extending his argument, I consider nationalism to be a discourse that mediates constructions of femininity and ethnicity in order to produce a particularly gendered notion of citizenship. In order to manage and control different styles and practices of citizenship, beauty pageants thus create imagined communities where nationalist discourse is produced as cultural tradition. Pageants confront national tensions about gender and race and, through performances of "diversity" and femininity, "resolve" these tensions. In this way, they are similar to other cultural traditions and rituals in contemporary U.S. nationalism: they do not necessarily attempt to erase existing inequalities (whether those of class, race, ethnicity, or gender) as much as they perform the function of confronting those inequalities (albeit on very particular terms), incorporating them into a common language and practice, and ultimately providing some sort of idealistic resolution.

Of course, in a diversely constructed society like the United States, the practice of "managing" citizenship always carries with it the potential for disruption or disjuncture. Historically, one of the tasks of nationalist rituals and discourses is to demonstrate the ability to contain disruption, to subvert potential crises, and to incorporate disjunctures onto smoother, less conflicted ideological landscapes.[14] Thus if contemporary forms and practices of femininity present a crisis of identity in the national imagination, and if the very real material and cultural conditions of an increasingly multicultural society produce in turn a crisis of racial and ethnic identity, American national identity in the 1990s can be (and has been) characterized as experiencing what amounts to an "identity crisis." But rather than stymie or even contradict the development of national consciousness, this national anxiety presents precisely the necessary context for its development. Within the site of the beauty pageant, the opportunity arises for the presentation—or the invention—of a national crisis and also for the possibility of containment or conversion. This promise, or these conditions of possibility, are offered through the vehicle of the female body, which comes to "represent" nationalism in terms of a particular image of femininity. This same female body, however, also "represents" the nation in terms of a particular culture or community.

This in itself is an important development in studies of nationalisms: an idealized concept of the "nation" actually *needs* women to sustain its cultural and political currency. The "nation," especially in the United States, is formulated as an abstraction, and one is not necessarily compelled to fight for, to place beliefs within, or to give up one's life for an abstraction. Rather, we are compelled by desires. Thus any concept of the nation must incite particular desires in its public to remain a legitimate institutionalized system of beliefs and practices. As we can see by a mere glance at the popular press and television programs, idealized figures of femininity have long been understood as a lucrative avenue for desire. Who better to incite legitimating desire than Miss America, the woman who performs on a popular cultural stage, expertly weaving desirability with respectability, and sexuality with morality?

The "America" in Miss America signals not only nation, but citizenship, and the "Miss" in the title calls attention to a particular representative of the nation, a specific kind of ideal, universal citizen (always keeping in mind that it is "Miss" America, not "Mrs." or "Ms."). Feminist critiques of pageants have questioned this relationship between femininity and nationality, exposing the implicit premise that the "ideal" American female citizen is defined in terms of heterosexual or subordinate femininity. Although this is a good starting point, it questions the relationship between gender and nation in a particular and limited way.

What these critics have not accounted for are the other dynamics at work in beauty pageants. Pageants are not only about gender and nation, they are also always (and increasingly visibly) about race and nation; more specifically, they are about gender and nation as racialized categories. When we take into account these facets of the specific cultural work that is performed and actualized within beauty pageants, we automatically disrupt the simple equation of woman = nation. Once the category of citizen is broadened to include multiple ethnic and racial categories, the equation no longer balances in quite the same way.

The acknowledgment that race, gender, and nation are interconstitutive categories is key to disrupting any simple examination of nation, gender, and popular culture. That is, though particular constructions of the nation function as a moral reminder about conventional gender relations and institutions, femininity itself, as a social practice, operates in a constant state of flux and potential disruption. Dominant norms and conventions of femininity are constructed within the borders of a precarious balance: women simultaneously "need" to be protected and exploited, must be publicly displayed yet privately consumed, and are considered both the guardians of national morality and the largest threat to this moral foundation simply because of their gender.

Within beauty pageants, these long observed contradictions of femininity are even more complicated by the newly visible presence of nonwhite contestants. The nonwhite body functions as a specter—the marked other—against which the ideal female citizen is defined. And the pageant's history of celebrating universal whiteness has become increasingly obvious as pageants are forced to confront contemporary demands that they reflect racial and ethnic diversity. Although "difference" is assimilated in the pageants, the assimilation process has been imperfect: despite efforts to uphold a universal standard of beauty for all women, the representation of women who have been historically excluded from this standard renders beauty itself an unstable category of experience. Moreover, an increasingly multiethnic and multiracial society threatens the traditional function of pageants as sites for the control of nonwhite identities through the enforcement of dominant, universal norms of beauty.

What occurs, then, on the stage of the national beauty pageant is the enactment of a particular kind of national dilemma, one that must continuously attempt to resolve tensions that characterize dominant practices of femininity and an increasingly diversified society—even as the pageant simultaneously celebrates and reinvents precisely these categories of experience. The categories of race, gender, and national identity seem at all times fixed and stable but are in fact always shifting. Thus the potential for disruption over the viability of dominantly constructed categories of race and gender always exists, lurking beneath the seemingly stable horizon. Because of the physical and national enactment of ethnicity and gender to which pageants are dedicated, these spectacles represent both a potential for national crisis and a source of national stability. In an increasingly diverse configuration of the nation, accompanied by an increasing absence of the notion of a universal citizen, pageants in the 1990s' United States uniquely respond to moral panic over the current state of national identity. The performance of feminine subjectivity that comprises the celebratory heart of the beauty pageant functions as national assurance that despite the threats posed to dominant culture by fluctuating racial and gender codes, the pageant successfully manages and disciplines the construction of national identity, femininity, and ethnicity.

FEMINIST DEBATES
OVER BEAUTY AND REPRESENTATION

Though many respond to a project on beauty pageants by automatically relegating pageants (as well as research focused on pageants) to the realm of "low" culture, perhaps the most prevalent academic reaction to my work has been to automatically assume that my feminist analysis will follow in the footsteps of other feminist analyses of beauty pageants. The presumption is that the goal of my work must be to "expose" beauty pageants as repugnant rituals of feminine objectification.

This feminist position has a long history. The feminist protest of the 1968 Miss America pageant is often noted as heralding in the second-wave of liberal feminism in the United States, where the tossing of bras, high-heeled shoes, and other "instruments of torture" into a "Freedom Trash Can" was understood as a symbolic refusal of the constraints of patriarchal society.[15] The feminist argument that the Miss America pageant objectified and alienated women was at the forefront of the second-wave feminist movement, and, as Alice Echols has noted, importantly called attention to the way in which beauty practices and rituals constitute a particular kind of politics. This widely publicized protest led the way to a series of important feminist interventions to dominant representations of gender in the workplace, at home, and in the media. These interventions focused on the oppressive quality of dominant norms and standards of beauty and positioned various cultural sites such as assembly lines, corporate offices, advertising, pornography, and of course, beauty pageants, as harmful arenas, where the discrepancy between mass-mediated bodies of women and their "real" bodies was considered huge and damaging.

This critique of beauty pageants has been very powerful, and the overwhelming feminist consensus that pageants and other dominant norms and conventions of femininity are political practices that oppress and exploit women has made visible a wider range of choices for the construction of femininity. The analysis I develop throughout this work is indebted to feminist critiques of beauty pageants, but I nevertheless argue that this critique is formulated in simplistic terms and focuses primarily on the relationship between women and commodities, in particular the way in which pageants and other such displays of women construct women *as* commodities. For this feminist scenario, the objectified bodies of the contestants are the victims, and the pageant producers, directors, and public audience are the perpetrators. The theorizing of gender and the feminist assertion that women are in fact subjects has functioned as a vital opening to conduct research on beauty pageants, but it is an assertion that can take us only so far. We now need to complicate the picture by exploring precisely what kind of subjects are produced within beauty pageants and what practices and institutions not only sustain but work continuously to revise this production. As Susan Bordo, Sandra Lee Bartky, Teresa de Lauretis, and many others have demonstrated around other realms of femininity, theories of power and agency that understand gendered and raced bodies as effects and enactments *of* power rather than passive sites *for* power are required to generate a more complex understanding of productions of femininity—as both represented by dominant culture and self-representing within dominant culture. As these scholars have pointed out, a Foucaultian framework that calls for a reconfiguring of gendered and raced bodies on a political, social, and cultural landscape assists in analyzing the complicated and contradictory ways these bodies are disciplined and regulated.[16]

Judith Butler has argued that "[b]ecause there is neither an 'essence' that gender expresses or externalizes nor an objective ideal to which gender aspires, and because gender is not a fact, the various acts of gender create the idea of gender, and without these acts, there would be no gender at all."[17] The "acts" of gender make us, produce us, construct us—even as we enact and construct gender ourselves. In other words, gender is *performative*: it is a constant, repetitive production of the self, and yet not *performance* in the classical theatrical sense, the sense of playing a specific "role." Rather, a performative theory of gender proposes that the enacting of gender produces gender; it does not assume that gender already exists as a pregiven fact of nature, or an authentic core. Gender is a set of practices, which are historically specific and conditioned by race and class. Gender is not outside of how women dress, act, and speak but is instead constituted by these and other practices.

Thinking about the production of gender in this way moves beyond a dominant feminist approach to popular cultural forms such as the beauty pageant. Although challenging the objectification of the female body can be a liberating practice, it also simplifies how everyone experiences gender. Stories about "infiltrating" beauty pageants, where feminist "spies" pretend to act as contestants in order to sabotage pageants, are interesting and often liberating disruptions, but they also assume that somehow the disciplinary practices of femininity in which beauty pageant contestants engage are outside of how feminists themselves are constructed as female in U.S. culture. Dominant definitions of femininity—indeed, gender itself—are not tangible "things" that somehow exist outside of our "real" selves. Feminists who oppose beauty on the grounds that it is oppressive are not more authentic than beauty queens. Even in situations where pageants are protested and challenged, the protesters themselves do not step out of the relations of power of which gender is but an effect; on the contrary, gender is continually reenacted. To assume that nonparticipation in beauty pageants or other overt beauty rituals exempts a woman from dominant definitions of femininity not only obscures the ways in which gender both produces and is produced by a particular definition of the self, but also implies an illusory notion of choice.

This position also denies the pleasure and desire experienced by beauty pageant contestants as they participate in these popular cultural forms. The production of femininity is one characterized by pleasure, among other things, and the contestants' own accounts of their pleasure and desire when producing themselves as beauty queens should not be written off as mere acquiescence. The sheer excessiveness of a beauty contestant's version of femininity, complete with elaborate hair styles, exaggerated makeup, evening gowns, disciplined physique, and commitment to feminine virtues, is an excess that is threaded through and through with particular connotations of desire.

My resistance to an argument that insists that beauty pageant contestants are victims of false consciousness does not mean I embrace a "postfeminist" position. This position, largely represented by the very public

feminist personas of Camille Paglia, Katie Roiphe, and Naomi Wolf, takes
critical aim at the (perceived) recurring theme in much feminist work and
practice that women—and women's bodies in particular—are vulnerable
and in need of protection. It focuses on the notion that dominant feminist
discourse has produced a society of victims—a society of women who are
so focused on their own "victimhood" that they actually reinforce female
passivity and powerlessness.[18] This critique is even more limiting than a
narrow focus on objectified bodies, because it refuses to recognize power
as a key constituent in the production of feminine selves.

Situating feminist reflection and theorizing about beauty pageants
within current theoretical debates around issues of agency, subjectivity,
and resistance may allow us to sidestep both the liberal impasse of freedom versus protection and a more narrowly constructed feminist understanding of pageants; as a result, we may discover a more sophisticated
paradigm. What can we assume about the relationship between representation and the "real" when considering beauty pageants and beauty
pageant contestants? What subjectivities are created through and within
beauty pageants? Does the construction of subjectivity always imply or
assume a notion of agency? What of subjectivity that both caters to and
defines masculinist interests? Does such subjectivity necessarily mean that
there is a lack of agency—or an agency that is denied or suppressed—
among the contestants? Or does such a question already presuppose a set
of assumptions about "genuine" or "authentic" agency—namely, agency
defined by feminists?

METHODOLOGICAL DILEMMAS,
OR WHAT TO DO WITH "WOMEN'S EXPERIENCE"

To even begin answering these questions, we must theorize gender and
power in a way that entails understanding gender as a relation that not
only signifies but also is defined by power. As always, when one attempts
to understand the complexities of gender construction, one must address
the issue of methodology. What is the best way to account for the cultural
work that happens in beauty pageants? How do we understand the dimensions of power at work in these particular sites? Positioning myself

as a feminist means theorizing gender in terms that utilize a specifically feminist methodology.[19]

The tools I use in my research are intimately connected to my epistemological premise. I interviewed approximately fifty pageant contestants, producers, and directors, worked on the production of a local city pageant, and conducted detailed ethnographies of pageants, both smaller, more local productions and the more nationally significant televised spectacles. Because I think that self-representation is a necessary and crucial element in constituting gender, part of my work is an attempt to account for the experience of beauty pageant contestants. My choice to include the contestants' experience as evidence for the cultural practices that both sustain and construct beauty pageants is faithful to a feminist undertaking.

I am, however, faced with a dilemma: I must find a way to critique cultural discourses and practices that objectify, alienate, or otherwise fragment the female body without treating the contestants themselves as somnolent victims of false consciousness. This dilemma results from the distinction between my critique of gendered rituals and my own involvement within certain aspects of the dominant beauty system. It is crucial to recognize that this involvement can be a resource, not a limitation, in figuring the tensions and contradictions that characterize the production of beauty pageants.[20] To pretend that no dilemma existed would not only be intellectually dishonest, but also reproduce the precise feminist position I criticize—that of dismissively labeling pageants as "obvious" and "clear expressions of patriarchy."

My initial response to this dilemma was a committed effort to interview the women involved, to allow them space to speak about what they are doing, and to seriously engage with what they have to say. How do they account for and explain their participation in pageants? How, and in what ways, do they distinguish themselves as different from their major critics, feminists? Interviews with several beauty pageant contestants show clearly that these women do not consider themselves victims.[21] As one beauty queen commented, "We're not exploited. We're up there because we want to be up there. . . . You're up there and it builds confidence, it's not degrading, other women may think it is, well, okay, don't curl your hair."[22] Indeed, most other women do not consider themselves victims who participate, in one form or another, in disciplinary practices intended to produce a femininity both created by and reflected in dominant discourses.[23] Thus, although I find it personally difficult to place myself alongside Miss America, Miss Budweiser, or Miss Co-Ed as a product of a particular definition of femininity, I also find it too sweeping an indictment to claim that all women who participate in gendered disciplinary practices are victims, or as Stuart Hall has put it, "cultural dupes."[24]

My initial impulse to include women's experience as research evidence has remained only partially intact, but this methodological component to my work is nonetheless crucial for several reasons: including the contestants' experience belies any gesture toward a "genuine" feminist voice or standpoint, one that is only wrought from political struggle—in other words, this inclusion automatically rejects the distinction between false consciousness and "true" consciousness, or victim and critic. The experience of the contestants is also necessary to get at what de Lauretis calls the "potential trauma" of gender; in her words, gender is "not only the effect of representation but also its excess, what remains outside of discourse as a potential trauma which can rupture or destabilize, if not contained, any representation."[25] The only way to understand the processes of gender construction is to get at this "excess" of representation, to try to determine the ways in which excess is at odds with effects. As de Lauretis argues, the way to account for gender is to account for this tension: "The discrepancy, the tension, and the constant slippage between Woman as representation, as the object and the very condition of representation, and, on the other hand, women as historical beings, subjects of 'real' relations . . . are motivated and sustained by a logical contradiction in our culture and an irreconcilable one: women are both inside and outside gender, at once within and without representation."[26]

The testimony of beauty pageant contestants illustrates this slippage. The beauty pageant contestant cannot be conflated with her representation, and an account of her "experience" assists in theorizing how she, like all other women, is "at once within and without representation."

This important tension is brought into relief by the research methodologies of interviewing and ethnography. But what are the limits to legitimating "experience" as evidence? Joan Scott has argued that authenticating a notion of experience reconstitutes rather than challenges dominant discourse. As Scott argues, if feminists "take as self-evident the identities of those whose experience is being documented and thus naturalize their difference," the category of Woman is universalized (in much the same way as the category of feminist is universalized within feminist standpoint theory), and as a consequence, the "universal sex opposition" is naturalized.[27] The move to include experience—as I've outlined it here—as not only a viable but also a critical component in determining subjectivity can, according to Scott, "reify agency as an inherent attribute of individuals, thus decontextualizing it."[28]

What would be more fruitful is an examination of the testimonies of both feminists and beauty pageant contestants as a series of competing truths, one just as socially constructed as the other. Neither the rhetoric of beauty pageant contestants nor the rhetoric of feminists should be understood as self-evident or the truth; rather, both should be placed in the context of the production of subjectivity. In other words, how do the words of beauty pageant contestants help us to understand tensions between representation and historical, material lives? Can the contestants' accounts reveal the spaces in which the construction of the feminine subject is unpredictable and unstable? To understand not only the difference between feminists and beauty pageant contestants but also the ways in which this difference is constituted relationally, we need to "attend to the historical processes that, through discourse, position subjects and produce their experiences."[29]

One way that beauty pageant contestants have been positioned as particular kinds of subjects is through "free choice" rhetoric—the choice to enter a pageant, the choice to construct oneself within the bounds of a particular femininity. This rhetoric is one that has perhaps ironically been enabled by the efforts of feminists over the last two decades to pave the way for women to make new choices about their lives. As the popular press is wont to do, the politics of feminism have been completely obscured in a discourse that utilizes elements of feminism in a neutralized if not reactionary manner. Remarking on the popular construction of disciplinary beauty rituals such as makeup and fixing one's hair as "creative expression," Bordo observes:

> The one comment that hints at women's (by now depressingly
> well-documented) dissatisfaction with their appearance trivializes
> that dissatisfaction and puts it beyond the pale of cultural critique:
> "It's fashion." What she means is: "It's only fashion," whose whim-

sical and politically neutral vicissitudes supply endless amusement
for woman's eternally superficial values. ("Women are never happy
with themselves.") If we are never happy with ourselves, it is implied, that is due to our female nature, not to be taken too seriously
or made into a "political question."[30]

Instead of making women's feelings of inadequacy about their self-image
into a "political question," popular discourse instructs us to revel in the
creation of a new self, a self that requires particular disciplinary practices
in order to create a femininity that is exotic, novel, erotic, and fashionable.
If cosmetic changes, such as perming and bleaching hair, wearing colored
contact lenses, and plastic surgery help to create this new self, the beauty
pageant is merely the forum for the expression of these creative acts. This
discourse positions liberal notions of choice and agency as key elements
of dominant discourse about beauty and femininity. Beauty pageant contestants consistently claim that the "new experience" of the pageant was
their central motivation for entering; once in the pageant, when asked why
they are there, they answer, "I'm here because I want to be, I want the experience."[31] As one contestant said, "Hopefully, [participating in pageants]
helps you improve as a person. . . . You're not in competition with the other
girls, you're in competition with yourself, to be the best 'you' you can be."[32]

When examined through the lens of this framework, the pageant contestant becomes the enthusiastic defender of democratic values in the
world of "creative expression" and free choice. This cultural construction
of a pageant contestant as a liberal citizen dedicated to democracy and
self-agency lends even more credibility to the contestants' response to feminist inquisition: they point to their participation in pageants as examples
of "doing what I want to do." The fact that beauty pageant contestants
construct their feminine identities in relation to and because of power, not
because that particular identity was chosen from some grab bag, is not remarked upon by these contestants; the conditions that condition the
choices we all make (not only the ones beauty pageant contestants make)
are erased or obscured.

Exploring the construction of experience of beauty pageant contestants
also raises the question of subjectivity and identity. Scott's claim that "[i]t
is not individuals who have experience, but subjects who are constituted
through experience" historicizes experience and forces the contextual-

ization of the accounts of the contestants. It also compels me to take seriously constant critical self-reflection about my position in relation to the contestants. How I, as a feminist, would position beauty pageant contestants and historicize their experience is, in the words of Gayatri Spivak, "to make visible the assignment of subject-positions."[33]

The beauty pageant serves as a site in which these processes and their effects can be both marked and remarked upon. The pageant contestants embrace and resist different identities, identities that are constituted through the structuring of the pageant itself. And, through the words of the pageant contestants and accounts that rehearse why these women are participating in the pageants, we can understand the discursive processes that are both visible and invisible, and reactionary and potentially liberatory—processes that are part of the construction of the beauty pageant and, in the larger culture, of the beauty system itself.

THE AMERICAN NATION
AND REPRESENTATIONS OF RACE

[The success of the nineties' attacks on "Political Correctness"] activates a genteel white nationalism in which the red menace is directly replaced by the rainbow menace.

CHRISTOPHER NEWFIELD

The context of the 1990s and contemporary demands that all cultural forms reflect racial and ethnic diversity have forced pageants to confront their history of celebrating universal whiteness.[34] Appropriating the terms and language of diversity, the beauty pageant positions itself squarely in the center of national debates over identity and transforms the "crisis" of diversity—it accommodates diversity, performs and exercises toleration, and effaces any obvious signs of particular ethnicities or races. The nationwide debate around issues of diversity, which is situated centrally in fears about identity politics, is reinvented in the beauty pageant as a classic liberal tale about individual achievement in a land of opportunity.

"Political correctness" or "multiculturalism" has perhaps garnered more media attention than any other single cultural phenomenon of the early 1990s. Heated debates on these topics have largely focused on educational study, research, academics, and university curricula.[35] These debates, however, have also triggered a nationwide hysteria that finds a place in almost every political and popular cultural site: music, film, art, politics, and government. This hysteria has transformed into both the creation of and a response to what is being called a national crisis: a crisis of identity, a crisis of virtue, and a crisis of morals. The discourse of multiculturalism frames this crisis: as it is represented in the visions from the Right, the supposed cohesiveness of the "American identity" is rapidly disintegrating under the tyranny of identity politics and the assertions of "victimization" by numerous historically marginalized groups. As syndicated columnist George Will proclaims, "One way to make racial, ethnic or sexual identity primary is to destroy alternative sources of individuality and social cohesion, such as a shared history, a common culture and unifying values."[36] Multiculturalism's threat to the so-called common culture is perceived by the Right (as well as by some on the Left) as the "Balkanization" of U.S. society.[37] Balkanization results in the loss of the unified "American" identity as subcultures emerge and develop through the claiming of particular marginalized identities.

What is clear about the multicultural debates is that the term *multiculturalism* is the new code word for race in the United States, a code that Hazel Carby argues is just as effective "as the word 'drugs' or the phrase 'inner-city violence' at creating a common-sense awareness that race is, indeed, the subject being evoked."[38] In a historical moment characterized by a dismantling of affirmative action and national debates over presidential apologies for slavery, multiculturalism is situated in the cross fire. To flesh out the contours of the current moral panic in the United States, one must recognize that race is at the center of the anxiety. Indeed, race informs, constitutes, and shapes the crisis.

Combating and diffusing the Right's hysteria about multiculturalism has meant popularizing or democratizing the very notion that poses the biggest threat within the whole debate: the concept of "diversity." The language of diversity has been used in popular culture, in politics, and in academics as an indication that difference is recognized, as an identification with diverse demographics, and as an acknowledgment of a variety of subcultures. Not surprisingly, part of the practice of democratizing diversity has been to commodify it; retail corporations such as Benetton and Esprit routinely use images of diversity as hip new ways to sell cloth-ing,[39] and the cosmetics industry is capitalizing on an ever-widening new ethnic market. As *Vogue* magazine puts it, "Jesse Jackson's Rainbow Coali-tion may have been wishful thinking in the political arena, but in the beauty business it's become a reality."[40] The media widely uses "diverse" representatives in advertisements and television programs: children who watch public television are exposed to images of African American, Latino, and Asian children happily romping with huge purple dinosaurs, and public service announcements for children contain positive messages about combating racial prejudice alongside warnings about guns and drugs.

Thus, one of the various strategies involved in managing diversity is through the representation of difference. The body is, above all else, rep-resentation, and if displays of the female body—in the media, in film, and in advertising—are displays of black and brown female bodies, then di-versity is in fact represented. The African American model Tyra Banks and the Latina model Daisy Fuentes offer living, breathing evidence that di-versity sells and is equally captivating for consumers of all colors. Diver-sity becomes a commodity that is purchased through the representation and display of nonwhite feminine bodies (predominantly by white con-sumers who come equipped with an excessive dose of liberal guilt about race). Most white Americans want to believe that they are "tolerant" and that they legitimate the beauty of Fuentes or the musical talent of rap star Queen Latifah through consumption. Purchasing products that package diversity allows white consumers to believe that they are enacting toler-ance without the messy problems of actually redistributing resources or living the effects of affirmative action. Thus the ironic, unintended effect that characterizes the realm of representation becomes one in which white Americans *feel* more tolerant than ever, even as they continue to live in an increasingly segregated nation.

This language of diversity has resulted in anything but a recognition of diverse cultures and traditions. Rather, the use of "diversity" in popu-lar discourse has reduced the threat of identity politics by entrenching di-versity within commodity culture, within the language and politics of lib-eralism, and inside a circumscribed representation of the female body. As such, Carby's questions remain particularly appropriate: "Is the empha-

sis on cultural diversity making invisible the politics of race in this increasingly segregated nation, and is the language of cultural diversity a
convenient substitute for the political action needed to desegregate?"[41] The
slick, commodified image of diversity that is repeatedly deployed—by the
media and other forms of popular discourse—as a cover story for the material and cultural conditions of a society diverse in race, ethnicity, and
class assuages national tensions about race and legitimates the ideas of
people like Rush Limbaugh about the necessity of accepting the "American way." The mass-mediated debates over multiculturalism are both the
symptom and the enactment of the anxiety caused by the new vision of a
multiracial social order—now posed as an alternative and critique of white
supremacy and male dominance.

The beauty pageant, and especially the Miss America pageant, needs
to be situated centrally within this context. The cultural work the beauty
pageant performs creates an idealized subjectivity that corresponds to a
1990s' version of hip diversity. Alongside its nationalist claims and its celebration of a particular feminine subject, it also offers the dialectic of racial
crisis and containment, where the potential threat of making racial or ethnic identity primary is made visible and then summarily converted to the
successful production of "self-defining participants in a free society."[42]
Miss America is the face who is simultaneously the face of America, the
face of womanhood, and the face of diversity. The presence of black and
brown female bodies on the stage does not dismantle the privilege of
whiteness that frames the pageant. On the contrary, this presence, harmoniously situated alongside white female bodies, works to include
whiteness as a key player in the game of diversity.

SO, THERE SHE IS . . .

Rather than understanding beauty pageants as simple, obvious expressions of male dominance, we must begin by situating contemporary
pageants within the political context of the 1990s. In particular, the context of the debates over multiculturalism provides a point of entry for analyzing pageants as sites for cultural work that produces national female
subjects in postindustrialist United States. Particular definitions of gen-

der and race always inform the construction of national identity, even as these definitions present the constant potential for transgression. The challenge is to balance the two, or discover a way to ease a nation's anxiety about itself, to stabilize national identity even while reflecting some part of the reality of what that nation looks like. The beauty pageant is precisely this balancing act; it pieces together an ideal from separate parts and manages not only to convincingly call that ideal a whole, seamless identity, but also to spectacularly demonstrate the pleasure of power.

Taking into account the pleasurable and productive aspects of power, while simultaneously acknowledging the ways in which power—through both ideology and material effects—creates the feminine subject, is to understood gender as both representation and self-representation. This understanding entails more than merely considering the different cultural representations of the female body. Kathy Davis urges "feminists to recover the body as a locus of ongoing political struggle, a site of feminist practice in relation to the practical lives of women's bodies. Feminists need to pay special attention to the 'collusions, subversions, and enticements through which culture enjoins the aid of our bodies in the reproduction of gender.'"[43] Davis's project on the practice of cosmetic surgery serves as a useful departure point for thinking through issues and dilemmas regarding beauty pageants. Like Davis, my central question within this project has been framed in simple terms: why do women participate in beauty pageants? What is it, exactly, about these events that continue to motivate women, even in the face of various critiques? It is not so difficult to imagine why contestants so easily dismiss feminist critique, given the popular construction of feminism as hysterical and overly paranoid. But it is more difficult to explain contestants' continued participation in the face of criticism from various commentators on both the Left and Right, commentators who decry the supposed inherent vacuousness of the event and, by extension, of the contestants.

Davis's solution to her dilemma about cosmetic surgery was to take "the member's point of view," where, "without forgetting feminist critical perspectives of women's involvement in the feminine beauty system, [she] bracketed the notion that women and their bodies are determined or colonized by this system in order to see if (and how) [she] might find a way to believe the explanations they themselves had."[44] I found a similar way to reconcile, or at least negotiate, my own dilemma of privileg-

ing beauty pageants contestants' experience while simultaneously critiquing cultural discourses and practices that produce beauty pageants
and certain manifestations of the female body: I look at the thematic use
of classic liberal stories of individual achievement and pluralist tolerance
within the pageant. In other words, rather than merely dismissing these
liberal tales as part of a powerful system in which women and their bodies are "determined and colonized," I situate the pageants, and the ways
in which liberal discourse is operationalized within pageants, in a particular historical context. Making the connection between the various available cultural narratives about individualism and diversity or pluralism—
drawn from feminist discourses, popular discourses, political discourses
(with a particular eye toward the recent spate of neoconservative "feminists" such as Peggy Noonan and Arianna Huffington)[45], and discourses
about race and ethnicity—and the reliance upon liberal notions of individualism, equal opportunity, pluralism, and the like within beauty pageants allows us to conceptualize pageants and the women who participate within them as neither complete victims nor entirely free agents. We
need to begin by considering the pageants' and contestants' claim that
beauty pageants are important sites for the construction of national feminine identity, and that constructing national identity in the United States
means not only being a particular kind of woman, but also embracing a
specific definition of diversity.

Beauty pageants are occasions for the construction of a particular feminine subject that corresponds with these kinds of discourses and practices. In line with this, my original overly simplified question—"why do
women participate in beauty pageants?"—must be amended to include
a more complicated set of issues: in this current cultural and political climate, what is the distinctively "feminine" way in which women can wield
power (a way that does not simply recuperate the dismissal by radical feminists that women with power are merely women in masculine positions,
acting like men, because power is only configured as masculine)? In order to answer this question, we need to take seriously contestants' claims
that beauty pageants are a step toward an individual woman's experiences
of embodiment. We need, in other words, to take another look at the construction of feminine identity in U.S. culture in the 1990s, to situate and
contextualize claims of postfeminism and diversity rather than dismiss
them as reactionary and accommodating discourses.

If beauty pageants provide a space through which women can realize an experience of embodiment and the possibility of agency, one of the ways they realize this is, ironically, through a particular construction of the female body. The female body is situated in a cultural and political climate that has become increasingly hostile to various feminisms and feminist claims, a climate where postfeminist spokespersons such as Camille Paglia and Katie Roiphe have transformed feminist thought (at least in mainstream media) into something which is "psychologically motivated," "old-fashioned," or simply paranoid.[46] Beauty pageants in this context belong to a "set of social practices which evoke strong reactions and heated debates about what constitutes an appropriate or adequate feminist response," and through these tensions, pageants find a place within postfeminist rhetoric and practice.[47]

The 1990s' postfeminist call has been to urge women to "return" to the body, to explore its multiple pleasures, and to revel in its creative possibilities.[48] "Returning to the body," however, does not mean passively accepting a masculinist definition of the female body as empty and at the same time all-encompassing, that common experience women have of being *nothing* but a body even as they are made to understand that the body is *everything*. On the contrary, the feminine body is popularly considered as both a site for pleasure and an active, thinking subject. And so beauty pageants, rather than operating as simple showcases for displaying objectified bodies, are actually a kind of feminist space where female identity is constructed by negotiating the contradictions of being socially constituted as "just" a body while simultaneously producing oneself as an active thinking subject, indeed, a decidedly "liberal" subject. Beauty pageants produce the feminine body as a site of pleasure. This particular identity, argues Davis (paraphrasing Iris Young), is one of "feminine embodiment," which is the condition of "being caught between existence as just a body and the desire to transcend that body and become a subject who acts upon the world in and through it."[49] This notion of being an actor in the world, of both existing as a body and transcending that body, is the relentless theme of beauty pageants.

In fact, feminism played an indirect role in shaping how beauty pageants are now defined. Contestants have appropriated elements of (mainstream) or liberal feminist discourse as part of their self-presentation.

Interviews with contestants are riddled with statements about self-confidence, assertiveness, the importance of careers, and perhaps most important, "individual" choice. The pageants themselves change according to changes in dominant collective notions of gender, notions that are influenced by (and occasionally give credit to) mainstream liberal feminist discourse. For example, at the opening of most beauty pageants, each contestant offers a short, introductory autobiography. This goes hand in hand with the pageant being a scholarship competition: these brief histories inevitably reference career and education as the most important personal goals of the contestant. This is a shift in the image of Miss America, the "ideal" American woman who was "able to shoulder the responsibilities of homemaking and motherhood."[50] The idea that this woman would consciously choose a career over family, even if temporarily, is an important result of feminist movements in the United States.

Beauty pageant contestants perform an elaborate balancing act between representing themselves in terms of liberal personhood and individual achievement and participating in a competition dedicated to the display and maintenance of an ideal feminine form. The fact that the swimsuit competition within beauty pageants recently changed its name to the "physical fitness competition," and that some pageants no longer require contestants to wear high heels with their swimsuits, does not eclipse the fact that the swimsuit competition is just that: a competition where women parade in front of a panel of judges in a swimsuit. But this apparent paradox of feminine embodiment is precisely what allows pageants to maintain popularity in this political and cultural climate. The pitting of the swimsuit competition's object against the interview's subject reflects the popular sentiment of being sexual and serious at the same time—a sentiment that finds its way to Virginia Slims ads as well as Naomi Wolf's theoretical musings. In other words, the pageant attempts to accommodate the contradictions of constructing oneself as a feminine subject in U.S. culture in the 1990s.

ABOUT THE BOOK

The televised Miss America pageant that millions watch every September is really the end product of a highly complex process that involves regional and state volunteers, chambers of commerce, local sponsorship, and thousands of contestants. *The Most Beautiful Girl in the World* begins with an investigation of this process and with a consideration of the various strategies and material means that are necessary for contestants to compete on the Miss America pageant track.

In situating the Miss America pageant as a highly commodified, mass-mediated feminized spectacle, chapter 1 demonstrates that the pageant has vigorously defined itself, practically from its inception, as a civic event that is about respectable femininity and "typical" American beauty and morality. The strategies employed by Miss America officials, from the constant chaperoning to a strict no-alcohol policy to a commitment to charity organizations, have functioned to establish the pageant as an annual American ritual set apart from other beauty pageants. Thus chapter 1 suggests that the Miss America pageant has for most of its history been dedicated to making a claim on national feminine identity.

After this description of how both producers and pageant contestants conceive of the beauty pageant, chapter 2 explores the anatomy of the Miss America pageant itself. It begins with a description of what is perhaps the most (in)famous element of the spectacle, the swimsuit competition. Then the chapter describes the contestants' own understandings and sentiments about this event, focusing on their complex reconciliations about participating in the swimsuit competition (an event in which many of them feel uncomfortable participating) and their obvious enthusiasm for the rest of the pageant.

Chapter 2 details the various negotiations involving the contestants' discomfort with the swimsuit competition by framing their comments within a discussion of other pageants that focus more intensely and more singularly on the female body. At the same time, this chapter situates the swimsuit competition as an event that is about the physical and moral disciplining of women's bodies. In other words, the swimsuit competition requires the contestants to wear swimsuits that are designed to never come in contact with any body of water and are strictly regulated in terms of how many inches of skin may be exposed, and the chapter argues that it is precisely this disciplining that makes the swimsuit competition an absolutely necessary element of the Miss America pageant. It is necessary because it is the performance of the female object, a performance that is then juxtaposed to the interview and talent competitions, which are performances of the female subject.

The third chapter of *The Most Beautiful Girl in the World* details these performances by focusing on the interview and talent competitions. The chapter begins with a discussion of the pageant interview and describes the various expectations the Miss America pageant places on this event. The interview competition has two distinct elements. The first is the main interview, conducted with every contestant in front of a panel of judges in a closed space, which takes place before the public viewing of the pageant. The second component involves only the top five finalists in the pageant and focuses on the chosen "issue platform" of each finalist. In chapter 3, the contestants discuss the typical questions asked in the main interview, the questions' significance in terms of revealing personality, "poise," and career and educational goals, and the various strategies undertaken to "give a good interview." The chapter details the importance of the interview, not only as a means to establish the Miss America pageant as a respectable event that is fundamentally about personality and intelligence (and thus not beauty), but also as a crucial element in the self-construction of pageant contestants as modern liberal subjects.

Chapter 3 also explores the talent portion of the Miss America pageant. The talent competition is worth 40 percent of a contestant's total score and is uniformly thought of by pageant participants as the most important element of the entire event. This chapter suggests that the talent competition establishes the pageant as a "middlebrow" event; as such, it demonstrates through the performances the contestants' commitment to moral virtue and gestures and women's investment in what are usually thought of as high cultural forms. The popularity of vocal and instrumental numbers, and the relative failure of talents such as stand-up comedy, ventriloquism, and popular contemporary dance, offer evidence that the talent competition is a performative space in which contestants establish themselves as members of a particular cultural elite. The chapter further argues that the talent competition is a fundamentally racialized event, one in which every talent (especially those performed by women of color) are culturally and socially coded as white. This sets the stage for chapter 4's discussion of the pageant's strategies for accommodating difference and diversity in light of a long history of racial exclusion—a history during which, until the late 1940s, each contestant was required to list their genealogy as part of their biographical profile.

As a way of framing this discussion, chapter 4 focuses on the story of Vanessa Williams, who was crowned the first African American Miss America, for 1984. This chapter contextualizes Williams's reign—which abruptly ended after ten months when *Penthouse* magazine published nude photographs of Williams and another woman—within the cultural and political climate of the 1980s. Arguing that this historical moment was characterized by the extreme demonization of people of color in the mass media on the one hand, and the emerging recognition that celebrating diversity was a lucrative marketing and political strategy on the other, this chapter situates Williams's "fall from grace" as one that reinvigorated dominant stereotypes of black female sexuality as insatiable, wanton, and indiscriminate.

Chapter 4 further argues that the Miss America pageant, like other popular cultural forms, establishes clear conditions through which the representation of race occurs. In the particular case of Vanessa Williams, the condition through which race was filtered (and thus obfuscated) was sexuality. More specifically, the fact that Williams simulated (heterosexual-defined) lesbian desire in the pages of *Penthouse* diverted attention from her race and focused on the ways in which her apparent sexuality disrupted the heterosexual matrix of the pageant.

Although chapter 4 focuses primarily on Vanessa Williams, it also argues more broadly about the pageant's troubled history in representing racialized identity. Drawing together the themes of race, gender, and the nation, it discusses how the Miss America pageant offers a performance of feminine subjectivity that manages and disciplines the construction of national identity, despite the threats posed to national culture by fluctuating racial and gender codes.

As chapter 4 identifies these cultural processes as they are framed by Williams's troubled reign, chapter 5 situates two other extraordinary Miss Americas as particularly appropriate representatives of the nation. These two—Bess Myerson, Miss America 1945, and Heather Whitestone, Miss America 1995—were crowned in part because they provided safe answers to national questions about idealized American femininity. The chapter argues that Myerson and Whitestone represent a kind of embodied national community, one in which female icons of the nation assuage fears about ambivalent definitions of who and what a nation should be.

Bess Myerson was crowned the first (and only) Jewish Miss America—a significant event in its own right, but the historical moment of 1945 U.S. society lent even more importance to her selection as a national representative. Myerson was a figure of femininity that the nation needed symbolically at that particular moment—a need that hasn't expressed itself in quite the same way since, at least within the Miss America pageant.

Heather Whitestone, crowned fifty years after Myerson, also responds to national concerns and questions about feminine identity through her difference. Whitestone, who is deaf, is the first Miss America with a disability. Her deafness is constructed by the pageant as an obstacle Whitestone was able to "overcome," and as such represents a subjectivity that accommodates, rather than highlights, difference. In the cultural climate of the 1990s, when hysteria over identity politics and difference seems to continually reach new heights, Whitestone's innocence and purity, characterized by her deafness, trumps the politics of identity and offers a revitalized version of American femininity. The chapter further argues that the visual regimes of the nation shifted with the televising of the pageant, and that Whitestone, who dances ballet by feeling the beat of the music through her feet, responds uniquely to this shift by offering a feminine subjectivity that is visually and ideologically innocent.

In an attempt to discover whether there might be an international corollary to the Miss America pageant's efforts to establish a national feminine identity, chapter 6 turns to international pageants such as Miss World and Miss Universe. By showing that similar strategies of defining femininity are used in pageants such as Miss India and Miss Tibet, the chapter suggests that international pageants are also dedicated to establishing a feminine national icon that can be situated in a "family of nations." However, despite the similarities between the Miss America pageant and international beauty pageants, a westernized understanding of idealized femininity is not a universally shared condition. Chapter 6 concludes with a consideration of the possibility that although pageants may have format and structure in common, feminine sexuality plays itself out differently in different contexts and within different sets of national politics.

The book concludes by considering the implications of its methodology and findings for future investigations of feminized spectacles in late-twentieth-century U.S. culture. I suggest that the Miss America pageant appropriates liberal feminist rhetoric and is situated as a postfeminist space in the late 1990s—and although the pageant is not necessarily the road to feminist reform, this road itself is a complicated one, full of excess and contradictions. The pageant attempts to reassure national tensions about femininity, but because femininity is an unstable and unfixed category, the pageant cannot accommodate all of these tensions. In fact, the Miss America pageant does complex cultural work in terms of race, gender, and the nation.

CHAPTER 1 "A CERTAIN CLASS OF GIRL"

RESPECTABILITY AND THE STRUCTURE
OF THE MISS AMERICA PAGEANT

> Maligned by one segment of America, adored by another,
> misunderstood by about all of it, Miss America still flows
> like the Mississippi, drifts like amber waves of grain,
> sounds like the crack of a bat on a baseball, tastes like
> Mom's apple pie, and smells like dollar bills. Miss Lib-
> erty, looking out, away from the land, has never been
> quite the same since the McCarran Act, and Grace Kelly
> no longer calls Philadelphia home. But good old Miss
> America still talks like Huckleberry Finn, looks like Patti,
> LaVerne, and Maxine, and towers over the land like the
> Ozarks. She really is the body of state, and the country
> is in her eyes.
>
> FRANK DEFORD, *There She Is*

Every year at least 7,500 beauty pageants in the United States are franchised by either the Miss America Scholarship program or the Miss USA
pageant.[1] Several thousand other beauty pageants, ranging from beach
bikini pageants to Miss Budweiser and Miss Tulip, are produced on a
small-scale, local level. The question this book begins with is deceptively
simple: What is a beauty pageant? As is true when querying all forms of
popular culture, there is more than one answer to this question. Though
the actual structure of pageants varies depending on the context, most
have a familiar, recognizable format: female contestants enter a competitive event, where they are judged based on beauty, personality, talent, and
the ever so elusive "poise." A panel of judges evaluates each contestant,
and the woman who garners the most points in the various events of the
pageant—often including swimsuit, evening gown, talent, and interview
competitions—wins and is crowned "queen."

But what is this competition *about?* Is it, as feminists have eloquently and persuasively argued for decades, a "meat market," where women are reduced to judgable body parts, and the overt message is that women are sexual objects? Or is it, as much of dominant discourse has maintained, simply a traditional entertaining event, where women enjoy a sense of feminine community, and the covert message is that women are sexual objects? Or is it something more complicated than that?

This book does not discuss all of the beauty pageants that occur in the United States each year; rather, it focuses on one, perhaps the most famous beauty pageant of all, the Miss America pageant. And it argues that, although contestants are constructed as objects on the beauty pageant stage, the pageant is not merely, or even most importantly, about sex. The Miss America pageant certainly rests on an indefatigable grid of heterosexuality, and the swimsuit competition is clearly an event that both encourages and legitimates sexual objectification. But the swimsuit competition does not stand for the whole event. The Miss America pageant does not define itself in terms of sexuality, but rather promotes a self-production that relies on a more complex interweaving of two themes of femininity: typicality and respectability. This chapter explores these themes as central forces in the production of the Miss America pageant and focuses on the considerable efforts of this pageant to separate itself from other beauty pageants as an event that is not about sex or even glamour, but is instead about the ordinary, respectable American woman. More specifically, this chapter focuses on how the category of respectability mediates constructions of and responses to sexuality.

This part of the self-production and self-definition of the Miss America pageant is urgently important in the late 1990s. This historical moment is characterized by an increasing public awareness of the sexual objectification of women and girls in pageants—a moment fueled in 1996 by the media frenzy that surrounded, and continues to surround, the rape and murder of six-year-old JonBenet Ramsey, a child active in the children's beauty pageant circuit. With a variety of news magazine television programs and magazine exposés devoted to critically challenging the long-standing pageant claim that beauty pageants contribute to women's and girls' self-esteem and confidence, the status of pageants as entertaining events that benefit those involved is increasingly under attack. The

Miss America pageant, however, remains the beauty pageant least damaged by this attack; as the largest source of scholarship money for women in the United States and the only pageant circuit that emphasizes (and judges contestants on) both talent and charity work, the Miss America pageant vehemently maintains that it is an event that showcases feminine respectability and morality.

AT THE BEGINNING: THE MISS AMERICA PAGEANT

There are various claims about the origin of the modern-day beauty pageant; stories and legends detail ancient public spectacles that in some way resemble the Miss America pageant. Clearly, ancient tales such as the Greek myth of Paris and his golden apple, or stories about Queen Esther, Shahrazad, or even Cinderella, provide the modern-day beauty pageant with historical roots, and there are no doubt many other tales, legends, and fables about the competitive judging of women that could be considered the pageant's "origin."[2] Though it is interesting to trace these histories, it can also be said that women have nearly *always* been "judged" with respect to their physical appearance. One can just as easily interpret the colonial harem system or certain practices of arranged marriages or even promenades down fashionable London streets in the eighteenth century as precursors to beauty pageants. More fascinating than an origin story is a detailed exploration of the history of the one pageant that clearly lacks precise antecedents: the Miss America pageant.

In her historical study of the shapes and forms that characterize a specifically "American" construction of beauty, Lois Banner suggests that early-nineteenth-century festivals and celebrations that were borrowed from Europe appealed to the American public's lingering romanticism about medieval pageantry and European monarchy.[3] May Day celebrations, tournaments, and Mardi Gras festivals not only incorporated the pageantry of knights and kings, they also explicitly selected female queens as part of the joy and revelry.[4] Despite the historical and cultural context of Victorian conventions that prohibited public displays of femininity, the selection of queens at these various festivals attracted little protest. Banner argues that this unusual tolerance was the result, in part, of the influence of French analyst Maurice Chevalier, who "pointed out the need for festivals to invoke civic pride and affirm community values. They would complete the national character and 'thrill the fibers of democracy.'"[5] The selection of queens added to this "thrill" precisely because then—as now—middle-class white women were widely considered the moral guardians of the American spirit. And so, as Banner asks, "what better way was there to symbolize enduring community values and future utopian expectations than by choosing women as festival queens?"[6]

It is true that Victorian norms and conventions concerning the public display of women relaxed—so long as this display took place within middle- and upper-class festivals such as May Day celebrations and tournaments. When entrepreneurs conducted contests for profit, there was widespread public outcry over what was considered "appropriate" displays of femininity. In the United States in the mid 1880s, photographic beauty contests—which were originated by P. T. Barnum and quickly adopted by the mass-circulation dailies—appealed to a wider spectrum of classes, including the working class, and consequently were seen as an outrage by the upper strata of society. Beauty contests became popular only with those women and men who frequented the "questionable" sites in which they were held: dance halls, dime museums, carnivals, and fairs.[7] Subsequently, because of the connection with commercial entrepreneurs, the beauty pageant seemed destined for a lifetime of base immorality. It took both the growing middle-class acceptance of popular entertainments and the commitment of the Miss America promoters to invent a spectacle that "successfully combined the features of lower-class carnivals with upper-class festivals and thereby fused energy with refinement in a natural and national setting that celebrated the young American woman as a symbol of national pride, power, and modernity."[8]

In the early twentieth century, commercial culture emerged as a novel form of authority among the middle class, and many women, now situated as consumers of fashion, cosmetics, and other things, discovered a new form of social and cultural acceptance.[9] In fact, the first Miss America pageant was conceived largely as an effort on the part of Atlantic City businessmen to draw attention away from their resort competitor, Coney Island.[10] But the ties of beauty pageants to commercial culture go deeper than tourist gimmicks. The use of women's bodies as an incentive to buy commercial products has much to do with the changing ideologies and behavioral patterns concerning women in the early nineteen hundreds. The first Miss America pageant was held during a time when women were gaining a new acceptance and independence in American society: women's suffrage was granted in 1920, and it was increasingly common for women to appear more independent and defiant, both physically and politically. The traditional behavioral and physical constraints based on Victorian ideology continued to relax, which gave women more freedom and independence in their political and cultural lives. This independence became evident in the legitimation of women's place in the business world, where professional models began to represent commercial products. The image of a beautiful woman fast became essential in most advertisements, from the marketing of patent medicine to the publicity for department stores. Models and chorus girls also helped popularize and legitimate the display of the seminude female body, which entrepreneurs soon realized was a lucrative symbol to sell their products.[11]

As professional modeling and dancing in chorus lines became respectable professions for young middle-class white women, the initial moral outrage regarding the display and judging of women based on their physical appearance eventually diminished. A "proper" image of a beautiful woman was newly considered a symbol of "national pride, power, and modernity," and beauty pageants found their niche as legitimate public events. The first Miss America contest was a "bathing beauty" contest held on the beaches of Atlantic City in September 1921.[12] The idea was conceived by the Hotelmen's Association as a way to keep tourists (and their money) at the resort past Labor Day, the traditional end of summer.[13] Although there were only eight initial contestants, by the next year the number of contestants had increased to fifty-seven, and the best-known beauty pageant in America was officially inaugurated.[14] The Miss America pageant was well on its way to becoming a legitimate and celebrated public event in the United States.

PUSHING TOWARD RESPECTABILITY

The very first Miss America pageant began with the arrival of a man dressed as King Neptune on his seashell barge, surrounded by seven "mermaids." The mermaids were the "Inter-City Beauty Contestants," coming

from cities such as Washington, D.C., Philadelphia, Atlantic City, and Pitts-
burgh. The festival, alternately named "The Atlantic City Pageant" or the
"Super Carnival," lasted several days and included a boardwalk "Rolling
Chair" parade, a night carnival, a costume ball, a beauty contest, and a
"Bathers' Revue" that included men, women, and children.[15]

The first few women to be crowned Miss America were young, ranging in age from fifteen to seventeen years old. The first Miss America, Margaret Gorman, was a winner in a newspaper contest, where readers were
asked to submit pictures of beautiful girls. According to *Sports Illustrated*
writer and former Miss America judge Frank Deford, a member of the original pageant committee, Harry Godshall, randomly chose the initial eight
states and cities that would be represented in 1921.[16] Publicity releases is-
sued weeks before the pageant promised that "[t]housands of the most
beautiful girls in the land, including stage stars and movie queens, will
march in bathing review before judges in the Atlantic City Fall Pageant."[17]
The production was an instant hit, and the second year of competition inspired local preliminary eliminations, prompting an increase from eight
contestants in 1921 to fifty-seven in 1922.[18]

From its inception, the Miss America pageant wrestled with its self-
production and definition; not content to remain a mere part of the Atlantic City festival, the pageant worked to become a sophisticated event
in its own right. In 1922, preliminary eliminations were officially introduced, and the evening gown competition was formally included. Not
only did the number of contestants increase—in 1923 there were seventy-
four, and in 1924 there were eighty-three—but they eventually became recognizably mature and experienced adults. During these early years of the
pageant the rule that only single women could enter was institutionalized. The Atlantic City pageant continued to increase in scope and scale
throughout the 1920s, during which time the judge's panel was comprised
mainly of artists and illustrators, including Norman Rockwell, James
Montgomery Flagg, and Howard Chandler Christy.

From the beginning, the Miss America pageant (a name that was apparently coined in 1921 but not used until much later) was funded through
sponsorship. And despite the Miss America pageant's insistent self-construction as a nonprofit organization, it was clear that the spectacle had
initially been produced to extend Atlantic City's tourist season by draw-

ing more people and more revenue to the "World's Playground." The public display of women in bathing suits proved, as always, to be an extremely profitable venture; as historian A. R. Riverol argues, "Besides the promise of diversion, potential customers were tempted to Atlantic City by the mystique of what proved to be the gimmick with staying power—the Inter-City Beauty Contest."[19] Though the festival's other events continued alongside the beauty contest, the selection of Miss America was clearly the event that the crowds eagerly anticipated.

Unfortunately, it was this apparent enthusiasm, as well as the pageant's questionable association with tourist revenue, that led to its early and, of course, temporary demise. Although Victorian norms and conventions of womanhood and femininity more or less relaxed during the 1920s, other freedoms that women sought—such as the vote and new forms of employment as well as shorter skirts, shorter hair, and other changes in fashion—led to a general nationwide anxiety over the apparently loose morals that middle-class women were adopting, and this anxiety extended to the Atlantic City beauty pageant.[20] In fact, the first sponsors of the pageant, the hotel operators, reversed their initial positive outlook on the spectacle and called for its elimination because they felt its presence led to poor profit: "[The pageant] was condemned by civic and religious organizations for not only being indecent, but also because the contest exploited women for pecuniary purposes, while at the same time corrupting them through rivalry and competition."[21] Before they could even contemplate reinitiating the pageant, Miss America officials needed to conceptualize an event that truly did celebrate "the young American woman as a symbol of national pride, power, and modernity," within a context of solid respectability and moderation.[22]

In 1935, Lenora Slaughter, a member of the St. Petersburg Florida Chamber of Commerce staff, was hired to help produce the pageant. Slaughter had coordinated a highly successful "Parade of the States" in Florida the year before and, based on this success, was hired by the new Miss America executive director, Eddie Corcoran.[23] Slaughter's directorship over the Miss America pageant would last until 1967 and would bring the most significant and lasting changes to the pageant's structure. She was hired specifically to (re)produce the pageant as a respectable and legitimate event. In the 1930s, women's groups (along with hotel operators and other sponsors) attacked the Miss America pageant as a base, immoral spectacle, and Slaughter began her crusade with these organizations. She chose women's groups because she sought to revise the pageant precisely in their terms: on a moral basis. The pageant, insisted Slaughter, needed to be transformed from a "leg-man's" spectacle into a respectable civic venture:

> The director . . . was running these pageants all over the country in amusement parks, fairs, things like that. . . . In the state contests they had the girls parading around in swimsuits in front of the theater before the pageant. It was awful. I wanted to throw out all the cheap promotions. I said I believe I can get civic organizations to run the pageants and we can get the class of girl that we should have.[24]

The 1935 pageant marked the beginning of the Miss America pageant's self-construction as an event that energetically sought the appropriate "class of girl" to represent the nation through the most suspect and "inappropriate" means—displaying the feminine body to the public.

The question was how to overcome this seeming contradiction, how to forge what Robert Allen, in his study of burlesque, has called "the battle between the felt need to uphold the inviolability of pure womanhood and the libidinous pleasurability of watching women onstage whose costumes and demeanor were sure signs of their impurity." Allen details the struggles in the burlesque industry in the late nineteenth century, focusing on both the "loss of respectability that invariably accompanied a woman's appearance in the leg business onstage" as well as the obvious pleasures derived by this same appearance.[25] In many ways, this discussion over the struggles inherent within the burlesque industry mirror the difficulties surrounding the efforts to define the Miss America pageant as a respectable forum for civic virtue.

These efforts were conceptualized and exercised by Slaughter, who instituted specific changes in order to revamp the pageant. In addition to structural changes concerning preliminary eliminations and awards for discrete, separate events, such as the swimsuit competition, Slaughter stipulated new rules that directly influenced and constructed the aura of respectability for which she so desperately worked. In 1937, for example, a rule was instituted that banned all contestants from night clubs, bars, inns, and taverns, an obvious antecedent to the current rule that insists that reigning Miss Americas cannot be present in any establishment that serves alcoholic beverages.[26] Related to this new discipline of surveillance that monitored the pageant, a nightly curfew was established for all contestants, as well as a regulation that promised disqualification if a contestant was seen alone talking to any man—including, incredibly, her father—during pageant week. This particular rule was enforced by a new pageant convention that was to become institutionalized over the years: the hostessing system.

The hostess concept was developed in response to the Federated Women's Clubs of New Jersey. As journalist Susan Dworkin argues, Slaughter initiated the system in the 1930s in response to women's clubs, "which were . . . attacking the Pageant as an obscene and disgusting degradation of American girlhood. Her plan was to out-women's club the women's club."[27] To do this, she solicited the "society ladies" of Atlantic City—many of whom were members of the Quaker elite—and enticed them to chaperone the contestants, which meant spending every waking moment in their presence and overseeing their behavior. Adrian Phillips, one of the earliest members of the pageant board, argued that institutionalizing hostesses served to "protect" the contestants:

> In the 1920's and 1930's the contestants were selected by the newspapers and the radio stations as a circulation promotion gimmick. We had girls who represented amusement parks and so on. You got a weird variety of females. Some were professionals and others were not yet dry behind the ears. Then you began to have this influx of so-called agents, some of them legitimate but most of them questionable. These agents would make prostitutes of the girls, lead them into entertaining in cheap bars. It was pretty bad. It became obvious that we had to take some responsibility here for the protection of the girls. From that need to be protective, we got the hostess situation.[28]

The Miss America pageant rapidly became unlike any other beauty pageant or contest in the country in its relentless policing of femininity and behavior. This was precisely the effect that Lenora Slaughter sought in her crusade to construct the pageant as a rare entertainment venue for "respectable" girls. Histories of the Miss America pageant are riddled with tales from former contestants recalling their fear of Slaughter. Sometimes called "Mother Superior" and sometimes "the dictator," Slaughter assiduously and thoroughly regulated the contestants' behavior, insisting that they call bathing suits "swimsuits" and threatening disqualification for every real and invented mishap, whether it was speaking to one's father or "wearing falsies." As Bess Myerson, Miss America 1945, remembers it, Lenora Slaughter spread fear in all the contestants by warning them that they could be disqualified without notice for any "sinful act" during the entire pageant week. In other words, a contestant could find herself in the competition but have absolutely no hope of victory.[29] Notwithstanding these grim stories, and however she was regarded, it is clear that Lenora Slaughter irrevocably changed the construction of Miss America. She established the pageant as a respectable civic ritual and paved the way for future directors to confidently embrace the pageant as an event dedicated to modest and honorable American womanhood.

One of the most significant changes of the 1930s was the initiation of the talent competition. Introduced in 1938, the talent competition continues to be an important element of the Miss America pageant, and it is often noted that talent is the element that sets the Miss America pageant apart from other beauty contests that are more overtly dedicated to face and form.[30] During this same year, the contestants were required for the first time to represent a state, key city, or geographical region. Before 1938, many contestants represented amusement parks and fairs, so that Miss Coney Island competed alongside Miss New York or Miss California. In yet another effort to sever all connections with places associated in any way with "questionable" morals, Lenora Slaughter formalized the rule of state representation. The pageant became officially limited to young, single women; only women between the ages of eighteen and twenty-eight could enter the pageant, and only then if they had never been married, never divorced, or never had a marriage annulled.[31]

By the end of the 1930s, the current structure of the Miss America pageant had, for the most part, been set in place; the pageant was no longer held in low regard by most of the country, and its popularity was soaring. In fact, in 1938, the crowning of the new Miss America, Marilyn Meseke, was witnessed by approximately 112 million moviegoers in the newsreel *Movietone News*.[32] The Miss America pageant, unlike other feminized spectacles, maintained that its contestants—and especially the winner of the pageant—were about national pride. The pageant, then as now, was thus characterized by a kind of defensiveness; because it looked so much like other public spectacles of femininity, it worked hard to "prove" its difference, and this difference lay in its appeals to respectability and typicality. Miss America has to sell itself as a legitimate public event, one that is entertaining yet much more than that: the pageant self-consciously defined (and continues to define) itself as a showcase for amateur female talent, a symbolic form that demonstrated not glamour and sexuality, but wholesome typicality and respectable femininity.

In her study of working-class English women, Beverley Skeggs argues that respectability, a signifier of class, "would not be something to desire, to prove and to achieve, if it had not been seen to be a property of 'others,' those who were valued and legitimated." She continues by arguing that respectability "is rarely recognized as an issue by those who are positioned with it, who are normalized by it, and who do not have to prove it. Yet for those who feel positioned by and position themselves against the discourse of respectability it informs a great deal of their responses."[33] It was this discourse of respectability that the Miss America pageant positioned itself against through various changes in the format of the event.

In 1940 the pageant became officially known as the Miss America pageant and was incorporated as a nonprofit civic corporation with a board of directors comprised of eighteen business leaders. In 1941 the federal War Finance Department approved of the pageant after Lenora Slaughter promised a nationwide tour complete with Miss America selling war bonds.[34] Miss America 1943, Jean Bartel, embarked on the national tour and sold over one million dollars in Series E bonds.[35] It was on this trip that the idea of offering a scholarship to competitors was first conceptualized; the same logic that went into the hostessing campaign was employed with the scholarship—Slaughter believed that a scholarship would attract an even better "class of girls":

> I never went to college. I wanted to go to college more than anything in the world, but I didn't have the money. Now I wanted my girls to have a scholarship, something constructive. I knew the shine of a girl's hair wasn't going to make her a success in life, and I knew good and well that the prizes Miss America had been getting were a joke . . . a fur coat that couldn't have been worth more than two hundred dollars, the Hollywood contract that they got for fifty dollars

a week—why, they couldn't even live on that in California. To get through to a better class of contestants, I had to raise money enough for education and training, for the opera, to be a judge, a doctor.[36]

In order to offer a scholarship to Miss America, Slaughter had to come up with the money, and in keeping with her ongoing assault on the pageant's initially "questionable" funding, she canceled sponsors such as radio stations, newspapers, and amusement parks and instead solicited funds from the more respectable Junior Chambers of Commerce (Jaycees). She apparently considered the Jaycees' members to be the male counterparts to Miss America and therefore a perfect funding match: "What better than to have the ideal men of America run a pageant for the ideal woman?"[37] After the various Jaycees agreed to sponsor the state pageants, she solicited well-established commercial corporations in an effort to wrest enough money to form a scholarship. She eventually received five thousand dollars from five companies: Catalina Swimsuits, Joseph Bancroft and Sons Company, the Fitch Shampoo Company, Harvel Watches, and the Sandy Valley Grocery Company.[38]

MODERN-DAY MISS AMERICA

The Miss America pageant survived the post World War II years, the so-called golden years of the pageant.[39] It also survived a growing feminist movement, even as it provided the forum for the first major protest of the second-wave feminist movement in the United States.[40] Although the viewership is certainly not what it once was, the second Saturday in September remains a recognizable date to many Americans: it is a time to sit down in front of the television and watch fifty contestants perform and compete for the title of Miss America. The old adage about all little girls wanting to become Miss America may not resonate for a 1990s' audience, but Miss America as an icon of femininity continues to prosper, just as the Mattel Toy Corporation continues to successfully produce its Miss America Barbie doll, although this Barbie is no longer only blonde or brunette, but may also be redhaired or blackhaired or distinctly African American or Latina.

The contemporary structure of the pageant remains fairly consistent with its past: the contestants are judged based on their participation in the swimsuit, evening gown, and talent competitions, as well as the interview portion of the event. An important addition to the contemporary pageant is that each contestant in the Miss America pageant must have an "issue platform." This platform centers around a political, social, or cultural issue to which a contestant dedicates volunteer time and effort. The success the contestants have with their particular issue or its viability as a social cause, which is measured by the size, funding, and longevity of the particular volunteer organizations, is factored in as part of their total score.[41] Most of these issues can be characterized as "women's issues," or rather, issues that are relegated to the private sphere and that entail nurturing, emotionality, and morality: childcare, handicapped children, AIDS and other health issues, literacy, and domestic violence. In this sense, the politics of the Miss America pageant dovetail with early, first-wave liberal feminism in the United States, where, in many cases, voluntarism formed the crux of political activity (indeed, one of the key assumptions behind early feminists in the United States was that women were the moral custodians of society).[42]

The host of the pageant has changed several times over the last decade; gone are the days when Bert Parks, in a simultaneously paternal and sexual tone, would introduce and interview his "ladies." For the first part of the 1990s, Regis Philbin and Kathie Lee Gifford, hosts of a popular daytime television talk show, hosted the Miss America pageant. The presence of these popular celebrities give the pageant a "modern" touch. Kathie Lee Gifford, once a pageant contestant herself and still known as "America's Sweetheart," offers genuine testimony to the pageant's claim that this is more than a meat market—she is smart, savvy, and successful. Contemporary Miss Americas remain public figures; during their one year "reigns" they travel up to twenty thousand miles per month, visiting various states, attending public events, and speaking about their platforms. Indeed, much of the year is spent attempting to situate Miss America as distinctly different from other beauty queens. Whether Miss America is speaking with former first lady Barbara Bush on literacy, or advocating AIDS awareness, or calling attention to the nation's problems with domestic abuse, she consistently and forcefully establishes herself as an icon of respectability, someone much more than a mere beauty queen.

SCHOLARSHIP PROGRAMS VERSUS "BOOBS AND BOUNCE" PAGEANTS: THE CHOICE OF MISS AMERICA

Although Miss America is certainly the U.S. beauty pageant with the longest and most well-known history, the Miss USA pageant, the affiliate pageant to the Miss Universe competition, is also well-established in popular culture. The Miss Universe pageant was created by Catalina Swimsuits in response to Yolande Betbeze's (Miss America 1951) refusal to pose in a swimsuit—a swimsuit that, coincidentally, was supplied by Catalina. Although Lenora Slaughter supported her decision—after all, it was yet another step toward shifting the pageant's reputation from a "cheesecake competition" to a respectable showcase—Catalina Swimsuits responded to what they regarded as Miss America's prudishness by withdrawing their sponsorship from the pageant. The president of Catalina at the time, E. B. Stewart, created a new pageant that was initially called Miss United Nations until Universal-International joined Stewart in his venture and the pageant became Miss Universe.[43]

From the beginning, the Miss Universe pageant constructed itself in entirely different ways from the Miss America program. Perhaps most significantly, the Miss Universe pageant never claimed to be anything but a beauty pageant, and a commercial enterprise at that; indeed, as Deford points out, "It was declared [by the Miss Universe pageant] that beauty was the girls' 'only talent,' and each U.S. entrant—33,000 in 42 states—was required to purchase a Catalina suit."[44] For the pageant that "makes no bones as to what it really is,"[45] there was none of the complex architecture of respectability that Lenora Slaughter was so instrumental in constructing, no pretensions toward talent or education, and no ambitious expectations as to future careers. The Miss USA pageant eventually became a subsidiary of the Miss Universe pageant, and the two U.S. pageants—Miss America and Miss USA—remain, as they began, in competition with each other.

Despite this competition, it is clear that the Miss America pageant sets itself apart from the Miss USA pageant. The political and economic context or complex infrastructure of the Miss America pageant that Slaughter helped to create situates the pageant in very different ways from Miss USA. The Miss America pageant's status as a nonprofit civic ritual, rather than merely another commercial venture in which women's bodies are on constant display, also distinguishes it from most other popular cultural forms. And although both pageants make the claim that the contestant chosen each year best represents the "ideal American woman," the Miss America pageant is more politically dedicated to constructing the ideal female subject as she is situated in American culture. As the pageant itself claims, the members of the "pageant family" are "citizens who value good community projects and who, above all, believe in the youth of America. They understand the importance of affording young women a 'showcase' to display their talents—to voice their opinions and their ambitions—and to gather together and share a mutual experience which will increase their poise and their self-confidence."[46] The Miss America program loudly and relentlessly insists on the primacy of its scholarship agenda; indeed, it currently enjoys the status of being the largest scholarship program for women in the United States. Every contestant competing in the Miss America pageant must demonstrate concrete evidence that her ultimate goal is to be an educated woman, and each contestant must either already be enrolled in a college or university, or be preparing to enroll. The winning contestants are well rewarded for their commitment: the winner of the Miss America pageant receives a thirty-five thousand dollar scholarship (to be used only for formal education), the first runner-up receives twenty thousand dollars, the second runner-up receives fourteen thousand, the third runner-up receives eleven thousand, and the fourth runner-up receives eight thousand. In all, every year over eighteen million dollars are available to young women at the local, state, and national levels of the pageant.[47]

In contrast, the Miss USA pageant offers the winner a comparable amount of money, but it is disbursed in both cash and prizes that include a car and a fur coat. A contestant's decision to participate in one system or the other is informed by a clear understanding of the different goals and expectations of the two pageants. For example, one woman I interviewed commented on her decision only to enter Miss America-affiliated pageants or those sponsored by scholarship money:

> The first [pageant] I decided to take up the offer was the Miss American Co-Ed pageant, and the reason I decided on that one was because it was heavily weighted on interview, you had to have a certain GPA

[Grade Point Average] to get into the competition, and the reward
was scholarship money to the winner. So, I thought it was a little bit
different than what I like to call the "boobs and bounce" pageants,
where they did care about the person inside. They were looking
for poise and appearance as well as intelligence and someone
who communicates sufficiently.[48]

As this contestant demonstrates, there is clearly a great deal at stake for
the contestants regarding their association with either the Miss USA or
the Miss America pageant. Those women who participate in both tracks
are called "crossovers" by other participants, and it is more common for
a contestant to stick with one type of pageant or another.[49]

Another important difference between the two pageant systems is, as
mentioned, the issue "platform" that is required by the Miss America
pageant. The Miss USA pageant has no such requirement, and the substance of the Miss USA interview segment focuses much more on a contestant's specific career goals and vague ideals. The Miss USA pageant,
however, does spend more actual stage time on the interview competition. Rather than one lengthy question and answer period, there are three
separate interview "events," including the "judge's questions." This is a
competition staged among the top five finalists: each contestant chooses
a judge's name from a bowl, and that particular judge asks the contestant
a preformulated question. The final interview event in the Miss USA
pageant occurs in the last minutes of the pageant, when the top three finalists are each separately asked the same question (while the other two stand
in a sound-proofed cubicle). Their score on that final question determines
their place as second runner-up, first runner-up, and Miss USA.

A final important contextual difference between the Miss America and
the Miss USA pageants is the political economy in which these events are
embedded. Miss USA, along with Miss Universe, formerly owned by
Universal, a private, for-profit entertainment corporation, changed ownership in the 1980s to yet another entertainment corporation, Madison
Square Gardens, Inc., and has since changed again, and is now owned
by Donald Trump and his partners.[50] Miss USA is constructed according
to an entertainment tradition with an emphasis on spectacle and display
and has a "game-show" or "quiz-show" quality to the final round, complete with the heightened suspense of an audience watching the contes-

tants squirm. In contrast, Miss America is its own corporation—the Miss America Program—and is nonprofit and organized as well as directed by volunteers. Its commitment to voluntarism and education construct the Miss America pageant as both a more plausible and a more convincing site for the production of the liberal, female subject, as well as a more complicated and complex popular cultural form.

MAINTAINING NONPROFIT STATUS: VOLUNTEERS AND SPONSORS

The Miss America pageant uses its nonprofit status as a strategic defense against pageants such as Miss USA and as a major justification of its claim to be about "brains not beauty." The historical assumption that "money corrupts" holds as true for the Miss America pageant as for most other forms of popular culture. In fact, Frank Deford, a former Miss America judge, believes that the reliance on volunteer labor is the "salvation of the institution." In Deford's words: "If some promoter could come into town and make a quick profit on a beauty show, it would be all too obvious in most communities that there was a high correlation between sex and remuneration—and also, ultimately, surely, municipal depravity. Under such a light, pageants could not long survive, for respectable girls would not enter them, and respectable citizens would not support them."[51] Many of Lenora Slaughter's early efforts to establish the Miss America pageant as a respectable venture had to do with obtaining the "appropriate" kind of funding. "Appropriate" in this case translated as volunteer labor. Not only is the entire event produced by volunteer labor, but those companies and corporations that provide the necessary sponsorship for needed elements such as televisual production costs, the rental of Convention Hall, and judges' fees are well-established, reputable organizations such as Clairol, Chevrolet, and Cheer.

Sponsorship begins on a local level: contestants participating in local and regional pageants who cannot afford entry fees, clothing, and other accessories solicit sponsors for support.[52] Funding for the actual pageant production is partially obtained by selling tickets to the pageant itself, or selling raffle tickets for prizes donated by local companies.[53] In addition, the sponsors buy advertising space in the pageant program, where individual companies are visually depicted alongside photographs of "their girl." Finally, many of the contestants' families support them. As Alice, a nineteen-year-old pageant contestant commented, "Sometimes people are very wealthy, they have wealthy parents, a lot of times it's easier . . . depending on their positions at work, sometimes their company will sponsor them if their company has money for that type of thing. Usually it's tax deductible, so they're more likely to do it. I would say that a lot of [contestants] either have their parents or themselves as wealthy enough to do it."

Unfortunately for Alice, she did not happen to be in this position. In order to enter the pageant world, she needed to find a reliable funding source. For the first pageant in which she participated, the Miss American Co-Ed competition, the entry fee was 350 dollars. Although her parents supported her emotionally in her endeavor, they could not support her financially, so she traveled to various car dealerships and solicited sponsorship. The entry fee, however, is merely the beginning of an extremely complex system of required fees, as Alice described:

> Eventually, you get into big money, but when you get into like
> the Miss America pageant, if you win a city pageant or a regional
> pageant, they'll pay for your fee into the Miss California pageant,
> and the Miss California pageant will pay for the entry into the Miss
> America pageant, and usually if they don't finance it fully they'll at
> least finance it partially, like an evening gown. Because the original
> expense of 350 dollars doesn't count the swimsuit competition or
> the evening gown, and they have gowns that are upwards of one
> thousand dollars, so there's a lot of money involved and by the
> time you get to the Miss America pageant, there's a lot of money
> to be won, but they've invested so much time and money into win-
> ning that pageant. And you don't know how many times they've
> tried to win the regional before they get to the state.

Learning to navigate her way through this complicated arrangement of funding sources seemed an entirely acceptable process for Alice—as long as the pageant itself had a solid reputation and was on the "up-and-up." In fact, as I detail more fully in other chapters, most of the women I interviewed made a clear distinction between those pageants that are profit-oriented or "in it for the money" and those pageants, like Miss America, that seem to have a more altruistic goal of being "in it for the girls." Alice was particularly concerned with this distinction; several times during our interview she clarified exactly how funding was obtained and who was responsible for offering it. She was particularly wary of those pageants who were "in it for the money." She explained:

> And you have to be really careful, because there are a lot of those that are asking 350 to 400 dollars, and there's a ticket requirement, you have to sell so many tickets at twenty dollars each in order to be in the pageant after that. And what they provide for the girls in terms of prizes, you know that they're not putting all that money into the actual pageant and they do it for a profit. And a little bit of profit is fine if that's what they do to put on the pageant, but if they're doing it solely just for profit and the girls aren't getting anything out of it . . .

Nothing resolves this dilemma in a more perfect way than an educational scholarship. One reason that Miss America continues to successfully construct itself as something other than "just" a beauty pageant is the very real fact that, unlike the Miss USA pageant, Miss America officials cannot survive financially based on their involvement in the event, so they must be in it for something else. It depends on the official whether that "something else" is promoting a "higher class of girls," seeking an appropriate national representative, or genuinely desiring to see more women in education. What remains constant is that, in terms of financial gain, being the chief executive officer of the Miss America program is a thankless job.

LOCAL, REGIONAL, AND STATE PAGEANTS

For most Americans, the Miss America pageant is solely comprised of the two-hour televised production of the pageant, a competition that involves only the top ten finalists. Sprinkled throughout the production are vague references to the week-long competition that determined these top ten, but the "big event" entails only the competition between ten women. What the program also does not make visible are the thousands of local, regional, and state pageants that precede the Miss America pageant—including the several hundred thousand young women who participated in these events. In order to reach that coveted place on the stage in Atlantic City, each contestant must first win a local or a regional pageant, and then a state pageant.

The Miss America pageant grants a state franchise to one "responsible" organization in each state—usually the Jaycees. That particular organization then conducts the state finals in accordance with all Miss America pageant rules and regulations, including having a judge's panel comprised only of Miss America-certified judges. For the state pageant, part of accepting the responsibility of conducting state finals includes the reciprocal enfranchising of "responsible" organizations within the state to sponsor official local or regional pageants. Thus, although there are hundreds of pageants produced in San Diego County each year, only those winners at local pageants enfranchised by the Miss San Diego pageant can participate in the Miss America-affiliated pageant. And there may be several Miss San Diegos—Miss San Diego County, Miss Greater San Diego, Miss Fairest of the Fair—but only the "official" queen can participate in the Miss California pageant, which culminates in the Miss America pageant.[54]

The women I interviewed were all involved in local or regional pageants, with the exception of three victorious contestants who went on to state and national pageants. Depending on the region, the pageants I observed were either constructed as elaborate productions or as mundane civic events. Most of the Miss America regional pageants—pageants where, for example, contestants representing a particular zip code in the city of San Diego would compete—took place in high school auditoriums. Again, depending on the region's funding and commitment to the pageant, a local dance instructor will typically choreograph the event, and interested community members or members of the local Jaycees will assist in directing it.[55] Most of these smaller pageants draw a limited audience consisting of friends and families of the contestants with the required one or two visiting "queens."[56] At the city level, the pageants become more elaborate, but even here the production quality is usually poor to mediocre; at the Miss San Diego pageant in December 1993, the sound quality during the talent segment was so poor that the audience could not hear the accompanying music. At this level, when many of the contestants discover their "talent" only weeks before the pageant, and when the performer needs to rely more on the music than her own voice, it is especially humiliating when the music is inaudible. However, various people involved in pageants—from the contestants to the directors and producers—seemed to take most mishaps in stride; it is clear that what motivates the preliminary, local pageants is the promise of spectacle held by the more nationally significant state and national pageants.

For the Miss America preliminaries, the rules and regulations of the local pageants exactly follow those at the national level. The rules of a local San Diego pageant state that contestants:

> must be female, single, have never been married, never been a mother, and must be of good moral character.
>
> must not have been convicted of a crime of moral turpitude.
>
> must not have appeared nude in any photo, movie, video, publication or event and must agree not to appear in such during the year of competition in the Fairest of the Fair/Miss San Diego County competition.[57]

As these rules illustrate, pageant contestants must never have had a child and must be single in order to have a "good moral character." In other words, in order to be considered a good or proper "representative," contestants must not bear evidence of having had sex. Pageant rules and regulations also reinforce a definition of American women as moral, self-sacrificing, noncompetitive, and unambitious. But to be a beauty pageant contestant *is* to compete, and to desire to win. The ambition of beauty pageant contestants must be veiled so that they remain well within the boundaries established by the pageant's rules and regulations. Contestants need a cover story to explain their ambition, an "alibi" that tells of voluntarism, an unshakable moral foundation, and strict behavioral codes.[58] This cover story is necessary both to mask and to dilute the ruthlessness that often occurs in the competitive atmosphere of the pageant. One contestant describes the tension of maintaining this illusion: "It's extremely competitive. You think that you just go up there, and it's no big deal, and usually when I enter, it's like 'we're all winners' and you try to have that attitude, or we wouldn't be here, but by the end, you really want to win. And there are girls out there that will slash their hose, I've been in

pageants where they are stuffing their bras, so there are all types of contestants out there."[59] This woman assures herself—and me—that there is
a specific "attitude" required to enter a beauty pageant, a particular moral
character that says "we're all winners." But of course, only one woman
can win, and the implications of this reality threaten the perceived conception of beauty queens—hence the need for and constant maintenance
of a cover story.

In terms of rules, perhaps the most important concern at the local level
is the authenticity of a contestant's address and the length of time she has
lived there. Many districts will not accept applications from local college
students if the woman has not lived in the town or city for a certain length
of time before entering school; competing in a pageant while living in the
city less than the required time is called "state-hopping" or "crown-chasing."[60] Another contestant I interviewed related her story of a "scandal"
that frequently occurs: when she won a local event, her first runner-up
accused her of living in a neighboring zip code. This "scandal" grew to
enormous proportions—as Mary tells it:

> My first runner-up had been in [the pageant] three years in a row
> and had not won and she was really resentful towards me because I
> had just come in, I was new, I had raised the most money, and I took
> it all away. I took everything. And she was just resentful. . . . There
> was a large scandal with my first runner-up. . . . [She] learned of my
> address and she didn't know about the maps, and her mother—we
> all thought she was on drugs—went to the fair board, threatened to
> go to the press, told the fair board that [this zip code] was not going
> to be represented, if her daughter was not going to be in the pageant
> she'd protest, and put it in the press. The title was rightfully her
> daughter's, etc. . . . [This] had come out two weeks before [the pag-
> eant] and she had sent a letter to the Kiwanis threatening to go to
> the newspapers, and you know how newspapers eat that up.

Of course, part of this "scandal" has to do with marketing: if community businesses donate time and money to the pageant, they want to be
sure that the person crowned queen will reciprocate by advertising for
them in the community. As Mary's tale reveals, the connection between
commerce and a definition of community for the contestants is an important one. Although the pageants attempt to both construct and maintain a definition of *community* that best suits their contestants, there is no

actual community in the way pageants define them. Zip codes are the best means the contestants have for determining such boundaries. As a marketing device, zip codes work to establish other kinds of boundaries: merchants decide where to advertise and establish franchises according to the profitability implied by the demographics of the zip code zone. Nonetheless, this episode presented itself—and was presented—to Mary as a very real scandal, one that hurt her in the later judging process. During her interview, she commented that she had been told that the judges at her pageant were instructed not to choose her as the winner because the pageant "cannot be involved in a scandal." Despite the fact that the entire scandal consisted of misinformation about a zip code, it took on monumental proportions because it dared to question the authenticity of not only Mary's representative status but also her own personal integrity.

The sense of community that seems so palpable each year in the Miss America pageant is more slippery for the local and regional pageants to keep hold of. Various efforts are made to project an image of a particular community to the local pageant audiences—for example, another contestant defined the community for which she was a queen in a similarly commercial fashion. When asked what it meant to be representative of a particular community, she answered, "You have to know a lot about the city. When I was Miss X County, I knew exactly how many pools there were in X, and how many golf courses, and things like that."[61] Despite the claims that the Miss America pageant and its preliminaries represent a deep community life and representation, at the local level, the definition of a community is primarily formed according to its zip code and its commercial consequences.

THE "OBJECTIVE" PROCESS OF JUDGING: SCORING FEMININITY

In a standard American beauty pageant, women are judged according to their performance in several categories: the personal, offstage interview; the talent, swimsuit, and evening gown competitions; and the "spontaneous," onstage interview.[62] The judges in the Miss America pageant are usually solicited from the entertainment and communication fields. In the early years of the pageant, the judges were primarily artists and illustrators, in part because such men—and they were all men—were considered to have the best "eye" for the beautiful feminine form. In more recent years, efforts have been made to attract judges who represent the various facets of the pageant.[63] In other words, there is usually at least one judge who represents a classical musical tradition (commonly involved in the dance, opera, or orchestra fields) so that the talent portion is adequately evaluated by other than popular standards. Several judges from the various entertainment fields are also seated to ensure that the winning contestant can appropriately represent herself in the public eye, and at least one former Miss America contestant or pageant director is included, a person who apparently can best judge the "whole" contestant's ability to serve as a proper pageant representative. To give an idea of the composition of a local pageant's judge's panel, the 1994 Miss San Diego panel consisted of the following professionals: a field director for the Miss California pageant, a professional writer and public relations executive, a president of a local Jaycee, a former Miss California contestant, and a Miss California Travelling Companion.[64] As the pageants become more nationally significant, it is easier to entice famous celebrities to serve as judges; the Miss America pageant always includes a currently popular television or musical star as one of its judges. Deford argues that a "majority coalition at Miss America is virtually always formed by the producers, actors, singers, and dancers. There are few educators, and virtually no peers of the contestants."[65] The celebrity status of the judges ensures their unquestioned authority and credibility, and it is understood that those best qualified to evaluate a contestant's ability to present herself in public or speak publicly are those who have had personal success in these and related fields.

The actual judging is widely considered by both contestants and pageant producers to be simultaneously an arbitrary and a clearly calculated process. In fact, there are gestures made in both the subjective and the objective directions: despite the universalization of beauty norms and standards, the definition of beauty is acknowledged to be constantly in flux and often shifting. The judging, however, is determined based on an "objective" numerical scale, in which each contestant is judged in different categories. In the preliminaries, the judges usually vote for the top five contestants in each stage division—swimsuit, talent, evening gown, and interview. These scores, which determine the finalists, are then discarded, and the judges begin anew with the top ten. The final five contestants are then ranked according to their answers to an onstage "spontaneous" interview question.

The necessarily subjective quality of pageant judging is often invoked as one of the most common ways to console a losing contestant. A sentiment frequently expressed at pageant time is the reminder that "with a different group of judges, a different girl would win every time."[66] As Alice explained during her interview:

> You never know. It's all the disposition—what that person thinks, what they think is beauty, what they think is talent, and it's all subjective—you know, there's no scantron to fill out the answers for these. You really have no idea. They could be sick that day, and look at you right before they sneeze, and get mad at you because they sneezed, and so you have no idea about their dispositions, or the choice of judges. It could be a different winner every time.

As I mentioned, this sentiment is expressed unproblematically alongside the notion that the judging is a fairly "objective" process—the fact that the judging process is considered subjective (because beauty itself is subjective) does not indicate that the process is completely arbitrary. There are rules and regulations for judges, and the Miss America judges must be "certified." According to a local pageant director, this means the judge must attend training classes and receive a judging certificate according to the regulations of the Miss America Program; in other words, his or her vision must be "trained" to recognize the appropriate markers of femininity needed for a Miss America. And in the early days of the pageant there were strict point systems for the judges in an effort to determine which contestant was genuinely the most beautiful. For example, in the 1923 Miss America pageant, there were seventeen artist judges, including Norman Rockwell, James Montgomery Flagg, and Howard Chandler Christy. The judges evaluated contestants according to a hundred-point body breakdown:

construction of head:	15 points
eyes:	10
hair:	5
nose:	5
mouth:	5

facial expression:	10
torso:	10
legs:	10
arms:	10
hands:	10
grace of bearing:	10

Although this system proved to be too confining for the judges, it is clear that it is the ancestor to today's numerical scoring.[67] And, although there is now only one category for "body"—the swimsuit competition—the "grace of bearing" category seems to be reflected in both the interview and the evening gown competition.

In order to further encourage the "objectivity" or the "science" of judging, the televised production of both the Miss USA and the Miss America pageants includes a sidebar where one of the hosts explains the judging system to the audience. As each finalist in the Miss America pageant parades down the runway during the swimsuit competition, her offstage interview score is superimposed on the screen. In the Miss USA pageant, immediately following each competition, there is a breakdown of the scores of the top ten finalists as well as an accompanying analysis offered by the previous year's Miss USA.[68]

Clearly, the judge's panel is intended to be somehow representative of society; after all, the woman selected as Miss America apparently "represents" the nation, so the judges must adequately mirror that nation. Interestingly, whether they do has rarely been a question for public debate; although some contestants complain about the favoritism of the judges, and although there were many in-house rumors about the pressures Lenora Slaughter placed on judges to select her favorite contestant, these sentiments usually escape media attention. Instead, like many of the various facets of "science"—whether popular science or academic branches of science—the objectivity of the judges is unquestioned, and the anachronism of having a panel of men and women "judge" a woman who performs before them is rarely acknowledged, except by pageant critics.

A typical Miss America pageant is a blend of components borrowed from other traditional public events: the talent competition is in the grand tradition of carnivals, and pageants clearly resonate with parades through both the array of women on stage and the actual parading of bodies (see plate 1). They are also reminiscent of sporting events, because competition is always their focal point.[69] What is clear is that from its inception, the Miss America pageant went to great lengths to establish itself as something other than a beauty contest, something different than "girl-watching." These efforts have truly paid off: the Miss America pageant, despite criticism and ridicule, remains an important civic ritual in the United States and continues to be a vital source of knowledge for many young women about the disciplinary practices of femininity.[70] The various interventions made by Lenora Slaughter and others—instituting a chaperone and hostessing program, installing various rules that regulate the "respectability" of the contestants, and, most important, institutionalizing the scholarship program—maintain a particular construction of femininity and American womanhood.

The pageant, situated intractably within commercial culture, becomes what Robert Goldman and Stephen Papson have called a "legitimation ad" for a particularly idealized vision of the nation. Like advertisements that legitimate corporate control and power, the Miss America pageant addresses general themes about the relationship between a feminized morality and the public trust. Like other corporate strategies, the Miss America corporation offers its viewers-consumers a slick package and spends a great deal of time on spin control. In doing so, the Miss America pageant both simplifies and typifies its version of femininity and offers its definition couched in "taken-for-granted assumptions about the arrangements of our lives and about what we value."[71] The rhetoric of ardent sincerity and moralism adopted by the Miss America pageant attempts to convince the American public that its spectacle is about reaffirming values—it is not about girl watching, or base sexuality, or even beauty in a glamorous sense, but is rather about typicality and respectability. The Miss America crown is thus held up to be supremely attainable; this crown, like commercial success, like the American dream, is there for those who try. The Miss America pageant slips between the individual and the image—it is all-inclusive and depicts a national community of which we are all part.

CHAPTER 2 ANATOMY
OF A BEAUTY PAGEANT

THE SWIMSUIT COMPETITION

> Most of [swimsuit competition rehearsal] is dedicated
> to the choreography part of it, but they do teach you
> how to walk, they like you to wear really high heels for
> some reason, and nude shoes because they make your
> legs look longer, and when you walk you're supposed to
> take one foot exactly in front of the other, you're taking
> large steps, but with one foot exactly in front of the other
> so you're walking in a line. And you keep your shoulders
> down in back and your neck up.
>
> DIANA,
> *Pageant contestant*

> The act is broken down into its elements; the position of
> the body, limbs, articulations is defined; to each move-
> ment are assigned a direction, an aptitude, a duration;
> their order of succession is prescribed. Time penetrates
> the body and with it all the meticulous controls of power.
>
> MICHEL FOUCAULT

In the Miss America pageant, 15 percent of each contestant's total score is
determined by her participation in the swimsuit competition (see plate
2).[1] During this competition, each contestant traces the same prescribed
figure eight, wearing a standardized "competitive" swimsuit—a suit that
is designed never to come in contact with any body of water. The labeling of the suit as "competitive" signals to the wearer that it is to be used
only in competition; in fact, it is suggested that contestants never wear
their swimsuits outdoors, because the climate might fade or otherwise
damage the suit.[2] As they trace the figure eight, soft music plays in the

background, with a voice-over of either the master of ceremonies reading a short biography of the contestant, or the women's own disembodied voice relating personal information. These voice-overs are precisely timed so that the last word is spoken at the moment of the contestant's last step. This coordination between voice and step produces a homogenized, seamless display of women parading down a runway, and judges are asked to evaluate each contestant based on this meticulously practiced routine.

In pageant culture, this disciplined routine is seen as evidence of "physical fitness." It is this commitment to being physically fit—routinely translated from current standards of a feminine ideal—that has compelled feminists to target the swimsuit competition as perhaps the most damaging moment of the entire beauty pageant.[3] Indeed, the sight of ten or twelve female bodies lined up to be judged and evaluated according to how closely they approximate this ideal provides a stunning illustration of the objectification and the resulting commodification of women's bodies.[4] But interestingly, feminists are not the only ones to voice critiques of the swimsuit competition. Pageant contestants themselves have questioned the validity of this event within the Miss America scholarship pageant—prompting the Miss America corporation to sponsor an unprecedented event immediately before the 1994 pageant: the pageant commission asked American viewers to call a toll free number and vote whether the seventy-three-year old pageant should retain the swimsuit competition as a part of the judging process. An overwhelming 73 percent of the viewing audience voted that the swimsuit competition was a crucial factor in the decision-making process leading to the crowning of Miss America.[5]

The pageant commission's unusual decision to allow viewers to determine the fate of the event made the pageant and its legitimacy as a national cultural form vulnerable. But it also managed to market or to commodify the ambivalence structuring the swimsuit competition, a move that generated increased publicity and further legitimized the pageant as an event that celebrates the minds, not bodies, of the contestants. The Miss America pageant became "our" event in a much more profound sense than ever before, and the call-in vote implied that the audience is the "real" judge of the pageant. In other words, the contradictory presence of the swimsuit competition within a larger spectacle whose self-described true aim is to give college scholarships to smart, talented women was acknowledged by the pageant commission, who asked the public: Do we need it? This reliance on the legitimacy of consumer sovereignty preempted suggestions that the pageant was sexist and close-minded, and the American public answered: Yes, we do need it.

With this strategy in place, the stories circulating about contestants who felt uneasy about the swimsuit competition were refigured as predictable complaints about a perhaps "uncomfortable" but necessary element to the Miss America pageant. And so, given this relentless self-definition of the Miss America pageant, it is no surprise that some of the more recent contestants quite keenly feel the hypocrisy of the swimsuit competition. Leanza Cornett, Miss America 1993, went public with her complaints and questions regarding the "appropriateness" of the swimsuit competition within the pageant, and one woman I interviewed, Grace, winner of a California Junior Miss pageant, refrained from entering the Miss America program because that pageant includes the swimsuit competition as part of the total score.[6] In fact, she decided to stop participating in pageants, despite her vast success, because she could not bring herself to compete in a swimsuit. For her, the transition from Junior Miss pageants (limited to sixteen-year-old and seventeen-year-old girls) to the more well-known and even more lucrative pageants that include swimsuit competitions is framed in terms of a "loss of innocence" that resonates with the transition from girlhood to womanhood and the accompanying relentless focus on the woman's body:

> But I couldn't bring myself to parading in a bathing suit in front
> of. . . . I have a hard enough time at the beach, let alone in front of
> big crowds. So I guess Junior Miss is maybe the baby of the pageants,
> you know it's not so extreme where I don't have to trounce around,
> it's more trying to make the girls . . . innocent and young and keep
> that cutesy [look]. . . . It was mainly just your stage appearance and
> how you projected yourself and your talent, and that's what I liked.
> I liked the fact that it wasn't focused so much on the women's body.[7]

The notion that this contestant could not "bring herself to parading in a bathing suit" in front of both a live and a mass-mediated audience signals her resistance to commodifying her body in this particular way; it also signals her resistance to the spectacle of the swimsuit competition, where her unease at "trouncing" around in "front of big crowds" demonstrates her unwillingness to watch herself in the mass media, even as she participates in watching the media itself.

But why the dilemma for Grace, Cornett, and others? After all, isn't the Miss America contest a beauty pageant? It is, but the disjuncture between beauty and scholarship, or body and brain, and the apparent incompatibility between these two subject positions, destabilizes one of the stories that beauty pageants tell: the transformation of women into objects for viewing. As the contestant pointedly noted, unlike the talent competition, the swimsuit competition is not a performance but a *spectacle:* it is about visual consumption of bodies, about homogeneity, and about containment. It is a spectacle of "femininity" on display. The nonspeaking female subject on display—the contestant—disciplines her femininity through the precision of her movements, and the intensity of her smile functions as an indicator of her accessibility and her availability. Again, unlike the talent portion of the pageant, which is a performance of personality, artistry, and female subjectivity, the contestants' participation in the swimsuit competition is almost totally devoid of subjectivity except in the sense that the body is read as a marker for a particular kind of feminine subject.

I witnessed a clear demonstration of the spectacular nature of the swimsuit competition at a local San Diego pageant. In this pageant, the contestants were asked to do the unthinkable: they were required to give a short autobiographical speech while participating in the swimsuit competition. In this particular case, the discourse of respectability that structured the pageant and the act of speaking and displaying one's body at the same time was almost too much to bear for these contestants. Each contestant was required to perform their disciplined figure eight in a swimsuit, but instead of finishing the competition by walking offstage, they ended up in front of a microphone where they then gave their speech. In most cases, the contestant was so visibly embarrassed and uncomfortable with giving the speech that words were stuttered, sentences were forgotten, and, in one case, the contestant completely froze and could not give her speech at all.[8] The immediate contradiction between the acts of performing subjectivity through speaking and performing femininity through displaying the body proved to be too much for most of the contestants to negotiate simultaneously. The humiliation of those contestants who attempted this feat is quite instructive. Witnessing this failure helped me to understand the logic of the fragmented pageant, for only when the speaking subject is distinguished from the speaking body in time and space can the contradiction be successfully hidden and negotiated.

At another local pageant, the swimsuit competition required the contestants to walk a short figure eight while the master of ceremonies (MC) gave their name. However, the MC initially misunderstood his instructions, and the first contestant was forced to remain frozen on stage while the MC read an entire biography of her. After the first contestant, he realized his gaffe and continued by merely reading the names of each contestant. The first contestant, however, was furious and felt that the MC had ruined her chances.[9] This seems odd. Why would remaining on stage—and thus receiving more "airtime" than the rest of the contestants—do anything but *increase* one's chances? Unfortunately for this contestant (as she was well aware), the amount of time spent on stage not moving silenced her too much and worked to "thingify" her completely. The swimsuit competition is only successful if timed well to display the body without dwelling on it. The totally silenced, objectified woman is not what the pageants desire as a representative. Rather, they seek women who are skilled in the ability to let their body speak for them, but who are also expected to speak for themselves. Too much in either direction results in disaster.

These experiences are humiliating precisely because they work against the pageant's attempt at constituting the female liberal subject by compartmentalizing different "selves" into one whole self that is appropriate to represent "American womanhood." By both speaking and displaying the body, two "selves" are brought together that have fundamentally conflicting effects—both on the audience and on the contestant herself. The swimsuit competition works in the face of internal conflict and controversy precisely because it denies her a chance to speak and thus contains and controls (at least for the most part) the contestant's potential humiliation.

However, having said this, the intention of this chapter is not to enter the well-documented debates over whether the swimsuit competition is good or bad for young American women. Rather, the aim of this chapter is to explore the ambivalence that is both reflected within and produced by the swimsuit competition, as the preceding examples demonstrate.

That is, I suggest that this ambivalence is not only about the actual swim-suit event itself but is part of a much more complex and contradictory set of meanings offered by this event and other contemporary concepts of femininity. These meanings shift and take particular shape over a period marked by contested definitions of racial and gendered identities, shift-ing conceptions of the feminine body, and the growth of consumer soci-ety and commodified popular cultural forms. Specifically, I suggest that the swimsuit competition both mirrors and invents standards for the "av-erage" American body (an average that is inextricable from current fem-inine ideals) and that these standards are and have always been connected to histories of nationalism and racial purity. The swimsuit competition offers evidence to the Miss America audience that the spectacle of it all, the bodies parading in front of a panel of judges, is in fact about feminine achievement—or, more precisely, the achievement of femininity. Part of what makes Miss America such an appropriate national figure in late-twentieth-century capitalist culture is this achievement, paired with the appearance of an appropriately raced and gendered body and a relent-less commitment to consumption and commodity culture.

Two questions underlie this chapter: What part does the swimsuit com-petition play in the construction of national identities for American women? How does the swimsuit competition serve to "crystallize some of the predicaments of femininity and feminine bodies in late-twentieth century North America?"[10] To get at these questions, we need to consider the swimsuit competition as an instance of the commodification of gen-der, where gender itself becomes a commodity.[11] The swimsuit competi-tion can be understood as offering one particular—but nonspecific—brand of gendered body: like national advertising, gender as it is produced and offered by the Miss America pageant is appealing in its universality, its nonspecific qualities, and its egalitarian promise. In this way, the bodies of Miss America contestants are structured using logic similar to another less animated but no less complicated or contested American icon, Bar-bie. Jacqueline Urla and Alan C. Swedlund, in their study of Barbie dolls, argue that "playing with Barbie serves not only as a training ground for the production of the appropriately gendered woman, but also as an in-troduction to the kinds of knowledge and social relations one can expect to encounter as a citizen of a post-Fordist economy."[12] Extending their argument to real live, thinking human agents—who are no less idealized—I suggest that participating in the Miss America pageant (either as contestant or as audience member) is a critical element to the production of "appropriately gendered" women and importantly functions as the kind of introduction for which Urla and Swedlund argue, an introduction to the knowledge and social relations that are expected of a national icon, or, at the very least, a U.S. citizen. All of the different events that comprise the Miss America pageant work toward this same goal, but all function differently and through different means.

REGULATING THE BODY

Michel Foucault articulates how bodies are disciplined through complicated and circulating discourses of power that function in particular ways to produce all bodies as "docile" bodies. Despite Foucault's crucial contribution to the formation of individualism and invented notions of the independent body, many feminists have observed that his discussion of bodily discipline does not take into account that gendered bodies are disciplined differently according to disproportionate stakes.[13] Women are *produced* as feminine subjects through disciplinary practices. Disciplinary practices such as dieting and other beauty practices are assumed by most women as femininity; the practice *is* the production.[14] The Miss America pageant, as with all beauty pageants, is clearly embedded within these dominant conventions of femininity. Nancie Martin details the disciplinary routine that contestants must undergo before competing in a local beauty pageant: "Many of them go to charm or beauty school to be instructed in the difficult art of walking in a bathing suit in high heels, which is a never ending chorus of 'Stomach in! Derriere tucked! Relax your shoulders! Look up and out! *Glide!*'"[15] The sheer discipline involved in performing this elaborate act—walking gracefully, not breathing, every muscle in the body tensed, and yet looking extremely cheerful and relaxed (in other words, walking as if one is *not* walking)—is not considered by pageant contestants as some bizarre act of torture, but rather just another step toward a more perfect femininity. In *How to Win Pageants,* Genie Polo Sayles asks contestants these questions: "What does your body communicate about you? Does your body in a swimsuit communicate that you treat your body the best it can be treated? Does it reflect the healthy self-care of self-respect? This is the communication the judges are looking for in a swimsuit."[16] The contestants—as well as the audience and the judges—correctly translate the question of "healthy self-care of self-respect" into "does my body closely resemble the body of the current feminine ideal?" Achieving this ideal demands strong discipline, in any sense of the word.

Practicing the "healthy self-care of self-respect" is a neat way of resolving the ambivalence produced by the faulty logic of the swimsuit competition. Again, the emphasis on education reveals an internal contradiction in this "scholarship program," where winning the money for education requires a strong and disciplined commitment to an industry and ideology that celebrates women not for their minds but for their bodies and appearance. Navigating this contradiction requires intricate processes of justification for appearing in a swimsuit on a public stage. For example, one contestant, Lisa, complained during our interview that most college scholarships are offered on the basis of either strict academic merit or financial need. Her family was not in dire financial need, and her grades were good but not spectacular. So she turned to beauty pageants: "[Pageants are] a good way to get a scholarship, because I couldn't really get any [other] scholarships. . . . So I decided I should try something that I *could* get a scholarship as."[17] This contestant believed that her distinguishing feature is clearly and unproblematically her body. This comment also reveals the deeply entrenched identification that many women have *as* bodies; this woman could get a scholarship as a particular construction, *as a female body.* Sayles gives advice that contributes to this identification: "Many pageant winners are girls who might not have had other opportunities due to limiting circumstances in their lives. They are girls who have only themselves as their asset, but who have the desire to take that basic asset of themselves and to better it."[18] Beauty pageants contribute to this reduction process by asking women to take those "basic assets of themselves"—their bodies—and construct them for display. The pageant illustrates that women's natural "asset" continues to be primarily located in and through the body, whereas men's natural assets include talent, intellect, and entrepreneurial ambition.

Disciplining oneself as a particular kind of body entails the necessary other side to this practice: humiliation. Denying a contestant her voice and requiring her to parade in front of a panel of judges is perhaps one of the most crass and brutal processes of reduction—and, as I mentioned at the beginning of this chapter, there are times when humiliation subverts the logic of competing in this way. In fact, many of my interviews were riddled with stories of embarrassment or humiliation (either inflicted upon themselves or other contestants) when the contestant didn't discipline her body enough: "[The pageant trainers] put you on an exercise program, personal nutritionist, personal trainer, and they are extremely, well, honest. The girl I was in the pageant with . . . was a little overweight, and they would seriously tell her, 'Don't eat that, your thighs are too big,' right there, and they would embarrass her, so she wouldn't eat, because they really wanted her to win, whatever it took."[19] The disciplinary practices involved in the "training" of this contestant not only insist on the conscious refusal to eat, but also involve public humiliation— "whatever it took" to get her to win. Another woman, interviewed during her reign as a beauty queen, confided in me with dismay, "I've gained so much weight since I won my crown!"[20] Yet another contestant offered this insight: "In other pageants I've been in, the girls watch their weight, that's a big thing, unfortunately, that our society has, that they want a thin girl, they don't want, you know [overweight women]. So, a lot of girls watch their weight."[21] Gaining weight during one's reign is indeed a serious offense; in the Miss Texas beauty pageant, if a reigning queen gains more than two pounds, she is given two weeks to take off the weight or relinquish her title.[22] The popular press and tabloids devoted much space and time to Miss Universe 1996, Alicia Machado, who caused great controversy and threats of dismissal over her apparent twenty-pound weight gain during her reign.[23] These women, like most women in American society, practice and produce feminine identity within the boundaries of these kinds of regulatory practices. Weight is one of the most talked-about subjects for pageant hopefuls; when recalling her preparations for the state title, Lex Ann Haughey, Miss Texas 1979, remembered this: "'I wanted to perfect my figure, and in order to lose twenty pounds I swam six hours a day.' That sort of preparation, while admirable, seems like nothing compared to what a state winner has to undergo before going to Atlantic City. After winning Miss Texas, Lex Ann was placed in the care of a weight trainer, who helped her gain back the twenty pounds she had lost—but just in her arms, legs, and back."[24] In fact, regulating the body through the regulation of de-sire and impulse is feminine praxis; it becomes a predominant way of "supporting" young women through the difficult practice of construct-ing femininity. For example, a local pageant newsletter, "The Winning Edge," details the story of Miss San Diego County Teen 1993. Responding to the difficulty of competing with more than fifty other contestants, she explains that "she has all the support any young woman could ever hope for: 'My family, friends, and personal trainer, Pam . . . have all been there for me. In fact, Pam has helped me take one inch off my waist, two inches off my stomach and two inches off my thighs in less than a month.'"[25] The most notable support, at least at the time of the interview, is offered by this contestant's personal trainer and is precisely measured in inches—inches that are removed from waist, stomach, and thighs through strict discipline.

This self-surveillance clearly indicates the constant and consistent dis-play of the female body as a matter of being—to be a woman means to be judged, objectified, and fragmented. In a well-known passage, Sandra Lee Bartky articulates this process: "In the regime of institutionalized hetero-sexuality woman must make herself 'object and prey' for the man: It is for him that these eyes are limpid pools, this cheek baby-smooth. In con-temporary patriarchal culture, a panoptical male connoisseur resides within the consciousness of most women: They stand perpetually before his gaze and under his judgement."[26] One contestant I interviewed gave evidence for this panoptical surveillance in her detailing of the judging process. Diana had recently finished competing in a local pageant, and we discussed the swimsuit competition. For some pageants (at least in the preliminaries) the swimsuit competition is not a public event; only judges, parents, and the pageant directors are admitted entry. Describing her ex-perience competing, Diana commented on the strict surveillance of the judges:

> You had to do figure eights—we learned this in practice. You had
> to stop, look at the judges, walk down the ramp. The judges know,
> they watch you, if you make a mistake, they notice it. They judge lots
> of pageants, they have a whole circuit that they go on. So you have
> to be careful about making a mistake, because they're watching for
> it. . . . Swimsuit judging is completely closed. It's not in the dark, it's

all very well lit. They have to be able to see your body—you're scored on muscle tone and your physique.[27]

This description perfectly captures the power of the panoptical male. In the swimsuit competition, women are exposed and displayed in "the light" while the judges sit in the dark—faceless surveyors, whose gaze cannot be returned, relentlessly "watching" for mistakes.

The bodies of the contestants bear the burden of signification in their disciplined, rigid focus. The swimsuit competition is not about the sensual movement of the body: breasts are not supposed to jiggle, butts and thighs are to remain firm. Firm, rigid flesh represents and reflects the intense discipline of each contestant—and, importantly, firm flesh does not merely reflect the physical discipline it takes to create such a body. Rather, tight and contained flesh represent a tight and contained moral subjectivity. As Susan Bordo argues, uncontrolled flesh—"lumpy" buttocks and thighs that jiggle—function as a "metaphor for anxiety about internal processes out of control—uncontained desire, unrestrained hunger, uncontrolled impulse."[28] She continues, "The ideal here is of a body that is absolutely tight, contained, 'bolted down,' firm: in other words, a body that is protected against eruption from within, whose internal processes are under control."[29] This ideal, of course, is one that is sustained in beauty pageants even as it is reinvented from one year to the next. And, as Bordo argues, the contemporary anxiety about feminine bodies is organized around a "tighter, smoother, more contained body profile," so that the oft-repeated comment that pageants are "cellulite-free zones" are intended as compliments for the successful enactment of femininity.[30] One of the main "tricks of the trade" in pageants, along with gluing the swimsuit to the body with a sports adhesive spray, is rolling a rolling pin over the thighs to flatten cellulite.[31]

On the one hand, the desire to "control" oneself is a particularly liberal impulse. The control of "internal processes" is made visible on the exterior body, thus forming the connection between the inner and outer "selves." Controlled, rigid flesh emphasizes the liberal fiction of the unified "self," constituted through mastery over desire and impulse. On the other hand, in the swimsuit competition, having "internal processes" that are under control is doubly important, because this particular competition is vulnerable precisely because of its celebration of the feminine body.[32] The women I interviewed constantly repeated a refrain of "inner-beauty," even though other comments that they made directly—and apparently unproblematically—contradicted this. Most of these comments were made in the context of discussing the qualities of a representative. Diana, for example, stressed the importance of being "well-rounded." But clearly, part of being well-rounded is also being beautiful. Even though the "prettiest one" does not always win, every woman who competes must, of course, be pretty enough:

> When you see these people who are demonstrating that it's just about your face and your body, you can really disagree with them because a lot of hard work goes into it and you have to be a well-rounded person to be a queen. And I really think that beauty is not so much a part of it anymore. . . . I really don't think that, because depending on how many pageants you've watched, you can see that it is not always the prettiest girl that wins. . . . When you have a bunch of girls up there together, there are certain girls that are going to stand out because they are so beautiful, but you have to be beautiful on the inside too. You have to have a mind, you have to have your own opinions.[33]

Part of what the pageant provides is a place where women can negotiate a sense of self in relation to their bodies, and part of constructing oneself as an embodied subject is to somehow resolve the tensions that inevitably arise when participating in a swimsuit competition. It is necessary to be attractive, to discipline one's body, but "you have to have a mind, you have to have your own opinions."

One strategy for resolving this tension is proving one's commitment to embodied subjectivity through education. This commitment is seen by contestants as an explicit statement about the progression and modernization of the pageants—perhaps they used to be "meat markets," but now they reflect the contemporary woman, who is serious yet sexy, smart yet attractive. Alice, for example, stood out among the women I interviewed by her vehement insistence on this point. Our first interaction was a phone conversation where I was reprimanded for calling pageants "beauty pageants" rather than simply "pageants." From that point onward, she insisted that pageants were about so much more than physical attractiveness:

> It's not so much as it used to be when pageants first started out, decades ago, as the perfect measurements, they smile for the camera, that's it. They're so talented, they're so intelligent, most of the girls

are going to universities—pre-med, pre-law, almost all the winners
are going into some professions that require graduate degrees, etc. . . .
I think that not only are they beautiful, but they are beautiful on the
inside, and I think that that's important.

As I mentioned, this insistent claim about "inner beauty" merely situates
inner beauty as equally important to "outer beauty"—it never intends to
obliterate the necessity of the disciplined, feminine body. And sometimes
contestants accidentally reveal exactly how important "outer beauty" really is. Mary, for example, related the story of her first runner-up, a woman
who apparently thought that she, rather than Mary, should have been the
queen. In the midst of a story about her sympathy for her runner-up, Mary
made it clear that the judge's choice was the correct one:

> You can see a picture of "Tania" . . . she is NOT attractive at all.
> [Shows me a picture] She's just not pretty at all and she went to
> Miss California. . . . She was probably one of the ugliest ones there,
> and I'm not even kidding. I could give you the tape and you'd go,
> 'Oh my God, this girl looks like she just stepped out of the bathroom,'
> or something like that. She looks terrible. So, if she wanted to waste
> a thousand dollars on an entry fee . . .

In a more sympathetic statement, Miss Connecticut 1982, Kelly Slater, who
has judged a number of pageants, also revealed the (implicit) inanity of
the "It's only about inner beauty" mantra:

> These girls, some of them, I think it's great that they get involved,
> because it does a lot for their self-esteem and makes them feel
> better. There was one girl in a local pageant who must have been
> forty pounds overweight. But you know, she went on stage in a
> swimsuit, and she did her talent—I have a lot of respect for some-
> body who just went out there and did it and gave it her best anyway.
> She knew she wasn't going to win, but she wanted to try it once
> in her life, so she went ahead. And I think that's great.[34]

Clearly, it is essential that the body be read as a transparent statement of
the interior moral qualities of each contestant; even if Slater has "a lot of
respect for somebody who just went out there and did it" it was obvious
from the beginning that, because of her "overweight" body, "she wasn't
going to win." The reason it is so unproblematic for contestants to routinely make the inner beauty argument is precisely because of the dialec-

tic relationship between inner, profound beauty, and outer, superficial beauty. One reflects the other: the overweight contestant had no chance of winning because her body reflects an interior loss of control.[35] The body in the swimsuit competition must be contained and disciplined, effectively containing in turn the potential sexual transgression visible on the exposed body.[36]

Perhaps the most illustrative example of the way in which the bodies of contestants are restrained and standardized comes from the seminars that teach the "do's and don'ts" of competing in a swimsuit.[37] The convener of the seminar I attended was the owner of a swimsuit shop that specialized in pageant competitive swimsuits, ironically named "T & A Swimwear."[38] She began the seminar on the following note, "In the swimsuit competition there are two 'musts': you must wear cups in the bra of the swimsuit, and you must use Stick-Um spray in the buttocks of the suit."[39] The cups function to make the swimsuit opaque, so no trace of the contestant's nipple is revealed through the suit. Of course, a woman's erect nipple immediately and persuasively signifies sexual excitement and, as such, would be totally inappropriate for a beauty pageant, dedicated as they are to the repression of sexual excitement—of both the contestants and the (male) audience members. During the dress rehearsal of a local pageant one of the contestants asked me to adjust the bra-cup of her swimsuit, because she thought it made her breasts look "all lumpy," which would destroy any chance of a smooth, seamless silhouette.[40]

The Stick-Um spray to which the T & A representative referred is used to adhere the swimsuit to the body so that the suit does not "ride up" and reveal an inappropriate amount of flesh. Given the emphasis on control and mastery over oneself that is paramount in the swimsuit competition, the obvious constructedness or artificiality of the contestants' bodies—produced by Stick-Um spray, nipple cups, and in some cases plastic surgery—is not an issue within the pageant. However, the process of construction must not be evident: the "finished product" should perform as the natural or authentic body in a convincing way. Diana commented on the importance of this "finished product":

> The funny thing about the swimsuit competition is that they have this stuff called Stick-Um, it's a sports spray, you used it to make a swimsuit stick to our bodies so that when you're walking on stage

it doesn't get into areas that you don't want it, so you spray it up
around your breasts and your butt, so your swimsuit sticks. It
would have been really tacky if you would have had to readjust
in front of the judges.

The idea of readjusting her swimsuit in front of the judges was unthinkable to Diana, because it would have revealed the complex process of construction required to maintain and display her body. Disclosing anything
other than the ideal, finished product is regarded as "tacky." And tricks
and helpful hints abound for constructing the perfect body. Consider these
from a "how-to" pageant book:

> The smooth legs that extend gracefully from the swimsuits the semi-
> finalists wear on television are not the result of daily waxing . . . ;
> sheer hose are allowed, and even recommended, for the swimsuit
> competition. Most contestants find that a tan, either natural or out
> of a bottle, helps their chances in a swimsuit, and a coating of baby
> oil on the shoulders and chest gives the skin a nice sheen.[41]

The smooth, hairless body, glowing with a healthy tan, is clearly—and
knowingly—anything but a "natural" occurrence. This awareness does
not seem to be at odds with the pageant's insistence that the outer body
reflects the (natural) morality and grace of the inner body. The stage body
is one that is artificially constructed but "innocent" nonetheless:

> So who you are on stage—all sweetness and light—is not necessarily
> who you are in person, but just as long as you portray that image
> to the public again and again, then you're doing a job for them and
> that's what they want. There are all kinds of little tricks, like Vaseline
> on your teeth and hairspray on your butt to keep your bathing suit
> down, there are all sorts of little tricks that aren't necessarily bad.
> When you get into stuffing your bra and plastic surgery, you're
> getting into something that is borderline illegal. But those other
> things are innocent things that pageant girls have been doing for
> years.[42]

Clearly, the main concern of the contestants, as well as personal trainers and pageant advisors, seems to be not *why* but *how* her body is displayed. The boundary of what is "too much" in terms of artificially constructing the body is commonsense knowledge for the contestants—a
common sense that is not necessarily officially recorded in the pageant

rulebook. In yet another example, Sayles offers this advice for "taping" breasts:

> Many pageant girls, even full-bosomed ones, create glamorous cleavage by taping. This means you use duct tape underneath your breasts, bending forward, tightly pulling them together and up, creating cleavage. Your swimsuit is backless, so wrap back and forth under breasts. You can cinch in waistline and hips with tape, which, by contrast, makes your breasts look higher, fuller, rounder, larger, ample.[43]

Constructing "glamorous cleavage" by this method is obviously painful to deconstruct. Sayles suggests to the contestants, "If you are able to remove it in a shower or bath with liquid soap, do so, gently."[44] The actual application of electrical tape to one's breast, completely aside from the inevitable painful removal of the tape, is understood as a normative practice within beauty pageants. In fact, T & A Swimwear offers taping lessons for all contestants.[45]

The constructed body within the swimsuit competition represents in exaggerated form the various disciplinary practices women perform every day in order to approximate the current ideal. Bordo comments that "through the pursuit of an ever-changing, homogenizing, elusive ideal of femininity—a pursuit without a terminus, requiring that woman constantly attend to minute and often whimsical changes in fashion—female bodies become docile bodies—bodies whose forces and energies are habituated to external regulation, subjection, transformation, 'improvement.'"[46] Nowhere in the beauty pageant is this quest for "improvement," this acquiescence to external regulation, more evident than within the swimsuit competition. I witnessed perhaps the most potent—and the most disturbing—realization of this regulation during the swimsuit competition at a local beauty pageant. I happened to be backstage during this competition, and an assistant was preparing each contestant to enter the stage. In classic assembly-line fashion, the contestants lined up to go on stage. Just before she crossed the boundary between backstage and onstage, each contestant passed a kneeling assistant who fiercely tugged each woman's swimsuit upward, exposing as much skin as possible. The assistant then vigorously sprayed Stick-Um spray on the contestant's cheeks, yanked the suit back down, and with a gentle pat on the butt, sent each woman on her way.[47] I couldn't help but be struck by the factorylike repetition of both the assistant's motions and the final results of her work. Although this insight resonated with the many critiques of pageants that focus primarily on the construction of female contestants as "simply" commodities in a capitalist marketplace, it also provides insight to the transformative aspect of the pageant. In other words, there is a transcendental quality to the swimsuit competition that has as much to do with transforming the "inner self" as it does with external regulation of the body. And perhaps the most salient element for successful transformation is to regulate desire. It is to these practices that I now turn.

THE INNER SELF: REGULATING SELF AND DESIRE

The structure of the beauty pageant is organized in terms of fragments of femininity: individualism is celebrated in the talent competition, ambition and independence are reflected in the interview, and commitment to a middle-class status is demonstrated through the selection of a career goal and an evening gown. Although each of these different events contributes to the constitution of a national icon, the focus of each is on how these characteristics—ambition, individualism, and independence—explicitly construct feminine bodies. So where does the swimsuit competition fit in? The swimsuit event is ultimately about the reassurance of tradition. It reassures the audience that despite the commitment to abstract liberal values such as individualism and ambition in the other parts of the pageant, the carefully performed display of bodies in the swimsuit competition recoups the crucial materiality of femininity: the seemingly changeless female body, fixed in age and the embodiment of heterosexual desire.

The swimsuit competition presents a temporary resolution to the contradictions and tensions of femininity in late-twentieth-century consumer culture: its celebration of the silent, sexualized, white body remains powerfully and immutably fixed and homogenous while the contestants' performances of self in the interview and talent competitions demonstrate both malleability and heterogeneity. By displaying the female body in a way that obviously and forcefully signifies a current cultural representation of white femininity, the swimsuit competition reaffirms the central difference between men and women—namely, that women "possess sex" in the way Bernarr MacFadden argued in 1901: "The word 'woman' does not indicate solely a certain form or condition of body: it indicates the possession of *sex*, and unless the body has been developed sufficiently to bring out and emphasize the instincts and powers of sex there is no real womanhood."[48] In the context of the pageant, "possessing sex" indicates a particular sexual doubling, where the contestants anchor their bodies in and through a conventional notion of sex at the same time as the pageant in general is dedicated to a particular usage of sex, one that is bound up in a history of nationalism and racialization.

But how is sex used in the pageant? How does it contribute to the constitution of a national icon? Sex is forcibly called up through the swimsuit competition, not only because of the sexualized body that is evaluated, but also because of the silence of the contestants. Voices may be heard during each individual parade in front of the judges (and the voice may even be the recorded voice of the contestant), but the contestant herself does not speak during this particular competition. Her status as a nonspeaking subject is absolutely crucial to the logic of the swimsuit competition— and to the processes of containment that ensure its success within the larger pageant. The celebration of the body, separated from the other pageant competitions, factors in as part of a constituted yet separable whole. Fragmentation of this kind is characteristic of the engendering of women in U.S. liberal society; women experience this "dismemberment," couched in the language of the "well-rounded" individual, as a daily, lived experience. Consider the following remarks from a pageant participant about what the judges look for in a winning contestant: "They [the judges] are looking for the well-rounded girl who's attractive, intelligent, and has a talent. Usually they say that the three categories are poise, personality, and appearance. They never come right out and say beauty, they never come right out and say body, it's usually poise, personality, and appearance."[49] Clearly, these characteristics are mutually constitutive: "poise" only makes sense with a particular kind of appearance, and personality is situated only in relation to poise.

This fragmentation works in conjunction with the voicelessness of each contestant, where denying the contestants their voices contains the female body by reducing it to an isolated sexuality, one with no voice and no chance to talk back. It is, in other words, a body spoken for or on behalf of.[50] The body that is evaluated in the swimsuit competition is, borrowing again from Foucault, an "intelligible body," a body that explains sexuality to the mass-mediated audience. In the swimsuit competition, the intelligible body is represented in terms of a particular idealized feminine body, the body that must speak for itself a particular story of sex, even as it is presumed to be inextricably linked to the "human" qualities of independence and individualism.

But as Foucault so astutely observed, the intelligible body makes sense only in context of its other "register": the useful body.[51] The same cultural representations that constitute the intelligible body work to produce a useful or docile body. In other words, ensuring the construction of the properly sexualized and racialized feminine body in this middle-class context means applying a particular set of practical rules: disciplined movement, commitment to capitalism and consumer society, and most important, a studied lack of voice. Bordo elaborates on these kinds of rules by arguing that in order to achieve the aesthetic norm of the "intelligible" body, a specific feminine praxis is required. Clearly, this praxis includes disciplining one's physical body, but along with that discipline comes another: mediating the alienation that is characteristic of both the female subject and the liberal subject within capitalism. Foucault argues that the intelligible body and the useful body mirror each other, and the discipline necessary for these two registers "dissociates power from the body . . . on the one hand, it turns it into an 'aptitude,' a 'capacity,' which it seeks to increase; on the other hand, it reverses the course of the energy, the power that might result from it, and turns it into a relation of strict subjection."[52] In the swimsuit competition, the alienated body characteristic of liberal society represents the capacity of the contestant to become this subject, yet the potential power that might be granted by occupying this subject position is refracted and redirected into the creation of a nonspeaking, docile, feminine body.

Given that every woman's body is both intelligible in terms of an aesthetic norm and useful in the sense that this norm requires a particular praxis for its construction, we must determine what, in the context of the swimsuit competition, do bodies actually *mean?* How does the swimsuit competition enable the feminine body, and how does it disable this body? Rather than engaging in a debate about the danger of this kind of feminine praxis, we can use the opportunity the swimsuit competition offers us to explore the meanings embedded within the beauty pageant as whole—what it means to participate in this sort of competition as opposed to others. The swimsuit competition minimizes the potential threat that contestants pose as intelligent speaking subjects by insisting that they are also bodies, also women. The coherent anatomy of the pageant makes it clear that the contestants are both "only" bodies and also future scholars and career women, thus rendering invisible the tension between woman and subject while producing a feminine subject that both wants to save the world and wants to show off her body—but does not want to save the world *by* showing off her body. This balancing act is also the reason the contestants need to be autonomous; they are poised between dependence on family and dependence on a husband (granted, it's a false autonomy, given the chaperoning and other disciplinary regulations that are imposed on the contestants, but the appearance of autonomy is important).

The feminine body is also propelled by a discourse of objectivity that structures the entire pageant, especially the swimsuit competition. In the commodified context of the Miss America pageant, women are constituted as products with specific exchange values—and the swimsuit competition is structured as a site for what Gayle Rubin called trafficking in women.[53] The most obvious and direct way it constitutes them as products is through the objectification of women's bodies, where one body after the other is paraded in front of a panel of judges to be measured and evaluated upon a numerical scale. In fact, although all contestants would resist the characterization of themselves as "objects," the logic that legitimates the objectification of women is wholeheartedly approved and endorsed by the contestants with respect to the judging process; when all the "ingredients" for a winning contestant are considered "neutral" and natural, the judging process is seen as an "objective" process.

Not surprisingly, the objectivity of the judging process is clearly and historically situated: the contestants in the Miss America pageant are not *only* "women." The gendered identity of pageant contestants—as of other women—is constituted by the historically and culturally contingent foundations of "Woman" herself—Miss America contestants are judged "objectively" as women according to specific racial and class terms. The judges' decisions are formulated within these specific social contexts, and thus their evaluation, authorized by numerical statistics and meritorious performances, officializes the feminine body as racially coded.

But what about the pageant's claim that theirs is a multicultural stage? This claim is, on the one hand, preemptively undermined by the sheer dearth of contestants who are women of color. On the other hand, the pageant also constitutes whiteness in a way commensurate with other late-twentieth-century popular cultural forms: the swimsuit competition not only is a spectacle of homogeneity in terms of its standardized codes of femininity, but also participates within what Susan Willis calls "racial homogeneity." Racial homogeneity represents women—white women and women of color—as a uncolored blur; "a woman whose features, skin tone, and hair suggest no one race, or even the fusion of social contraries. She is, instead, all races in one."[54] This unitary racial identity that is presumably an amalgam of all possible racial configurations remains clearly and identifiably white: guess which "one" all races combined produce? But in keeping with other national icons of the late-twentieth-century United States (such as Betty Crocker), the national and ethnic origins of Miss America contestants are made deliberately vague in a gesture toward the egalitarian premise of the event. Clearly, this does not mean that the contestants are not racially marked; on the contrary, this event is one in which national figures produce themselves even as they are produced, where ideal American women respond to national ethnic shifts by emphasizing the individual within the homogeneity. It denies the possibility of material or cultural diversity by demonstrating egalitarian individualism, where diversity is understood and celebrated as an issue of choice, or even more in keeping with the Miss America's commitment to commodity culture, an issue of fashion, where "difference is only a matter of fashion."[55] In other words, the "uncoloring" of the Miss America contestants within the swimsuit competition does not deny the logic of whiteness that structure the event. Instead, whiteness is recouped by the sheer blur of bodies—and by the very speed of the event. The line up of bodies that comprise the swimsuit competition makes it possible to read this event as one in which there is homogeneity—before the audience has a chance to process a complicated racial configuration, the next body is presented. The swim-

suit competition is *the* spectacle of the larger spectacular event, and whiteness provides the momentum for the spectacle.

Indeed, the visuality of the swimsuit competition is clearly its most palpable feature—the spectacle of this event represents a configuration of visuality through which bodies are invested with specific social meaning.
Nonetheless, although the sheer materiality of the body provides both legitimation and titillation for this event, the visible economy of the swimsuit competition is inextricable from an equally important moral economy.[56] Recall Foucault's notion of the "useful" body, a register mutually
constitutive with the material or intelligible body. The useful body is also
governed by both formal and informal surveillance. At the time I interviewed eighteen-year-old Mary, she was right in the middle of her reign
as Miss J., representing a small town in east San Diego county. She took
her representative status very seriously, constantly connecting it with how
a female body is sexualized. Her comments are worth quoting at length:

> When I go out as Miss J., I'm representing ten thousand people
> and I'm that representation, I'm not going to go behind a building
> with my crown and banner on and make out with my boyfriend.
> I'm representing a whole town, and through that, I've got to watch
> everything I say, everything I do. But I consider that a lot of girls
> without their crown and banner on will go out and buy beer. But I
> think, even without my crown and banner on, if some little kid goes,
> 'Mommy, I recognize her from the paper, she's Miss J., why is she
> buying beer?' People watch you the whole year. You have the rest
> of your life to screw off, you're representing a lot of people, so you
> have got to act like it. I don't consider that a pressure, I mean you just
> got to be moral about it and not cause any controversy. So when I'm
> out, you have to be very nice. We had a . . . casino night, and it was
> a fund raiser, and a lot of the older men got drunk, and my boyfriend
> was there, he was my escort, and they would come up to me and try
> to pick up on me: 'Hey baby want to go home, let's go do the cha-cha,'
> and I can't slap them in the face and tell them to get out because I'm
> in the position to be cordial and to be polite and you've got to know
> how to handle yourself and say, 'Oh no I'm not feeling very well, I've
> got to go home now,' rather than blow them off.

For Mary, the act of representing indicates a kind of sexual surveillance:
she avoided "making out" with a boyfriend, doing the "cha-cha" with

older men, or even buying and consuming alcohol, a practice that, at least for women, is almost always sexually coded. Disciplining the body is clearly the reining in not only of one's hunger for food, but also one's hunger for sex; in short, disciplinary practices regulate and domesticate desire. It is also about politeness; she made a point of letting the men down easy rather than, say, telling them to get lost. Politeness, especially in the heavily regulated beauty pageant, is an important code of femininity.

So despite its spectacular nature, the swimsuit competition defies conventional codes regarding popular cultural events that display the exposed feminine body. This is clearly not any old bathing beauty contest—in part because it disciplines the audience. The audience is engaged as a respectable spectator: there is no hooting and hollering, no catcalls, and no conversation with the contestants. The display of female bodies is mediated by the short, disembodied autobiographies that detail things such as what it is like coming from a "one stoplight town," or the hope the future holds for American children. Though the separation of voice from body (or subject from body) highlights and exaggerates the display of the body, it also contains this very body through intense, disciplined focus. Surveying only the body in this competition transforms each contestant into simply a body and not an embodiment of sexuality, moral transgression, or aggression.

But perhaps one of the most efficient ways to minimize the sexual content of this competition is to compare it with spectacles that are considered more overt and distasteful in their display of sexuality. The concept of respectability sets the pageant's swimsuit competition apart from other corporeal spectacles. "Respectability" is structured within the logics and contingencies of race and class, and participating in the swimsuit competition in a beauty pageant has historically been considered a white, middle-class way of communicating desirability appropriately: as a matter of restraint, a nonexcessive display of the body. The way female bodies are examined and judged in the swimsuit competition during the Miss America pageant is considered by the contestants to be different than the ways in which female bodies are displayed in other, less "legitimate" competitions, such as bikini contests. Diana, a nineteen-year-old first runner-up in a local San Diego County pageant, directly referred to this element of "legitimacy" when recounting the various pageant regulations: "[Y]ou can't have posed for pictures. Actually, you can have been a model, but bikini pictures, like bikini calendars and things like that, they don't want you to do that, when you are Miss S. you are not allowed to go for Miss Budweiser . . . that's a definite no-no." What constitutes a "no-no" for pageant contestants is directly related to conceptions of respectability that both construct beauty pageant contestants and regulate beauty pageants themselves; in other words, the traditional ways in which women's access to and use of money has been restricted, ensuring that contestants themselves do not participate in competitions that are overtly about selling bodies and sex.

Ironically, the swimsuit competition serves as a crucial element of the pageant's moral structure, insofar as the emphasis is on the *authenticity* of this competition, as opposed to, say, bikini contests. In bikini contests, the contestants are competing only for cold "hard" cash, whereas in the Miss America pageant, the women compete for a more "refined" kind of cash: an academic scholarship.[57] This distinction is especially important because competing only for money exposes the commodification of the event, whereas for Miss America contestants, the money is controlled— they do not have a choice as to how they will use it. Another contestant, Lisa, a twenty-year-old former title holder and college student at a local university, referred to this distinction between the "kind" of money earned through beauty pageants. When asked how she felt about bikini contests, she replied, "Oh, that's a different story. That's definitely promoting, . . . that's for money. I mean, at least in the USA system [a mainstream beauty pageant system] you do get a car, but it is for the scholarship, and you tour the world, and you have this great experience, and you go to the Miss USA pageant and you get to meet different people. [Bikini contestants] are just wearing a string bikini, a g-string bikini." Not only is the academic scholarship important to this woman, but the pageant itself is framed as an experience that builds moral character by enabling its contestants to tour the world and meet a variety people. In contrast, bikini contests do not offer "experience"; they are crass venues for displaying the unclad female body. According to this view, the women who participate in bikini contests care nothing about cultivating a particular moral character and instead merely sell their bodies for money.

The women I interviewed all defended this class-based view that bikini contests were less "authentic" and, thus, less moral than the pageants in which they participated. Several contestants expressed a complete—and to me, stunning—denial that the typical beauty pageant swimsuit competition is a contest based solely upon the shape and conformity of the female body. For Alice, a nineteen-year-old psychology major who first entered the pageant world by competing in Miss Co-Ed, a pageant based primarily on academic achievement, the distinction between bikini contests and the swimsuit competition was absolutely vital:

> If people want to do that [enter a bikini contest], and they have a great body, . . . that's fine. But most of the pageants you find that are really *legit*, they have the regulation swimwear, where it can't be cut up too high or cut down too low. . . . I don't know, if you have a great body, and you don't mind going up there and showing it off and get some money in the process, I don't know, that's up to them. . . . But I think traditionally, if you're going to pursue it for what the pageants—I think—are all about, then that's not your best choice.[Emphasis added]

Alice made a moral distinction between "legit" pageants and bikini contests, a distinction based not on whether the sexualized female body is displayed for consumption, but upon a gendered discourse about display, where overtly displaying the body solely for financial reasons is somehow cheap and immoral, or "tacky," "sleazy," or "unprofessional."[58] In contrast, in the Miss America pageant the "regulation" swimsuits are not "cut up too high or cut down too low."[59] In fact, a regulation swimsuit does precisely that: it regulates the body and controls the body's display. This contrast is distinctly class-bound at the same time that it is framed explicitly as a matter of choice: entering a bikini pageant is both "up to them" and "not your best choice." This contrast resonates with class-based assumptions about constructing femininity, where working-class women and women of color are presumed to lack both taste and style and somehow overdo their performance of femininity: "they" wear too much makeup and clothes that are garish and too tight. Of course, the decision to construct oneself in this way is not considered a result of specific cultural and economic contexts but is understood as matter of choice as well as a lack of commitment in cultivating a particular kind of social taste. The class discourse that structures these "choices" is not limited to momentary participation in pageants—according to the contestants I inter-viewed, a decision to enter a bikini contest influences (if not determines) other life decisions. Alice made an even sharper distinction between beauty pageants and bikini contests with her focus on future career op-tions: "I think that the girls are usually approached in pageants to model afterwards by different agents. I think that the type of agents that would approach these girls [in bikini pageants] are sometimes different than what you find in the Miss America pageant, where you have Nina Blan-chard [a high fashion designer] approaching Miss America, whereas you have second-rate photographers interested in nude shots approaching the bikini pageants."

The unspoken but pervasive assumption underwriting this reading is clear: only certain kinds of women—working-class women and, by asso-ciation, those with little or no moral values—participate in bikini contests.[60]

The bikini contest, and its counterpart, the wet t-shirt contest, regulates gender identity as it simultaneously polices class identity.[61] This clearly is directly derivative of a dominant ideology that claims there are two main "types" of women, the virgin and the whore. Of course, the ideal woman should have characteristics of both: a common stereotype about men is that some might not want to marry the woman they have premarital sex-ual intercourse with, but they expect their wives to fulfill them sexually once they are married. In the opinion of many contestants, choosing to enter bikini contests is like choosing to become a prostitute. Like the bikini contest, the money that prostitutes receive for their work is seen as ille-gitimate, whereas the money many women receive through marriage—and beauty pageants—is legitimately earned. Even when a contestant rec-ognizes the similarities between the swimsuit and bikini competitions or allows the strict moral code to relax a bit, she always considers tainted the money received from bikini contests. Lisa, for example, insisted that the general public's reaction to both beauty pageants and bikini contests is similarly misguided:

> The reaction [to bikini pageants] is that these are kind of sleazy.
> But a lot of people also think pageants in general are, they really
> don't know what goes on with them. They think, you know, they're
> [pageants], just stupid. It's very hard. Even a lot of girls in the Miss
> Mission Beach pageant [a local bikini contest] aren't stupid. I know

> a girl who did a legs contest, and she's a medical student and she did it for the money because it paid her way through a lot of things, and she had good legs, so she used it. And she was definitely not stupid. She used it to her advantage. But a lot of the girls, I don't know why they do that, except for the money.

Even though Lisa seemed to reluctantly approve of her friend's choice to enter a "legs" contest, she distinguished morally between the monies earned through particular kinds of competitions; she based the distinction on what the money is used *for*. If one uses money won from a bikini contest to enter medical school, the respectability earned by becoming a doctor presumably overrides the illegitimate origin of the funds for that education. But "a lot of girls" participate in these competitive displays merely "for the money," an assertion that situates the bikini contest in a category alongside prostitution and sex work.

Another contestant, Grace, participated in the Junior Miss Pageant, a scholarship pageant for girls who are too young to enter the Miss America program. Grace was very successful in her endeavor: after winning her local pageant, she went on to win her state pageant and to then compete in the national Junior Miss (recently renamed Young Woman of the Year). All in all, she won twenty-three thousand dollars in scholarships, and she plans to use the money to pursue a graduate education after completing her undergraduate work. For Grace, the fact that the money she won was to be used specifically for education assuaged the tension of parading on display.

> I had an opportunity to try to get a lot of money to try to go to school. And it's not money. If I don't use it all, it's forfeited. So it's not like this, . . . that I wanted to put a down payment on a house, or buy a new car, I mean it's money for school. After I got done with Junior Miss I was going to go in to more pageants (like the ones that lead to Miss California) and that would have been for the money also, because you still win a lot of money that way, too.

In order to maintain the fiction that it is acceptable to win money for what, at least in part, constitutes a display of the feminine, sexualized body, sexuality itself needs to be disciplined according to particular sets of social and moral practices. In the beauty pageant, disciplinary practices domesticate female sexuality as moral and marriage-bound. Clearly, the discipline involved in constituting other visions of feminine sexuality operate according to different conditions and are perceived to produce not only different constructions of femininity, but also a diametrically opposed version of femininity. The reliance on this kind of oppositional politics is not incidental to the Miss America pageant; it is, rather, crucial for the pageant to define itself in opposition to more debased forms of popular culture for their own legitimation.

It is precisely these same politics of opposition that propel the racialized discourse produced by the swimsuit competition. The racial inscriptions of bodies proliferate as a series of cultural determinations about the women who participate in the swimsuit competition. Whiteness is the great mediator here, working effectively through historical discourses of respectability and morality—recognizable tropes of the "cult of true womanhood," which demonstrate, as Robyn Wiegman has argued, "how widely prized was the white woman for her civic roles and responsibilities, as her reproductive activities and domestic occupations were themselves crucial elements within narratives of social progress and national identity throughout the nineteenth century."[62] The nineteenth century held out a specific promise for white woman that was a product of that historical and economic climate. But the cult of true womanhood has clear staying power; we witness in the late twentieth century various manifestations and circulating images that could only be articulated in a society thoroughly permeated within and constituted by the mass media—and one central discourse activating contemporary gender identity is race.

The process of categorization in which beauty pageant contestants (as well as many other women) participate—that of good, moral women and 'bad,' immoral women—is always racially coded. Character designations such as "respectable" and "moral" that are connected with ideal femininity signal the unmarked, invisible designation of whiteness. Racial hierarchies are preserved in U.S. society in general and beauty pageants in particular through the reliance on whiteness as an unmarked, "neutral" category. And so, in this particular context, morality is framed not only as desexualized, but also as implicitly nonraced, constructed simply as a principle "good girls" adhere to. The discourse of racial homogeneity has a certain political efficacy within the boundaries of the beauty pageant because dominant conventions of morality are infused with racial politics. The swimsuit competition engages in a repressed fetishization of the skin, of appearance, and of fantasy; in the carefully monitored inches of exposed skin the limits of bourgeois respectability are on display.[63]

Earlier I discussed the different disciplinary practices within the pageant that create feminine bodies appropriate for the swimsuit competition. The physical body of each contestant must closely approximate the current feminine ideal in order to remain competitive. This current ideal of slenderness is, as Bordo argues, a body "suffused with moral meaning." Thus a deeper decoding process is indicated here, one that attempts to reveal "the psychic anxieties and moral valuations contained within it—valuations concerning correct and incorrect management of impulse and desire."[64] Given the sexist, racist society in which we find the swimsuit competition, this event has a misogynist logic and makes a kind of misogynist sense in its display of the alienated, sexualized female body. It is more than a story of misogyny, however. The efficiency of the swimsuit competition lies in its focus on the body; in that focus, it allows the rest of the pageant to define itself as dedicated to far more than that body.

CHAPTER 3 "IF YOU WERE A COLOR, WHAT COLOR WOULD YOU BE?"

THE INTERVIEW AND TALENT COMPETITIONS
IN THE MISS AMERICA PAGEANT

"This is *your* chance to impress the judges. In the interview and the talent section, you get to show them how smart you are, how poised you are, how confident you are—these are the most important parts of any pageant."[1] This advice was given by a pageant director for a regional California pageant in the Miss America pageant system while preparing the contestants for "Pageant Night," the final night of a pageant in the Miss America program, when the viewing public watches the ten finalists compete for the crown. Pageant audiences are most familiar with this part of the program, but several days or even weeks of competition lead up to Pageant Night, and it is during this time that the contestants participate in the bulk of the interview and talent competitions. During a rehearsal for this same city pageant, the twelve contestants spent the majority of the time practicing their performances for the talent and interview competitions, which the pageant director considered to be the most important elements of the entire competition. When I interviewed this director at length, she explained that the reason she was so involved in the Miss America system was because of the talent portion of the program; pageants, she argued, provided one of the only showcases for amateur female talent in the United States. The questions that concern me in this chapter involve this issue of "showcasing"; what else—besides talent and public speaking skills—are showcased in the interview and talent competitions in the Miss America pageant?

Both the interview and the talent competitions, as discrete events within the larger spectacle of the pageant, serve as the architecture for the construction of the contemporary ideal female subject. This subject is not at all like the vapid, empty beauty queen at which public folklore pokes fun; on the contrary, she is intelligent, goal-oriented, independent, feisty, and committed to individualism. Through performances in the interview and talent competitions, the contestant makes important gestures toward a liberal agenda—and often a liberal feminist agenda—concerned with equality of opportunity and equal partnership. That is to say, within these events, the audience witnesses the investment Miss America contestants have in the successes of feminism, especially in the feminist lessons about the value of independence and a strong sense of self (although few would actually go so far as to identify *as* feminists). Within the talent and interview competitions, contestants constitute themselves as active, self-possessed, and most of all, deeply embodied.

Both the talent competition and the interview competition are a continuation of the cultural work that the swimsuit competition performs, but with important distinctions. The swimsuit and evening gown events are clear spectacles: the display of standardized feminine bodies parading before a panel of judges is evidence not only of self-discipline, but also of the conformity that is produced by such surveillance. The swimsuit competition, like the evening gown competition, is a spectacle of homogeneity. In contrast, the interview and talent competitions are clearly performances. These performances restore heterogeneity among the contestants and thus testify to the individuality of the contestants. Both the talent and the interview competitions are constituted by performances of particular kinds of cultivated knowledge, which externalize the inner qualities and character of contestants.

In one sense, the excitement surrounding these talent and interview competitions derives from their "liveness," their spontaneity. But because this is a performance—and one that eventually takes place on a mass-mediated stage—the spontaneity demonstrated in the interview is meticulously rehearsed, and the talent performed for the talent competition is cultivated over months and even years of training and practice. The Miss America pageant has become a national event through its televised broadcast, and as such the pageant is transformed from a local, regional example of popular culture into an elaborately staged performance for a national audience. Not surprisingly, there is a specific rehearsal required for a media event of this scale—even (or perhaps I should say especially) one that is supposed to be a "live" competition. This rehearsal ensures that the women on that national, mass-mediated stage are not dim-witted proposals for a representative, but are smart, interesting women who demonstrate clear evidence of discipline and training. And, notwithstanding the dominance of simulacra in the world of beauty pageants, these events are part of an ever more encompassing media frame in which identities are formed and forged; beauty pageants constitute and are constituted by mass media and are crucial factors in representations of "American" women. If, indeed, as Suzanna Walters has argued, "in this society of the spectacle, it is women's bodies that are the spectacle upon which representation occurs," then all elements of beauty pageants, including the interview and talent competitions, must be considered to understand the cultural work this spectacle performs.

The performances, or "acts," that make up the interview and talent competitions importantly constitute the gendered and racial identity of the contestants; indeed, far from being mere theatrical demonstrations, the interview and talent competitions actively produce gender even as the contestants enact gender themselves. The rehearsed spontaneity and the acquisition of culture that constitute the logic of the interview and talent competitions can be seen as performative in the sense of a constant, repetitive production of the self. As Judith Butler argues:

> Gender ought not to be construed as a stable identity or locus of agency from which various acts follow; rather, gender is an identity tenuously constituted in time, instituted in an exterior space through a *stylized repetition of acts*. The effect of gender is produced through

the stylization of the body and, hence, must be understood as the mundane way in which bodily gestures, movements, and styles of various kinds constitute the illusion of an abiding gendered self.[2]

This performative theory of gender proposes that the enacting of gender produces gender. If we take as our starting point that gender is a set of practices that are historically contingent and conditioned by race and class, how does the beauty pageant, and, more specifically, the interview and talent competitions, figure in as crucial elements that structure these practices? Or, even more specifically, how does the Miss America pageant, and its claim that regional or state identities constitute an appropriately representative national figure, use these gender performances to play the game of national politics?

In this chapter I explore the sets of logic that underlie the performances of both the interview and talent competitions. The interview competition highlights the ways in which particular kinds of women are encouraged to speak within a liberal political framework, as well as the means by which the subversive potential of that speech is contained and regulated through enacting what I call rehearsed spontaneity. The talent competition, in contrast, is a demonstration of "culture." The talent competition, along with academic scholarship prizes, is what sets the Miss America pageant apart from other beauty pageants in the United States. Like the interview, the various talents performed by the contestants are carefully chosen and mediate the precarious boundaries between the reassuringly "modern" and the threatening, the independent woman and the feminist, and the serious and the banal. Because these two events are crucial in bolstering borders for "appropriate" gender representations, I focus most of my inquiry in this chapter on the ways in which these gendered events structure and inflect racial and national identity as well. What does it mean, for example, to be a national representative? How, and in what ways, does the interview competition mediate discussions of a multicultural U.S. society? How is the construction of racial identity understood as part of a broader liberal discourse of crafting selves and abilities to make choices? How does the talent show, with its emphasis on public musical performances, retrench or recoup historical notions about women, race, and performance?

SELF SEARCHING: THE INTERVIEW

Although the interview segment has been an informal part of the Miss America pageant since the late 1930s (the contestants then were interviewed at an informal breakfast meeting with all of the judges), the interview was first formally instituted within the pageant in 1947, when the contestants were officially judged in a fourth category called "Intellect and Personality." The judging in this new category was based on the contestant's answers to interview questions.[3] Since the institution of this category of evaluation, the interview competition has garnered 30 percent of a contestant's total score and has increasingly aimed to capture the construction of liberal characteristics of agency and choice-making abilities.

Interestingly, despite the purported intentions of this portion of the pageant, the interview competition is by far the most easily and commonly ridiculed element of the spectacle. The beauty pageant contestant answering onstage interview questions is an easily recognizable trope in contemporary U.S. folklore: contestants are represented as dim-witted and hopelessly naive, responding to "serious" questions with hugely false smiles and ridiculous or nonsensical answers that illustrate only simplistic understandings of complex issues and that offer grossly exaggerated projections of their own individual impact on the world. The impossibility (not to mention improbability) of saving the whales, working for world peace, and earning graduate degrees, all the while simultaneously maintaining a solid commitment to family, apparently legitimates the dismissal of pageant interviews proffered by critics positioned outside of this popular cultural form.

Indeed, and for very obvious reasons, those of us who are not currently participating in beauty pageants are suspicious of the vast and varied achievements to which contestants lay claim; answers that follow the preceding formula only add to the common stereotype of the beauty pageant contestant as the vapid, "airhead" female. I suggest here, however, that answers to the interview competition are not merely pat, vacuous, and rehearsed responses. They are, rather, part of a complicated series of acts that perform and thus constitute gender, and in this way the interview competition is both related to and distinct from other forms of national constructions of identity. Structured by the concept of rehearsed spontaneity, and following the lead of politicians or professional athletes, the contestants in the interview competition offer evidence of the (feminine) embodiment necessary for a national representative self.

For example, during the rehearsal I observed, the pageant director repeatedly expressed to the contestants the unofficial pageant mantra: "Be the best you you can be"—in other words, pick out a certain idea of a self and through hard work and effort, *become* that self. Alice, a pageant contestant who had recently won a local pageant and was heading for the larger, more significant city competition, commented on the importance of this motto:

> They say, basically, you're not in competition with the other girls, you're in competition with yourself, to be the best you you can be. That's another good pageant answer. You try to be the best you can be, and you can't compare yourself to the other girl, because she has nothing to do with how you're going to react. So, basically, you should concentrate on yourself instead of the other girl, which is going to help you win.

When analyzing the political framework of the interview segment of the pageant, it seems clear that the motto "Be the best you you can be" nicely captures these politics. This formulation relies on several complicated and contradictory assumptions, not the least of which is the self-awareness that repeating this motto is considered a "good pageant answer," even if it is also a strongly held conviction. The practice and training involved in cultivating good pageant answers while also maintaining a convincing and spontaneous air results in a particular skill for pageant contestants: rehearsed spontaneity. Like other public figures, beauty pageant contestants are constantly practicing performances of the self, where the motto "Be the best you you can be" assumes, in the liberal tradition, that the self can be made and constantly improved upon—that there exists somehow a best You out of all the possible "Yous," and you can choose to be it, become it, and have it, with work and discipline.

This You is constructed as one with a strong self-identity, but the construction takes place within a dynamic between a patriarchal context based on openly displayed competition and a logic that necessitates that women compete in a way that does not undermine their "femininity." In other words, the "best You" is one that expresses female liberal selfhood within patriarchal culture—which means that the contestants realize an identity that relies upon a construction of the female self in relation to others—specifically, in relation to men and children. Contrary to the opinion of many pageant critics, this does not mean that any and all "strong" notions of the female self are completely obliterated. Rather, the female liberal self as it is constituted in pageants is a subject constructed according to the *promise* of patriarchy and as such is constituted by the possibility and the realization of female agency.

The interview competition gives pageant contestants an opportunity to express their desires and goals in terms that are about taking control, about self-determination—and, crucially, about speaking for oneself. When contestants were asked what they gained most from pageants, the answer was almost invariably the ability to "speak" or to conduct oneself in public. Alice, for example, competed one year in the Miss Colleen Pageant, a local San Diego pageant produced by the Irish Congress. This competition is open only to women with Irish heritage, and one of the requirements is to write an essay detailing this heritage. When I asked Alice what the onstage interview was like in this pageant, she answered:

> Basically they are not looking for, the example is "How do you make an Irish Stew," they are not looking for potatoes, they are looking for wit, almost a smart aleck, is what they said—because she'll be relating to the press a lot, on the radio, and they need someone who can talk. The press interviews them . . . on the radio before the parade, and they need someone who can communicate.

Alice points out that "knowing how to talk" is a specific skill with particular guidelines—merely answering a question will not do, one must know how to answer a question in a clever, witty way. Another woman, Rochelle, who had participated in several pageants over the past few years, offered this list of answers to a written question about the ways in which she had benefited personally from pageants:

1. Interact with public
2. Develop speaking skills
3. Deal with situations

4. Focus on personal, career, educational goals
5. Learn more about myself
6. Become better informed about the world[4]

At least four out of the six answers she listed have to do with presenting oneself publicly and, more basically, simply knowing how to speak. Lisa, who recently won a city title and was on her way to a major state pageant when I interviewed her, claimed that "being enthusiastic about interacting with the public helps make others feel you are genuine and friendly." Part of this preoccupation with relating to the public is both necessary and expected; after all, during a queen's average reign, she must adhere to a relentless schedule of public appearances. Pageants are also commonly understood by the contestants as a possible entry to a career in entertainment or professions such as journalism, acting, and modeling, where public speaking skills are a necessary asset.[5] But another part of the intense focus on speech involves the notion that speaking in public—and "knowing" how to do it—are particular skills that characterize a modern, independent woman, a woman who possesses a strong sense of self-confidence, self-determination, and agency (see plate 3). Many contestants felt that pageants, through their emphasis on public speaking, gave them an invaluable skill for any future career. And although learning how to speak is considered part of a complicated process that intends to naturally "reveal" the "best you you can be," the contestants were, for the most part, candid about how the skill of rehearsed spontaneity can be cultivated.

Grace, for example, won an extremely significant state pageant and continued on to a televised national competition. When asked what she learned from this unusually successful experience, she replied, "It's helped me to be able to speak in front of people. I felt that the interview part was so important so that when I go to a job interview, I feel that at least I will be basically articulate and be able to bullshit my way through it [laughs]. But I can get up on stage and I can talk in front of people." Of course, part of learning and cultivating "how to speak" is mediating between being "basically articulate" (which apparently includes bullshitting) and remaining both "natural" and spontaneous. Alice related a story about her sister, also involved in pageants, who had a conflict with another contestant. Alice's sister won the pageant, and apparently this other contestant did not take her setback lightly. Alice believed that the reason for her disappointing show-

ing in the pageant was her lack of spontaneity: "She was very upset that
my sister, who had never been in a pageant before, just came in and took
it away from her when she felt that she was perhaps more qualified because she had the training, almost like a job. She was submitting a resume
for a pageant, when all they were looking for was a nice girl who could
express herself." This comment reveals Alice's anxiety concerning a cultural narrative of the "overambitious" woman; the pageant not only allows
but encourages contestants to demonstrate their ambition and agency—
as long as these characteristics are regulated within the boundaries of a
"nice girl." Training is important but should not be so evident: the pageant
is seeking the "natural," spontaneous woman who can express herself.

Another contestant, Mary, echoes Alice's sentiment about contestants
who seem overtrained or too prepared: "One of the girls went in there [to
the interview competition], and she was real bitter about the . . . pageant
because she hadn't won the year before, and that totally showed to the
judges because my pageant director sits in on the interviews and she said
that this girl, her answers were too pat, because she had practiced them
and she just wasn't happy. She wasn't the carefree, the 'I'm just here.'"
Knowing how to speak is a carefully constructed practice that balances
expertise with spontaneity and know-how with naïveté. This construction mirrors the mainstream definition of what female agency looks like
in the 1990s United States, a definition that rejects the overambitious,
mean-spirited feminist stereotype who threatens and attacks. Instead, this
definition represents a strong woman as someone who can speak to her
public, who can express herself knowledgeably and naturally, in a professional manner, yet maintain an aura of "I'm just here"—as if not competing with anyone else. Most of all, contestants offer a self-definition of
"just having fun," where winning is not paramount.

Besides learning "how to speak," pageant contestants learn what kind
of questions to expect in the interview—and what kind of answers are appropriate. I would like to broaden a critique of pageants (not only by feminists but also by film directors, journalists, and other observers of popular culture) that claims that the questions and answers during the onstage
interview are obviously "cover stories" (and poor ones at that) for the
"real" purpose of the pageant: displaying the female body. Rather, there
is a clear political agenda framing the question-and-answer period. The
questions are carefully constructed to bring into bold and clear-cut relief

the pageant contestant as a thinking, political subject.[6] This is not to imply that all questions are overtly political—there is a wide range of questions, from "What is your position on sexual harassment?" to "What do you think the goal of a school teacher should be?" to "If you were a color, what color would you be?"[7] But with all questions, it would be a mistake to assume that just any old answer would be acceptable—even to the most seemingly banal inquiries. There are clear wrong and right answers, as well as appropriate ways to present an answer, and a contestant's ability to determine which answer is the correct one often determines whether she wins the crown.

Alice spoke candidly about learning how to recognize appropriate answers:

> You learn a lot as far as the standard questions, like if someone were to say, "If you could be anyone in the world besides yourself, who would you be?" and my answer to that is always "I'm very happy with myself and there's no one I'd rather be." If they ask you what your favorite color is, you are supposed to say the color of the dress you are wearing so there is no confusion as to why you are wearing that dress. And so usually you know how to answer a question. There are certain pageant answers that you say, and I can watch Miss America and hear a question and say, "That's the answer you should give," and she'll give it most of the time.

The knowledge it requires to immediately and "spontaneously" answer appropriately is not understood by the contestants as dishonest or disingenuous—the fact that blue might not be one's favorite color despite her blue dress does not constitute an ethical dilemma for Alice. Instead, it is merely seen as part of the process of constructing oneself as a competitive pageant contestant, of learning rehearsed spontaneity. And when I asked Alice if she ever felt dishonest when she answered interview questions, she immediately answered, "It's not that it's phony, but there are certain things that you know how to say, and certain things that you don't [say]." Another contestant, Diane, commented that part of learning the right answers was watching other pageants: "We watched a tape of last year's pageant so that you could learn—you know, they ask you a question on stage—so you could see the other girl's responses, see how they carry themselves, what they wore, you know, it's just a real good learning experience to watch the last year's pageant to know what to expect in every aspect of it."

Obviously, neither Alice nor Diane felt that rehearsed spontaneity was an oxymoronic practice. Rather, such training was a clear and well-defined strategy—one that most people employ constantly in their every-day lives. Alice continued her discussion of the interview questions, and it is worth quoting at length:

> The questions are basically standard, what they might ask on a college entrance exam, what is your goal in life. Again, the answer to what is your goal in life is not I want to pursue psychology, but that I want to be successful in whatever I try, so they know you have a positive attitude and everything. It is honestly that I do want to be successful, but my goal is probably psychology or academics, but to say I want to be successful or, unfortunately now they want you to say career but they also weigh heavily on family, they're really looking for the woman that wants to have the career and have a family, not just I want a career and that's it. And so, I might not want to have a family at this point and I'm only thinking of my career, but it will probably help in my favor, especially if there are men in the audience, older men, to say "Yeah, I want a career but a family is very important to me." You never want to say you hate your father on stage! So, it's just that you kind of bend the truth a little, I guess you can out and out lie, but there are just some answers that are better than others. And you get to know those the more you're in pageants.

Hate your father? Even while recognizing that there are some who "out and out lie," Alice made a clear distinction between dishonesty and bend-ing "the truth a little." Making this distinction is crucial for her targeted theme: that of balancing a family and a career. The expectations placed on contemporary American women to negotiate these two lives are high, and there are different strategies that constitute the balancing act: one never wants to say she hates her father in public, never wants to admit that career ambition takes precedence over maternal instinct, and should always consider that there are men in the audience, regardless of how in-significant or how vast that audience might be. Strategically positioning oneself in this way is not, according to Alice, living a "false life." It is, rather, simply being a woman in the context of the pageant.[8]

The training involved in perfecting the art of rehearsed spontaneity takes place on various fronts: Mary, a nineteen-year-old college student, religiously read a book called "The Book of Questions" to prepare for the interview, and Lisa suggested hiring a speech therapist or a coach. Pageant directors often distribute a list of commonly asked questions to the contestants, and it is recommended that all contestants read the newspaper every day so that their knowledge of current events is up-to-date. But perhaps the most important training comes during the actual rehearsal period before each pageant. During my fieldwork at the production of a local pageant, I was witness to the rehearsal process through which contestants learn and practice appropriate answers to such questions. These rehearsals took place once a week over a nine-week period, and the general format was as follows: each contestant would stand at a mock podium, in front of a group of other contestants, the pageant producers, and myself. The contestant was then asked to respond to hypothetical or "likely" questions posed by members of this small audience.[9] The questions were quite varied, ranging from timely, overtly political issues to more generalized, politically ambiguous questions.

The director and producer of the pageant offered advice and criticism after each contestant finished her mock interview. Most of the criticism was consistent with the tips of pageant "how-to" books, which are mainly toast-master-style hints: avoid "ummms," "aahs," excessive talking with the hands, and nervous laughter.[10] There were also, however, directed comments about appropriate and inappropriate responses. By way of giving advice, the director told a story to the group about a former contestant who had extraordinarily long hair. She was asked during the interview if she would cut her hair if she won the title and was requested to do so by the pageant committee. The contestant responded "No," because she couldn't see a reason why her hair would matter (a reasonable enough answer to me). The director, however, believed this to be an inappropriate answer and advised the contestants to remember what "it means to be a representative—you can't think only about yourself."

In another example, a contestant was asked about her involvement with her issue platform, "Children Having Children," a volunteer group dedicated to assisting teenage mothers. In her answer, she said, "I would advise teenagers: if you are going to have sex, please remember to use protection." The director immediately interrupted, directing the contestant to never "talk about *having* sex—talk about getting *education* about sex."[11] Both of these examples point to predominant themes that are expected in the answers: self-sacrifice, appropriate moral foundation, and commitment to education. The advice given by the director also steers the contestants away from overtly political issues (such as self-determination and sex) by way of offering safer, more palatable alternatives.

In fact, contestants consider "politics" to be appropriate content for the interview in the larger state and national pageants but unfair at the local level. In yet another curiously ironic move, contestants continually emphasize education and knowledge about current events as the only way to succeed in the interview competition, while at the same time they feel that any judge who asks a contestant to put this knowledge to use in an answer is somehow "out of line." Alice said during our interview that people are constantly surprised to sit down and talk with her, because she has opinions about particular issues such as environmental concerns and animal rights. But she added:

> In a way, we are more aware about things that are going on, because we have to be. We have to be up on news events. Hopefully, they won't ask you about your political views because they shouldn't put you in that position, but they could ask you what you wanted to change about the world and how you felt on environmental issues, but they shouldn't ask you which candidate you'll vote for, because the press might ask you that, but you're supposed to decline because you don't want to get into something political. But in a way, you are more informed because you have to be. You don't have any idea what they are going to ask you. And you want to be sure that you are well informed on the variety of things that they might ask you.

There are political issues that are widely recognized as more appropriate than others, such as environmental issues, a "safe" political realm regardless of one's personal politics, or "changing the world," which although overambitious is safely nonspecific. Other issues are not safe. Diane claims that for her pageant, the directors explicitly advised the contestants to avoid any conversations about current events:

> In city pageants they really try to stay away from things like religion and public events and politics. They really try not to get into those.

Because those are things that people have such high opinions about, so opinionated about, that it seems like it would be unfair for a girl to give her own opinion and contradict what the judges feel; it would really hurt her, so they don't do that.

The extent to which the interview questions may be formulated on a political basis seems to depend, at least in part, on the particular pageant and the specific judges. For example, in direct contrast to Diane's account, Mary, who also represented a small local area, claimed that the questions asked of her were explicitly political:

For the interview, [it's] knowing politics, knowing about your country, knowing some dates, just being educated. They might say, who is Nixon, Kennedy, and Bush—what do they have in common? They'll go totally off the wall too. They'll ask who's the president in nineteen-so-and-so. They get that specific. They'll even ask about news reporters. My friend said they asked her that, like who is Jane Pauley or something. And you have to know these people, so there is a lot that you have to study. Lot of politics, political things. Especially this year, about the [Gulf] war. You had to know a lot about it.

Of course, what Mary considers "political" might not be universal opinion: knowing who a popular news reporter is or a having a historical knowledge of past presidents could as easily be considered being "culturally literate." One thing is clear, however. As the pageants become more nationally significant, the interview competition becomes more and more overtly political. Grace details how this process accelerates as the pageants become more important:

At the local level, it started out like, "If I was a visitor in your town, where would you take me, what would you show me, what are the high points?" . . . "If your house was burning down and you could only take one thing out and it wasn't a person, what would you take?" You know, they were more like emotional. That one wasn't quite as hard, I left feeling good about that one. California got a little harder— who's your favorite novelist and why. National was definitely the hardest. It was right in the middle of Tiananmen Square, and all that, and so one of my friends was asked, she went in there and they asked, "Name all the leaders, all the pros and cons of Tiananmen Square." They asked me how I would solve the deficit if I were president. When you got up to a higher level, it was more political questions and awareness of the world around you, it was definitely political happenings—

"If there was a run-off between so-and-so and so-and-so, who would you vote for and why?" It was very political.

Grace's comments reveal the increasing importance of the notion of "representative." The woman who represents a small town needs to be equipped to sell the town to a visitor, to be a part of the Chamber of Commerce, or to prove herself worthy of the town in emotional and moral terms. However, the larger and more significant the geographic area that the woman represents, the more sophisticated and complicated the job of "representing" becomes.

Part of being considered an appropriate representative is the expectation that all pageant contestants will prove to be good role models.[12] In beauty pageants, the role that contestants are expected to play is the curious and rather contradictory role of independent femininity. In this respect and commensurate with liberal doctrine, thinking about gender as a series of roles indicates a commitment to a notion of the self that considers gender as yet another layer of identity that is mapped onto an essential core. This is the crux of the concept of "role models," a notion that we craft ourselves out of a composite of qualities that we and others find admirable. Of course, beauty pageants must be singularly dedicated to the concept of role models because, after all, Miss America is widely constructed as *the* role model for women in American society. Indeed, this vague ideal comprises almost the entire basis for the claim of "representativeness" to which pageant contestants energetically cling. This construction is maintained partly through a public, collective memory about individual identifications with Miss America, so to be considered a "good role model" means to police oneself in terms of dominantly enforced norms of behavior. One contestant I interviewed, Mary, claimed that her position as a role model for a small local community was what "made it all worth it" for her. She detailed the importance—and the self-regulation required—in being a good role model:

Once I was driving up to the . . . fair and I was in my dress and didn't have my crown and banner on, and my hair was all done. And I looked over and there was this little girl and she was pointing at me, saying, "You're SO pretty," like that, and I reached down and grabbed my crown and went like this [put it on her head], and she just went "Oooohhhh," and little kids in parades just go, "Mom, there's Miss America," and it's neat for little kids to look up to somebody who— I'm not going to go out and smoke behind the 7–11. I really really wish that the judges could see the girls when they're not at practice and they're not on stage and get to know what they are going to do the entire year of their reign. For the little kids. That's the most important part. A lot of older people don't care, but the kids do.

Mary, as well as most of the other contestants I interviewed, stated explicitly that wearing a crown and banner automatically put one in the position of being a role model, and therefore, as part of the "job," one must modify one's behavior to adhere to a dominant definition of precisely who and what this role model is.

But the concept of role models is constructed as more than an omnipotent surveillance device for crowned beauty queens. It functions as an important subject matter for many of the questions asked during the onstage interview competition. For example, in an interview during the Miss USA 1993 pageant, the following exchange took place:

Question: As times change, what contemporary woman do you think is the best role model for your generation, and why?

Answer: Hillary Clinton. As the president's wife, she's shown us that we can focus on our future, and be more concerned about our career and balance it with parenthood, and if '92 was the year of the woman, then the nineties could become the decade of the woman.[13]

Not surprisingly, Hillary Clinton is presented as a good role model for women with the necessary introduction, "as the president's wife." In another example, the contestant addresses the general importance of role models by choosing "positive role models" as her issue platform. Constructing a platform around role models legitimates this concern as a relevant social issue that requires immediate attention:

Question: It is important for young people to have positive role models. What can we do to have people for them to look up to?

Answer: I think that we need to remember that we are all heroes in some fashion. A recent survey said that 70 percent of Americans believed there were no heroes. But all it takes to be a hero is grace under pressure, that's what Ernest Hemingway said. I think we can be positive role models by just being heroes for children in their everyday lives. They need to see people who are hardworking, that aren't necessarily

Superman or Ninja Turtles or something like that, but real live heroes, and I think that's what we need to do to give them positive influence.[14]

Acknowledging the issue of role models not only establishes it as a noble social cause alongside AIDS awareness, homelessness, and care for the elderly, but also entrenches the importance of a figure like Miss America (as someone other than Superman, or a Ninja Turtle, or, more recently, a Power Ranger) in the minds of the audience. And, in a familiar strategy, this contestant uses statistics—and recognizably significant cultural figures like Ernest Hemingway—to establish her authority in these matters. She also draws on an important cultural construction in American society: the concept of "heroes." Although she doesn't give a specific definition of what—or who—these heroes should be, it is clear that in the United States, heroes are defined according to a particular democratization of valor where the "common man" is positioned as an everyday hero. For her answer, this contestant situates herself, the judges, and the audience within her answer, relying on the easily recognizable trope of the unique contribution of the hardworking liberal individual who overcomes obstacles and takes advantage of opportunity.

Even when interview questions seem unrelated to constructions of *any* recognizable identity, liberal themes eventually emerge. Liberal education, commitment to heterosexuality and family, and individualism are themes that inflect not only the contestant's interview answers, but also the structure and logic of the pageant itself. But the one theme that emerged as the most salient issue for Miss America contestants in the 1990s mirrored one of, if not the, most important issue engaging the nation as a whole in this decade: racial identity and multiculturalism. Not unexpectedly, a critique of racist policies and legislation is usually absent from the Miss America pageant. What is found is a commitment to democratic pluralism and a belief in the success of ethnic harmony as the heart of U.S. society.

As I've argued, a particular notion of "Americanism" in beauty pageants relies on a concept that selves are ultimately craftable—one need merely choose the most desirable self to be and then become it. It is obvious, in this particular tenet of liberal individualism, what kind of self is most desirable: the "American" self. This "American" self is not that of beat poets, or intellectuals, or even rock-and-roll stars. In this case, the "American" self is loosely tied to notions of national identity, identified by a particular ethnic mix. Americanism in beauty pageants is a conservative, idyllic version of the "melting-pot" and indicates a composite of what are considered the positive aspects of ethnic identity—a composite that results, through the dilution and obfuscation of identifiable specific ethnic characteristics, in the constitution of a self who is usually white and middle-class (or at least aspires to be both).

Obviously, though, ethnic or racial characteristics such as skin color cannot easily disappear. But because the scarcity of women of color on the Miss America stage dilutes the usual threat and fear that accompanies all people of color, skin color is then translated, within the beauty pageant, as the marker of authenticity, evidence that the pageant is a diverse event. For example, in the 1991 Miss America pageant, Miss New York, an African American woman, was selected as one of the five finalists and eventually made it to first runner-up. She was asked a direct question about racism, and it was clear that her answer was credited as being authentic because of her status as a black woman. Because the pageant is a predominantly white production—and because white people have little direct experience as the targets of racism—her very presence as a successful black American signals a progressive move to a (more) nonracist society, even as this same presence is exoticized and eroticized precisely because of her race.[15]

In a similar vein, many of the contestants are called upon during the interview competition to explain the benefits of being raised in a "multicultural" household. The pageant version of multiculturalism works, much like the world of commerce and corporations, to depoliticize the material conditions of racial inequality in this society; it glorifies instead a nonthreatening mystique produced by dominant definitions of race and ethnicity. Consider in this respect the following exchange:

Question: You have a bicultural background. What does that mean?

Answer: My father is Oriental—Chinese, and my mother is Polish.

Question: What did you learn from that?

Answer: Orientals have a strong honor system; they teach you at a very young age to respect elders in your family or community. There is love and understanding and respect instilled in me.

Question: How is your mom different?
Answer: My mom is sentimental, my father is the strong one. My mother looks to him for support, and he looks to her for sensitivity. . . .

Question: Who do you take after?
Answer: I'm a combination of both, I got the best of both.[16]

"The best of both" is perhaps the truest statement of melting-pot ideology and an implicit motto for a conservative utopic reading of 1990s' multicultural society. This contestant applies this composite logic of the melting pot to her own gender identity, thereby assuming the subject position of the liberal female, who is sentimental yet strong, supportive yet sensitive. In constituting herself as an individual, she merely selected the "best of both" from an apparently open and limitless set of options, and armed with these positive characteristics, she crafted a multicultural self. This move refracts and dilutes the material realities of a multicultural society. The following is another example of the flattening-out of the complexities of living in a multicultural environment:

Question: You come from a multiethnic background—your dad is American, and your mom from the Philippines. Was your household different from everyone else's?
Answer: Yes, we had rice, fish, and soy sauce every night, and we had to take our shoes off.

Question: What about dating procedures?
Answer: I couldn't date until I was seventeen, and I had to have a chaperone in my little sister.

Question: How did your parents meet?
Answer: Dad's in the navy, and mom was running for Miss Philippines—and she won![17]

Several stories are told in this brief exchange. There is, first of all, the reduction of a multiethnic identity to food and fashion. The assumptions in this exchange about Asian dating practices and female sexuality as something to be protected at all times (even though the restrictions on dating this contestant experienced are not atypical in white, middle-class households) hardly give insight into the uniqueness of a multiethnic background but do signal the orientalizing thrust of this exchange. Finally, the contestant legitimates her presence and participation, as well as the participation of all the other contestants in the beauty pageant, by offering the romantic tale of her parents as testimony to the sentiment that it is possible to find a husband if one knows the right way to be beautiful. In this sense, her mother has indeed "won"—not only the title, but the husband as well.

At first glance, it seems as though the latter two examples, in their focus on the specifics of multiethnicity, disrupt the impassioned plea of the previously mentioned Miss New York 1991 contestant, who, responding to how Americans should eliminate racism, asked all of us "to start acting like one people: Americans!" If we, however, take a closer look at these "specifics," we can see how the responses of each contestant assure both the judges and the audience that, despite their backgrounds, they are indeed Americans, complete with the enthusiastic embrace of such "American" notions as rigid, conventional gender identity, dating rituals, and the importance of marriage. Their Americanness is infused with difference, but it is a difference that has been domesticated, a racialization that is diluted by both literal and metaphorical tropes of whiteness.

The interview competition both sustains and is constituted by various representations and discursive formations of gendered and raced identities. These representations are enhanced by the "live" quality of the interview; theoretically, anything can happen, or any words be spoken, during this particular exchange. Because this segment of the pageant lacks the formulaic, homogenous quality of, say, the swimsuit competition, it is considered an event that truly celebrates individualism. The only other event within the Miss America pageant that restores heterogeneity in a similar way is the talent competition, which represents the sole space and time within the pageant where the contestant makes an autonomous (in a manner of speaking) decision about her performance.

STAR SEARCHING: THE TALENT COMPETITION

Introduced as a formal element of the Miss America pageant in 1938, the talent competition was perhaps the most significant change in the transi-

tion of the pageant from a simple bathing beauty contest to its more contemporary manifestation as a showcase for amateur talent. The talent competition of the Miss America pageant is both the pageant's claim on and
legitimation of a specifically "American" middlebrow culture, and it represents a struggle for control over a popular domain that has, to say the
least, historically been contested and unstable. The various talents performed on beauty pageant stages are efforts to connect popular arts and
middlebrow culture to "respectable" and "refined" traditions of art. Contestants singing arias from *La Boheme* or playing Mozart on the piano are
part of a conscious assertion of a cultural national identity on several
fronts: the performer's engagement with the material itself, thus legitimating her claim to be "talented"; the audience's engagement with the
particular performances; the judges' recognition that this particular talent is "distinguished" on an apparently universal scale; and, finally, the
contribution the performance makes to a national popular culture. This
is not to argue that the talent competition within the Miss America
pageant represents a struggle to contend for *the* national art form, but
it is to claim that this particular element of the pageant situates itself
squarely as an essential element for the "whole" American woman.

The question then becomes, if the Miss America pageant constitutes and
represents the American woman, what role does race, class, and gender
play in this configuring of nation? Insofar as all elements of the Miss America pageant figure the nation in popular cultural terms, the identity constituted is always an intersectional one, inflected by race, gender, and class.
This national construction is a process, not a fixed condition; it is the product of interaction between the past and the present—and the future. As
such, the national figure that is both invented and enabled by the Miss
America pageant involves boundaries, movement, and opposition—that
is, it progresses according to what it is *not* as much as what it *is*. How does
this work in the talent competition? In this part of the program, the gendered identities of the contestants are constituted according to a set of
boundaries that define the parameters of the appropriately feminine. The
racial identities of the Miss America contestants are constructed in terms
of opposition—what the talent competition obscures and disavows reveals
the underlying racial politics structuring the event. Finally, the contestants
produce particular class identities according to a logic concerning the tal-

ent competition's uplifting potential, focusing on the way in which talent is construed as the collection of cultural capital.

The notion that culture is something one can accumulate as a possession has a long and heavily contested history in the United States. The ruptures and changes in eighteenth- and nineteenth-century definitions of high, low, and popular culture, well documented by Janice Radway, Joan Rubin, Paul DiMaggio, Lawrence Levine, and others, emerged from new mass technologies and the shift in cultural production and reproduction brought on by the reorganization of capital. One result of this transition was the restructuring of the culture industries, including cultural sites such as parks, fairs, and museums. This revamping—and, really, reinventing—of the cultural industries continued throughout the nineteenth and twentieth centuries with mass-mediated technologies such as film, radio, and television.

And so, a coming to terms with the shifting divide between high and low culture, not to mention competing definitions of what constitutes the "popular," was manifested in different forms and social forces. One important cultural formation that emerged out of the "culture wars" was the creation of a new social class and aesthetic commitment: the "middlebrow." The debates over what constituted culture in the eighteenth and nineteenth centuries were motivated by a reinventing and retrenching of hierarchical boundaries between social classes, so that classes were no longer strictly vertically arranged but were conceived of as horizontal divisions between those who had "acquired" culture and those who had not. Pierre Bourdieu's important work on this subject explores the cultivation of social taste, or "distinction," and argues that this cultivation is acquired through education and not determined by social origin.[18] This cultivation of taste, or the collecting of what Bourdieu calls "cultural capital," partly determined the aesthetic and social boundaries of a burgeoning class distinction, the middlebrow. Not a part of the genteel elite, nor of an unrefined mass, middlebrow culture was about the acquisition of culture and the educating of oneself in social taste and cultural authority. This definition of culture, as something that could be achieved through both education and desire, was linked to the thinking of Matthew Arnold, among others, and was the result of pursuing "the best that has been thought and said in the world."[19] In this view, culture was a process, a matter of individual progress, perfectly in keeping with democratic values and principles concerning liberal education and equal opportunity.

Part of the debate that raged around Arnoldian views of culture involved the connection between commodification and culture. To commodify culture immediately and irrevocably situates culture as something that is no longer in the hands of the elite, thereby conferring a new status of availability and accessibility to this "property" that was once considered only available to those with either a natural ability or an elite social origin. The commodification of culture, or the accumulation of cultural capital, distinguished this social group from either lowbrow or highbrow and became the defining characteristic of the middlebrow class. As Radway argues, "Middlebrow . . . had to be coined to map a new taste culture or aesthetic formation, one that self-consciously appropriated the value of 'Culture' and 'the serious,' even as it linked those concepts and the objects that embodied them with new, highly suspect uses."[20] The new middle-class entrepreneurs of the nineteenth century engaged in the business of commodifying and marketing culture. Radway continues, "Culture, in their view, was less something offered for contemplation and study, a thing to be valued in its own right, than a sign of achievement and a mark of social position. It thus became fungible, a thing to be exchanged for ulterior purposes."[21]

The history of the construction and management of the cultural space of the middlebrow provides a context in which to situate the talent competition in the Miss America pageant. Situating this event in such a way, however, is not to commit the historical fallacy of reading the present into the past, but it is to identify a historical context for understanding what is often considered to be an anachronistic spectacle. Although the debates forged over what constitutes culture and cultural authority, made even more concrete in what Radway calls the "book club wars," continue to have force in contemporary society, the "scandal" over the commodification of culture loses significance in a society thoroughly permeated with mass-mediated definitions and articulations of cultural prestige and authority. The middlebrow is no longer as scandalous, depraved, or cannibalistic as it was considered by the elite class in the eighteenth and nineteenth centuries; it is, rather, the place where many Americans comfortably and confidently construct their national and cultural identities.

Which is not to say that the middlebrow is situated in uncomplex and insignificant ways in American popular culture, including within the talent competition in the Miss America pageant.

The Miss America pageant and other beauty pageants like it are commonly conceptualized by critics and the general public alike as exemplary instances of lowbrow culture, because of its anachronistic style and kitschy character. I am not necessarily interested in debating whether this is true; the more interesting question embedded in this formulation is why is the Miss America pageant still important for both lowbrow and middlebrow culture? Why is it that the pageant—and especially the talent portion—has not turned self-ironic, or burlesque, or parodic? Why hasn't the Miss America pageant made the postmodern turns made by so many other forms of U.S. popular culture?

At least part of an answer to these questions has to do with the way the Miss America pageant situates itself outside of popular culture. The Miss America pageant defines itself first and foremost as an institution of education. It is not a beauty pageant, its participants vehemently argue. Rather, it is an organization dedicated to the education and refinement of young American women. But what kind of education? In and for what are Miss America contestants—and their audience—educated? Surely the most obvious and present form of education that is offered by the Miss America pageant is a traditional one: college scholarships are awarded as prizes, and the organization donates millions of dollars each year for regional and state academic awards. But there are other edifying or educative practices and commitments that structure the pageant. The talent competition represents one such commitment: the educating of women in culture and refinement.

This kind of education is linked to the nineteenth-century views on both the acquisition of culture and democracy's role in this acquisition. The Miss America pageant is self-consciously dedicated to an egalitarian premise of "anyone can do it if you try." Like book clubs and programs, the talent competition presents to the pageant audience the cultured self—an identity or persona that is realized only after disciplining one's self in the pursuit of a genteel aesthetic (see plate 4).[22] The talent competition produces itself in direct opposition to kitschy mass culture, seeing itself as on a par with symphony orchestras, refined Broadway musicals, and the ballet. Obviously, the talent competition does not mistake itself for the New York Philharmonic, but it does situate itself in a similar category that involves strict discipline and training in the practice of recognizing and legitimating "worthy" art forms. All of the contestants work with professional trainers and coaches, and many express interest and commitment to continuing their education in their particular talent.

Despite this appeal to "high" culture standards, the talent competition understands the acquisition of culture to be a process deeply engrained in democratic principles. This availability of culture disentangles wealth and social origin from refinement and "distinction" and situates the talent competition as a crucial factor in the pageant's overall claim of democratic individualism. Indeed, it is within the talent competition that the contestants are most vigorously encouraged to be individuals. As Genie Sayles advises in her pageant handbook,

> There is no excuse for anything less than perfection in talent competition. Talent is the one competition you have more control over than any other. You may not have chosen your body structure or your facial features. You may not have been asked a single question in interview that you studied months for. You may not be able to afford a velvet and gold lamé dress for evening gown. But you— You—choose your talent! You also choose the costume you will wear in talent. You choose the image you will convey. And . . . you choose how flawlessly you will perform your talent. You CHOOSE that.[23]

This emphasis on choice is crucial: it not only underscores the significance placed on individual choice within the pageant as a whole, thus deflecting common criticisms of contestants as cultural dupes, but also recognizes individual choices within the talent program itself. Whatever talent a contestant chooses, it will be understood—by the other contestants, the judges, and the audience—to be an accurate reflection of the contestant's inner ability to demonstrate social taste and refinement. It will also be interpreted as clear evidence of training and discipline—namely, the disciplining of oneself in the practice of recognizing and performing signs of distinction. Andrew Ross sees this process as an "appropriation of distinctive cultural signs." He says that "this act of appropriation—showing 'good,' 'bad,' or 'mediocre' taste in the way in which we present ourselves to the world—depends, in each case, upon an individual's cultural competence, or mastery of the process of decoding/deciphering cultural signs."[24]

In the talent competition, Miss America contestants can demonstrate precisely this kind of "cultural competence." The cultivation of this competence, as Ross points out, is not only about the recognition of already established categories of social taste and cultural prestige; it is, in fact, involved in the *creation* of these categories. Thus the talent choices made by the contestants not only communicate a commitment to social taste and culture, but also create a specifically gendered component to these categories. If the rest of the Miss America pageant can be conceptualized as a popular cultural event, why bring in *any* gestures—no matter how superficial or transparent—to high culture? Gender provides the logic underlying the talent competition; the public performances that edify as well as entertain the national audience represent the "civilizing" tendencies of women for a national culture. In other words, the beauty pageant is a national event in which the bodies of women are asked to perform all of the functions of a nation, including its civility. There is a vast literature on the historical role of women in "civilizing" the nation, covering the gamut from voting to moral superiority to Republican mothering.[25] Where can we witness this process within contemporary popular culture, within the beauty pageant? Or, to put the question differently, why is it that culture is present in a rarefied form in the beauty pageant? The role of the Miss America contestants within the talent competition is to educate the nation in terms of civility and to demonstrate the moral qualities of women as national figures. Talent as cultural capital not only is about conferring prestige on those individuals who have mastered the particular talent, but also represents the constitution of contestants as specific national figures, those who possess the ability, by virtue of their gender and their class, to function as civilizing factors in the nation's progress.

Clearly, the beauty pageant is not about masculine prowess that maps the nation. Unlike the masculinity displayed in popular cultural events that ask men to perform the functions of a nation—boxing spectacles or body-building contests, for example—the femininity that so insistently constitutes the talent competition is not a crude display of power, but a refined performance of social taste and distinction. The model of middlebrow culture on which the talent competition depends refers to high or "legitimate" culture as it simultaneously makes these references palatable and accessible for a mass-mediated audience—and it does this on and through the bodies of women. In other words, if, as Ross claims, middlebrow culture is an "exemplary model of containment," what does it contain? Aside from reining in debates about the stultifying standards of traditionally high culture as opposed to the base quality of low culture, middlebrow culture contains the threat of women who publicly perform their femininity by retrenching and reconnecting this femininity with refined social distinction and civilizing and edifying tendencies.[26]

Obviously, then, within the Miss America pageant, any old talent will not do. And, not surprisingly, during the twelve-week rehearsal I observed, time not spent on interviews was spent focusing on talent choices. The contestants not only performed their talents in practice runs, but also discussed with the pageant director and each other whether their choices were appropriate. This discussion was truly relevant for only a few of the contestants—those who chose talents outside the traditional purview of the Miss America pageant's definition of *talent*. The majority of the contestants chose vocals as their talent; vocal performances are clearly the most popular choice in the national pageant. In the 1997 Miss America pageant, twenty-eight out of fifty contestants performed a vocal number, either a version of a Broadway musical, a popular song, or a classical or operatic rendition. And since 1990, five out of the eight winners of the Miss America crown chose vocal performances.[27]

There are clear definitions of what constitutes talent in the Miss America pageant, and because the talent competition sets this pageant apart from other beauty pageants in the country, much effort is expended to ensure that it is taken seriously. Taking it seriously means setting boundaries that are informed by cultural standards of appropriate entertainment for the contestants—even if the participants in the pageant consider these boundaries somewhat arbitrary. As Sayles laments:

> Pianists seem to follow vocalists in popularity, followed then by
> gymnasts and modern dancers. Over time, ballet dancers seem to
> do very nicely. Like classical vocalists, they seem to impress judges
> whether or not they are particularly good. There is a steeped-in,
> cultural snob appeal of these two art forms that can impress judges
> who know nothing about how they should be performed. The sad

truth is, really talented people who performed a folk talent beautifully have been passed over for a less talented person who poorly performed ballet or shrieked a wobbly high C, simply because the judges thought the "higher class" talent meant it was a better talent. Nothing could be further from the truth, of course, but those are the things we can't always control. It's a shame.[28]

Shame or not, the surveillance around the talent competition is understood as something "we can't always control," and therefore the boundaries are to be observed if one desires to win the crown. Needless to say, in the pageant rehearsal I observed, the contestant who chose to sing an aria from *La Boheme* made a clearly safe choice in her talent, as did the woman who sang a number from *Les Miserables*. The trickier performances came from those who ventured outside the safety net offered by traditional vocals (see plate 5).

One contestant chose a comedy act as her talent. She portrayed a ditzy waitress who uttered social commentary on every issue imaginable. Interestingly, her act mocked the stereotypical banal answers to interview questions within beauty pageants present in contemporary U.S. folklore; her representation of a waitress desired to resolve so many issues, from negotiating the North Atlantic Free Trade Agreement to freeing "Willy," that she was understood as imminently laughable. The pageant director, however, was clearly uneasy about her performance. Her unease was directed at two separate issues: one was that a performance of a dumb waitress shatters any pretension of taste and refinement. On this issue, Sayles offers these words of advice: "The points go to the cultural prestige acts and the socially approved ones. Anything that makes you look less than glamourous, intelligent, competent, and classy can be a mistake. Your imitation of a lame duck may be a favorite at home (and backstage with the girls, for that matter); but before the judges and audience, it could make you seem silly—not a Miss Wonderful."[29] This factor—silliness—was the focus of the pageant director's criticism. Apparently, in the world of pageants, to have a sense of humor (especially about oneself) is one thing; to be a buffoon is quite another. Given the precarious ground on which any live performance rests, it is essential to discipline oneself to look, as Sayles says, glamorous, intelligent, competent, and classy.

The pageant director was also concerned about another issue, the self-reflective and self-referential quality of the comedic performance. Issues such as animal abuse (or freeing Willy) or immigration often provide the quite legitimate basis for contestants' issue platforms in beauty pageants. To mock these issues—even in an exaggerated, comedic manner, even from someone on the inside—hits a bit too close to home. It reveals that the contestants' embrace of these issues may indeed be a laughing matter and hints at a degree of cynicism or hypocrisy that derails the logic of the pageant's structure. The judges in this pageant apparently felt the blow; this contestant scored quite low in the talent portion of the program.

There were two other performances in this particular pageant that challenged the middlebrow construction of the talent competition in important ways. The previous example highlights the way in which borders are set around the talent competition in an overtly gendered sense: there is a fine line between performing on the pageant stage as a refined beauty and performing on the pageant stage as a cutesy, silly "female." But there are other borders that organize the parameters of the talent competition. Public performances—especially musical ones—also entail the heavy policing of racial borders and boundaries. Women of color are positioned within the pageant in ways that retrench whiteness by means of addition; in other words, the femininities of women of color are added to an ever-broadening field of white womanhood without ever seriously challenging the boundaries of this field. The talent competition, with its emphasis on individuality and potential for transgression, becomes perhaps the most precarious stage within the pageant on which racial identity is performed. The primary representations of women of color within the Miss America pageant are African American women, and the connections between African American bodies and popular culture—especially music—have a long history. One important account of this history is Eric Lott's work on blackface minstrelsy, which emphasizes the negotiations and oppositions between black and white identities—indeed, emphasizes how blackness was essential in the formation of "whiteness"—in the early nineteenth century. Blackface minstrelsy provided a stage for the production of white identity that relied upon what Lott calls the "coupling" of racial fear and desire, or ambivalence and attraction, a dialectic that is always precarious and that threatens at any moment to subvert dominant norms of whiteness.

This fascination with difference as it constituted minstrelsy continues to inflect contemporary forms of popular culture. The practice of exoticizing and eroticizing bodies of people of color as the authentic practitioners of "native" popular culture has, as George Lipsitz powerfully argues, proven remarkably effective in terms of market and social value. But like the contestant who bravely attempted the comedy routine, the separation between "going native" and being a racial threat to the structure of the pageant is fragile indeed. It is acceptable within the Miss America pageant to position oneself as a mediator of ethnic identity if one has an "authentic" claim to this identity; this positioning enables the pageant audience's (if not the whole American public's) fascination with ethnic culture in its exotic-erotic form.

It is not usually acceptable, however, to perform race in a threatening manner. Another example clarifies this point. At this same rehearsal, the one African American contestant asked the rest of the group to help her decide which of two songs she should perform on Pageant Night: the Whitney Houston ballad "I'm Going to Run to You," or a version of Liza Minnelli's "Cabaret." This woman was quite talented and received accolades from the other contestants for both performances. It was clear, however, that "Cabaret" was the preference of those associated with the pageant. Later in the evening, this contestant approached me and asked me what I thought about the two songs. I replied that, like the others, I thought both were wonderful performances, but unlike the rest of the group, I preferred the Whitney Houston song. She replied that she too liked that song, but if she performed it, "The judges are going to look at me and say, 'She's just another black girl doing Whitney Houston.'"[30]

It was clear to both the contestant and the producers of the pageant that the Liza Minnelli song was considered more inclusive, which then situated the contestant outside the particulars of her race. This account exemplifies how contestants within the pageant are both representations and self-representations; the contestant herself was quite aware of the penalties for appearing too "black." The challenge, instead, was whether she could successfully pass for the "essence" of white. To be "just another black girl doing Whitney Houston" is a position of identity reserved for African Americans; quite obviously, white contestants never have to spend time on the particular quandary of whether they are performing beauty and femininity in a way that is considered "too white."[31] Put another way, this story illuminates the layered processes of self-construction experienced by all beauty pageant contestants. This particular contestant had to negotiate the effects of layering a "black song" over her black body, and she chose to avoid the danger that the judges would find the combination "too black." The performance of a "white" song presumed to have universal appeal appeared, by contrast, more appropriate—it worked to protect whiteness by rendering it invisible. There seems to be an implicit understanding (by both the black contestant and the white pageant producers) that the threat of being "too black"—or failing to pass—must be avoided by any black contestant who wishes to remain competitive. The apprehension felt by both contestants and producers reflects the danger that the politics of whiteness framing the pageant might become visible.

It is quite a different story to appear "ethnic" as opposed to "too black." For example, another contestant performed race in a different manner. Unlike the previous contestant, whose potential choice of talent could have signified her investment in blackness to her detriment, this contestant performed race in a positive and even uplifting manner. Her talent, which she called "traditional Middle Eastern dance," but which was quickly shortened by the other contestants to "belly dancing," involved a sensuous dance wearing an "authentic" costume from the Middle East. This contestant was skilled in this style of dancing and effectively claimed authentic status through the fact that she lived in the Middle East (where in the Middle East was neither specified by the contestant nor was she asked by the other participants; it was clear that the specifics of place made no difference on her claim of authenticity).

The "traditional Middle Eastern dance" was highly sexual; this contestant wore less and revealed more of her skin than any other contestant. Not once, however, was the sexual nature of the dance discussed or criticized. Rather, her fellow contestants responded enthusiastically to her talent, as did the judges: she eventually won the pageant, with the focus of the judges placed on her authentic rendering of the Middle Eastern dance. Clearly, race was inflected differently and understood differently for this contestant than it was for the contestant who wanted to sing the Whitney Houston song. The focus on the "folk," or the "native," invoked and construed the dance as authentic and therefore not only a legitimate but a potentially edifying talent to perform. This woman's race (her ethnic status was "partially Middle Eastern") was exoticized and eroticized; the success of her talent depended on what Lipsitz has called an "eroticization of difference and an engenderation of conquest."[32] In other words, the presence of this talent within the pageant clearly and unproblematically represented a world of the Other, and the orientalizing gaze of the judges accepted—indeed, applauded—this world as different, exotic, and exciting, but not threatening. In this instance, the difference was already accounted for before the talent was ever performed, so that it bolstered rather than disrupted a dominant representation of femininity. The authenticity of the dance derives from an invented historical representation of the Other woman, the sexualized, erotic, exotic woman. Her ethnicity was easily assimilated into the pageant's structure and ideology.

Perhaps the most important difference between these two racially inflected performances is that the woman who wanted to sing Whitney Houston's song is perceived as raced. Her self-awareness and wariness at becoming "just another black girl doing Whitney Houston" hints at this contestant's awareness of the perception and threat of "blackness" in contemporary U.S. culture. In contrast, the other contestant was perceived as ethnic: her performance offered a romanticized glimpse of an exotic and exciting ancestral past. As a contestant with an ethnic heritage but without identifiably ethnic markers such as skin color or accent, she both produces herself within and is produced by a conservative discourse of the multicultural U.S., where different ethnicities live harmoniously together. Adolph Reed Jr. has argued that the categories of race and ethnicity, rather than possessing a meaningful and independent difference outside of specific social and cultural hierarchies, are "just labels for different magnitudes of distance from the most desirable status on a continuum of 'okayness.'"[33] In other words, interpreting the Middle Eastern dance as ethnic brings this performance closer to whiteness and further from the stigma of blackness. Her performance can be considered by the pageant as one of the "positive" benefits to multicultural society, but one that recoups rather than disrupts racial hierarchies; it is part of what Reed calls "an application for a kind of contingent membership in whiteness, or for recognition of an ethniclike intermediate category of okayness—both gambits that only reinforce existing racial ideology and hierarchy."[34] The African

American contestant was interpreted more as an "objective" example of racial difference; her difference does not conjure up tales of exotic pasts and ethnic harmony but rather represents the scary and often disruptive present context of "blackness."

Although Sayles warns against the potential failure of performing what she calls "folk art," there are instances where a talent performance that relies on a dominant white perception of the authentic Other works to a contestant's advantage. Sayles says:

> Stay away from talents that make you look either country
> bumpkin or silly or cutesie or goofy or ignorant or crude—even
> if you can perform it accurately in its native form. You may be per-
> forming before judges who have no acquaintance whatsoever
> with your folk art as being art, just folk! If, however, you combine
> a native form with a classical form—such as Chopin with Dixieland—
> you'll stand a better chance.[35]

Her warning makes a certain kind of sense: social prestige and cultural value are usually awarded to talent performances that adhere to middle-brow cultural standards. However, as Lott has argued with regard to minstrelsy, the celebration of an "authentic" people's culture sidesteps the issue of high versus low culture and replaces it with the authority of the "folk."[36] The "traditional Middle Eastern dance" carries with it this kind of cultural authority, presenting a dialectic of fear and desire that results in a palatable exoticism rather than a threatening subversion.

Both of these examples are reminders of a powerful narrative surrounding racial identity, that of the opposition between talent and natural ability. It is clear that throughout U.S. history, African American talent has been degraded as something "natural." The skill of African American basketball players is seen as obvious evidence of African Americans' natural ability to play sports and constitutes the logic behind the film title *White Men Can't Jump*.[37] The "natural" ability that black people demonstrate in dancing or keeping rhythm is seen as "fact" in the United States, where the bodies of African Americans are considered somehow more corporeal than white bodies.

This ideology about natural ability is behind the African American contestant's reluctance to perform a Whitney Houston song. The choice to sing a "black" song would reduce her talent to "natural ability" rather than emphasize her training or her making and bettering of herself. Singing Liza Minnelli not only situates her outside the particulars of her race, it situates her within the particulars of class, where a definition of talent is inextricably tied to the bettering of self. It legitimates her as a contestant, because to sing a song outside the purview of what she is "naturally" predisposed to perform is incontrovertible evidence of training; it is the logic and the legitimation behind why white women in the Miss America pageant can sing Whitney Houston and why black women are praised for singing opera.

This logic is clearly inflected in the concept of middlebrow culture, where talent is an acquired skill, an acquisition that specifically works against the notion of folk talent. Though an individual may demonstrate a proclivity toward particular talents, the mastering of that talent is not embedded within oneself but is outside of the self, something one must work toward. This is precisely the logic that structures the success of the contestant who performed the Middle Eastern "traditional" dance. Despite this woman's claims of authentic Middle Eastern ancestry, her body and her femininity were explicitly coded white. And it is this whiteness that allowed the dance to be eroticized in a tolerable manner, because the acquisition of this talent is removed from her person. Her performance of the "folk" or the natural is acceptable because of her white body (in a similar way as Lott explains the acceptance of blackface minstrelsy in the nineteenth century); it is a skill to be mastered because that self—the Middle Eastern self—is *not* her.

This racialized argument resonates with a similar masculinist argument about the intrinsic "talents" of women. The gendered bodies of white contestants, their femininity, negates the possibility of talent that is obviously white. In other words, there is no "white talent" or natural ability that is coded white; it is, rather, a skill to be acquired and then mastered. The "white talent" of beauty pageant contestants may very well be "beauty"; it is clearly not, at least in this particular popular cultural form, maternity, which has been historically attributed as the talent of white women in the United States. Because all traces of maternity necessarily have been eliminated from the Miss America pageant (except for the trace of future certainty), it makes sense in the talent competition to acquire a particular talent, to project a skill that could be appropriately considered representative of the nation. How does this play against the racial formations of the pageant? The gendered identities of the contestants transforms the oppositional quality of black and white by focusing on the necessity of acquiring culture rather than possessing it "naturally."

In an article offering "Secrets to a Polished Performance," a pageant coach had these words of advice about the interview competition:

> Interview competition is an area which scares most contestants. "What will they ask me?" "What will I say?" "What if I get hiccups?" These are all questions that will make you nervous and of course, this is a natural feeling. . . . However, to win an interview competition you must be calm, collected and have the judges think that you have nothing else to do that day but speak with them. This is something which . . . must be practiced.[38]

This disciplined routine—rehearsed spontaneity—is part of a larger, more intricate performance of gender that produces an appropriate figure for the nation. Participating in the interview competition is not mere theatrics; rather, it is a set in a series of stylized acts of gender that constitute, retrench, and transform boundaries defining feminine national representatives.

Performances in the interview competition are not discrete events, situated outside and unrelated to the other aspects of the Miss America pageant. On the contrary, the interview competition and the performance of rehearsed spontaneity that comprises this competition are a crucial part of the accumulation of cultural capital structuring the talent competition. Indeed, the story told by the interview and talent competitions is that women—who are racially and class coded—provide a necessary genteel and civilizing element to the nation, embodied in the Miss America national icon. The talent competition gestures to "high" culture by setting firm borders that define degrees of appropriateness—borders that are tightly race- and class-bound. These same borders parameter the interview competition, where there are clear "good" and "bad" pageant answers.

I do not consider either of these events trivial, simplistic journeys into a world of overdetermined and uncomplicated gender constructions. Though I understand that dominant codes of gender are highly problematic and damaging, I do not see the Miss America pageant as a popular cultural event that is unusually complicit with these codes. As such, I find myself at odds with Richard Wightman Fox, who, in a scathing critique of the Miss America pageant, satirically commented on a recent contestant's interview, where she apparently expressed a sincere desire to "solve the solution."[39] What I have attempted to do in this chapter is demonstrate that the interview and the talent competitions are important, significant events in the pageant itself. There is reason to examine these particular components of the pageant more carefully and more critically—meaning not merely to be critical of the performances, but to critically engage with the content of the performances themselves in an effort to determine what exactly is being said about and represented as contemporary American women.

PLATE 1. The Miss America contestants make their entrance on stage at the Miss America pageant at the Atlantic City Convention Hall in September 1997. Courtesy AP/Wide World Photos, Charles Rex Arbogast, photographer.

PLATE 3.　Miss America 1996, Shawntel Smith, addresses the New Jersey State Senate on her "issue platform," a school-to-work program. Courtesy AP/Wide World Photos, Allen Oliver, photographer.

PLATE 2 (left).　Miss Hawaii 1997, Erika Kauffman, poses in the swimsuit competition. Nineteen-ninety-seven was the first year the Miss America pageant allowed the contestants to wear two-piece bathing suits. Courtesy AP/Wide World Photos, Charles Rex Arbogast, photographer.

PLATE 4. Miss North Carolina 1997, Michelle Warren, performs at the preliminary talent competition. The majority of the Miss America contestants perform vocals in the talent competition. Courtesy AP/Wide World Photos, Charles Rex Arbogast, photographer.

PLATE 5.   Miss Florida 1997, Christy Neuman, performs her rhythmic dance, "Robin Hood: Prince of Thieves." Talents in the talent competition range from traditional vocal performances to stand-up comedy. Courtesy AP/Wide World Photos, Charles Rex Arbogast, photographer.

PLATE 7. Vanessa Williams after winning the Miss America pageant, September 1983. Courtesy AP/Wide World Photos.

PLATE 6 (left). Miss South Carolina 1994, Kimberly Aiken, in the evening wear competition. Aiken was crowned Miss America 1994 later that evening. Courtesy AP/Wide World Photos.

PLATE 8.   Bess Myerson, in the traditional pose after winning the Miss America
title in 1945. The winners of the pageant no longer pose in their swimsuits. Courtesy
AP/Wide World Photos.

PLATE 9.   Miss America 1995, Heather Whitestone, the former Miss Alabama,
signs "I love you" to the crowd after winning the title in September 1994. Courtesy
AP/Wide World Photos, Tom Costello, photographer.

PLATE 10.   Former Miss America Tara Dawn Holland, top, crowns Katherine
Shinde Miss America 1998 at the Atlantic City Convention Hall. Courtesy
AP/Wide World Photos, Charles Rex Arbogast, photographer.

CHAPTER 4 **BODIES OF DIFFERENCE**

RACE, NATION, AND THE TROUBLED
REIGN OF VANESSA WILLIAMS

On September 19, 1983, headlines appeared on hundreds of newspapers across the country celebrating the passing of the crown to Vanessa Williams, the first black woman to win the coveted title of Miss America. The *New York Times* headline read, "To First Black Miss America, Victory Is a Means to an End."[1] Other newspaper headlines similarly rooted this unprecedented event in the history of the pageant, reading, "Black Leaders Praise Choice of First Black Miss America" and "Her Crowning Achievement. Vanessa Williams: A New Voice for Miss America."[2] Each of these headlines, and the articles that accompanied them, enthusiastically praised the style and panache that Vanessa Williams brought to the title Miss America. The day had finally come when a black woman had been selected to uphold the values deemed appropriate for "American womanhood" and thus serve as a role model for American women. Vanessa was different, the newspapers claimed, in more ways than her race. She was "outspoken on political issues, race, and beauty pageants," and she went public with her support for the Equal Rights Amendment and a woman's right to choose abortion. The executive director of the NAACP at that time, Benjamin Hooks, compared Williams's achievement to Jackie Robinson breaking the color barrier in baseball.[3] Like Jackie Robinson's, her achievement seemed to provide incontrovertible evidence that America was indeed a land of opportunity and that anyone could do anything if they but tried.

Ten months into Vanessa Williams's reign, the press had another field day with the first black Miss America. The headlines in the same newspapers that had less than a year before applauded the choice of the pageant judges now were somewhat less generous: "Miss America Asked to Resign: Pageant Officials Act after Learning of Nude Photos" and "Miss America Gives Up Her Crown."[4] The opinion columns were more revealing in their headlines: "Sleaze," "Missed America," "Pageant of Hypocrisy," and "There She Goes . . . ."[5] The ostensible cause of this change? *Penthouse* magazine published nude photographs of Williams that were taken in 1981 and that depicted her and a white woman in various sexual acts. The sales of that issue of *Penthouse* broke all previously held records, generating five and a half million dollars in profit.[6] Amid much controversy and debate among the Miss America pageant officials, feminist organizations, the NAACP, and other groups, Vanessa Williams announced that she would resign from her position, claiming that the "potential harm to the pageant and the deep division that a bitter fight may cause has convinced me that I must relinquish my title."[7] The first runner-up, Suzette Charles, also a black woman, was quietly crowned Miss America for the remaining two months of the 1984 reign.

Since 1984, there have been three other black Miss Americas, in 1990, 1991, and 1994. According to the pageant and the general public, the selection of black contestants to this title previously held only by white women attests to the growing understanding that the category "American womanhood" is a diverse one, comprised of many different "types" of women.[8] Even *Ebony*, a magazine that targets black audiences, quotes Kimberly Aiken, Miss America 1994, on the supposed racial harmony of the pageant: "We [Miss America contestants] all have different backgrounds, but it is as if we are all part of the same sisterhood" (see plate 6).[9] From this perspective, the selection of black Miss Americas is viewed as a stabilizing factor in an always precarious racial balance, a final step in achieving "true sisterhood." The crowning of Vanessa Williams is widely understood by pageant culture as the year that the Miss America pageant shed, once and for all, its stubborn and notorious racist past. No more protests that the pageant is a lily-white affair, no more reminders that the pageant's claims on "representative" status were fundamentally flawed and inaccurate.

Viewed from other perspectives, however, this tale of sameness within difference is not about sisterhood, but instead is indicative of racial politics of the 1980s and 1990s: Williams's presence and the presence of African American and other nonwhite contestants in recent beauty pageants both responds to accusations that pageants do not include women of color and reinscribes the primacy of whiteness celebrated within the pageant.[10] The presence of nonwhite contestants obscures and thus works to erase the racist histories and foundations upon which beauty pageants rest. Black contestants are evidence for what Herman Gray calls a "cultural sign for race and difference," a sign that mobilizes white fear and resentment at the same time as it contains this resentment through representations of blackness that are "both familiar and acceptable to whites."[11] As Gray pointedly argues in his study of race and the mass media, during the 1980s and under the political formation of Reaganism, blame for the deterioration of American society that was placed on people of color through proliferating representations of welfare dependency, crime, drug abuse, promiscuity, and immorality—in short, the black and brown menace—was not enough to mobilize white fears and resentment in the name of national rejuvenation. A positive image of people of color, an image of black people and Latinos who "acted just like whites," was needed for Reaganism to most effectively use racist representations of threatening black and Latino cultures. And so, "[l]ike their white middle-class counterparts, and yet distinct from the black poor, images of middle- and upper-class blacks with appropriate backgrounds, pedigrees, tastes, and networks were also part of the discourse of race articulated and mobilized by the new right."[12] Crucially, Reaganism, or the New Right, and the politics of race that legitimized that hegemonic formation, reconfigured and redefined notions of the nation and individuals within that nation. This process of reckoning with definitions of who and what America was and could be depended on cultural appeals from every medium imaginable, appeals that used representations of race to simultaneously incense and reassure white America about the fate of the(ir) nation.

I focus my inquiry in this chapter on Vanessa Williams, because the selection of Williams as the female representative of the nation functioned, with great political efficacy, as both an unprecedented entrée and a fearful reminder for the predominantly white pageant audience of the specter of blackness. More generally, the crowning of Vanessa Williams is a particularly visible instance of the politics of the 1980s and Reaganism. Vanessa Williams, like many other "First" black Americans, was truly situated as a test-site for the viability of competing racial discourses in the context of emerging multiculturalism and New Right politics. She, like Bill Cosby, Clarence Thomas, and others, was marketed as a race-transcending American icon, and the pageant itself participated in marketing diversity as it happened, thereby incorporating it—and Williams herself—as a crucial element fueling the national imaginary.[13] Could she unproblematically position herself as "just another contestant," competing on the "level" playing field of feminine beauty with the other forty-six white contestants? What kind of strategies were needed (and it was clear that strategies were needed) to deflect the "politics" behind the presence of Williams and the other three black contestants in the 1984 Miss America pageant?

THE RACE FOR MISS AMERICA

The positioning of Vanessa Williams not only as the lauded "First" black Miss America but also as bodily evidence of the diversity of the pageant mobilizes the desire of white America in the direction of commodities and markets. The discourses of power that underscore her crowning, as well as the way in which her racial representation reduced a complex array of race and representation to a limited set of preestablished categories and stereotypes, are indicative not only of variations of politics of Reaganism and the New Right, but also of the vicissitudes of the 1980s' and 1990s' economy. In other words, the white imaginary that was mobilized and titillated by Williams' crowning figures in relation to a specific market and commodity culture characteristic of that historical moment. The selection of a black woman as a feminine national representative makes sense only in relation to the pageant's history as a popular cultural event that routinely excluded blacks and other people of color: "'Rule Seven' of the Pageant's bylaws for nearly half a century restricted participation to 'members of the white race.' The first blacks appeared in the contest as 'slaves' in a musical number in 1923, and up until the 1940s contestants were required to list their genealogy as far back as they could."[14] African American women did not even participate in the Miss America pageant until 1970, and not until 1984 was there an African American Miss America.[15] In fact, several contestants I interviewed unwittingly perpetuated the racism embedded in beauty pageants by discussing the 1990 and 1991 African American Miss Americas as strategic ploys to incorporate race in the pageants. They viewed the crowning of an African American woman as a purely "political" matter; if they commented at all on the crowning of white women, they attributed that crowning to the women's genuine, natural, self-evident beauty. As one contestant put it, "In the Miss America pageant there's always one or two black finalists now and you never saw that before. I don't think that's a coincidence, I really don't."[16] This comment refers not to the notion that African American women are beautiful, but rather to the presence of African Americans in beauty pageants— this presence is understood as noncoincidental and purposeful. What is important about this comment is not necessarily the racism expressed by this contestant, but the truth the statement embodies. Once black women enter the pageant, the politics of the event are more exposed and more vulnerable. That is, what this comment reveals is that pageants have been political all along; the exclusive crowning of white women prior to 1984 was overtly political. The inclusion of black women forces awareness and struggle with the implicit definitions of both beauty and national identity, foregrounding the contradictions of the pageant as well as the politics of racial and sexual difference.

This forced awareness on the part of white Americans takes place within the context of an economic climate where representations of race, diversity, and difference are employed as successful signs in such forms as American advertising and televisual culture.[17] Racial and gendered identity occupy a specific national imaginary in the 1980s and 1990s, one produced in a historical and political context determined by a dialectic of persistent liberal ideals of personhood and individualism and a "hip" marketable diversity. Fueled by a moral panic over perceived threats to freedom and speech caused by "political correctness," U.S. political and popular culture has responded to this racial crisis with what Christopher Newfield calls "managerial democracy," where diversity and difference are encouraged and included within terms bounded and determined by tropes of whiteness. What a 1995 issue of *Newsweek* called "Diversity 'R' Us" was well on its way to becoming a general national definition of the American ideal in the mid eighties.[18] The diversity offered up as this ideal is diffused, flattened out, and managed by liberal politics so that racially specific identity claims are disciplined by a "well-governed integration." The beauty pageant performs the cultural work necessary to create this body of difference; alongside its production of a particular national imaginary and its celebration of a feminine subject, the pageant contains race through the promise of tolerance.

Williams's story is thus a crucial one to be told; the construction of Williams as a "First"—as in the first black woman to win Miss America— importantly functions in dominant discourse as a sort of limited opening: the selection of one black woman as Miss America undermines claims that the pageant is a racist production and supposedly throws the doors wide open for any other nonwhite contestant to win—provided, of course, she demonstrates the same moral and physical qualities as her white counterparts.[19] The specific historical and political context of Vanessa Williams's crowning marked a shift in racial politics, a shift that determined that within the Miss America pageant, the blackness of the black contestant is not to be denied; indeed, it is precisely this blackness that is crucial to the pageant's claim to represent diverse womanhood. This definition of diversity relies on representation or recognition of difference—achieved through the presence of nonwhite bodies—and so the physical representation of the few black and brown women on the pageant stage serves as testimony to the pageant's claim that it does indeed represent all American womanhood.

Yet, although black contestants are considered living proof of the progressive diversity of the pageant, it remains their job to represent their blackness in a way that does not bring to the foreground those dominant social narratives about the instability of the category "black woman," a particular sign of blackness that is used in the mass media, political culture, and popular culture to signify not only welfare dependence, crack cocaine addicted mothers, and shady characters, but also wantonness, sexual abandon, and indiscriminate promiscuity.[20] The pageant (like U.S. culture at large) must utilize strategies to control this instability, which through public and "spontaneous" performances of difference can potentially transition into crisis at any moment. Difference must be *managed* within the pageant as it is similarly managed in U.S. culture: black contestants continue to tell the conventional story of racial harmony, and the subjectivities of the black contestants are characterized by the tensions that result from attempting to assert that indeed "black is beautiful," but only when it can be shown to correspond to an historically "white" model of interior womanhood. In fact, when Vanessa Williams was crowned Miss America in 1983, she was repeatedly asked to pose for photographs with the three other black contestants, as well as questioned incessantly about "what it felt like to have a chance to become the first black woman to win the crown."[21] These requests by the press signify a move to "capture" diversity as it happens and to market the narratives of the lives of the successful black women who made it to the pageant as proof that diversity is truly alive and well in America. The photographs of the three black contestants and Williams aptly demonstrate "diversity" by self-consciously including and celebrating the four nonwhite contestants who participated on the national pageant stage that year.

In a commodified popular cultural form like the Miss America pageant, inclusion of diversity and the recognition of difference does not represent a radically destabilizing shift in politics or the material structure of the event. Difference is bounded by a heavily surveyed conception of "moral bodies" that is, in turn, tightly bound up in—indeed, constitutive of—discourses of whiteness. The bodies of the contestants are understood as direct reflections of inner character, which then functions as an implicit statement about and affirmation of racial identity. The contestants themselves construct this statement, as one contestant said to me: "I think that not only are [contestants] beautiful, but they are beautiful on the inside, and I think that that's important. There's a certain breed of girls that makes it. I mean, occasionally you find a hometown girl that makes it up there, but . . . you don't usually find a girl who just says, 'Oh I want to be in a pageant,' and just enters it without any training."[22] The language of "breed" and "training" employed by this contestant makes it clear that beauty pageants are about reading the female body's surface as direct visible evidence of interior, invisible qualities of womanhood. It is also a direct statement about representations of racial identity, in which breed, pedigree, and appropriate backgrounds are understood as necessary to possess "the requisite moral character, individual responsibility and personal determination to succeed in spite of residual social impediments."[23]

Reading the body in this way is only possible within a particular kind of normative framework, where the idea that moral character is rooted in the body allows for a proliferation of narratives that there are some bodies that are biologically destined to be socially disruptive or morally corrupt.[24] Indeed, the entry of black women in beauty pageants destabilizes the easy convergence between inner moral character and outer body that is traditionally assumed for middle-class white women. The appearance of the black body corresponds not with a morality and respectability considered appropriate to a Miss America contestant, but rather serves as a signal for the unknown, the threatening, and the chaotic. The job for black contestants thus becomes one of "proving" to the audience and to the abstract category of "American womanhood" that they are indeed the moral "sisters" of the white contestants. Black beauty pageant contestants must authenticate what Wahneema Lubiano calls a "cover story" in order to "obscure context, fade out subtext, and . . . protect the text of the powerful."[25] This particular cover story is told by engaging in the difficult process of controlling and containing the social meaning of blackness through the discourses of morality and respectability. Because dominant social narratives hold that the bodies of women of color are biologically determined to be corrupt and immoral, the visible body of the black Miss America contestant must pass as a cover for the invisible moral qualities of the white woman. In other words, in the context of the pageant, and in a perverse echo of Sojourner Truth's question "Ain't I a Woman?" black contestants must pass for women.

To thoroughly examine the cultural work that takes place within beauty pageants and to redirect our attention to the pageant as a site for both the enactment and control of national feminine identity, where individual women are placed, and place themselves, on the supposedly neutral

"field" of beauty, we need to consider in broader terms the different social practices that claim to level this field in order to make competition
possible. Through what structures of liberal democracy and meritocratic
society are fields of opportunity, including the opportunity to represent
American womanhood, made level in such a way that denies homogeneity
in the name of racial "diversity," while at the same time maintaining a
system that devalues and disempowers this diversity? In the context of
this question, Vanessa Williams's story must be reexamined or reframed
in a fashion that foregrounds what was really "exposed" in those *Penthouse* photographs and the public reaction to them.

UNCOLORING AMERICA

The beginning of Vanessa Williams's reign as Miss America illustrates
the ways in which her "difference" was specifically marketed and commodified by Miss America officials, the media, and Williams herself. The
press coverage of her initial crowning can be read as an elaborate and complex process of "uncoloring" of Williams as Miss America. Part of this uncoloring was figuring a way to transcend, or at the very least overcome, dominant social narratives about black women's sexuality and respectability.
She not only had to "pass" for white, but in doing so, because of the ways
in which whiteness is constructed precisely in terms of morality and respectability, and because of the "questionable morals" purportedly held
by black women, she also had to pass for respectable.

As we trace the construction of Williams's story through the mass media, we see that at the beginning of her reign, she managed to fulfill the
expectation of a "colorless" Miss America (which, of course, meant
fulfilling the expectation of a white Miss America). However, as I argue
later, when she was asked to relinquish her crown because of the public
exposure of nude photographs, it became clear that she could not maintain the fiction of race transcendence—the pornographic photographs immediately and detrimentally reinscribed her racial identity. Posing nude
with a woman signifies not only a failure of morals and respectability, but
a failure to occupy a particular definition of white femininity. In the context of eroticizing difference, by the ostensible evidence of Williams's un-

controllable desire, dominant social stereotypes and narratives about black female sexuality were reinvigorated and failed to adequately contain the fears about sexuality that frame the pageant. But before we get to how Williams ultimately became a site for the simultaneous mobilization and displacement of dominant racial fears, we need to examine how a particular concept of "diversity" was deployed at the beginning of her reign.

When Williams was crowned Miss America, the news media, like other popular discourses, relied on two dominant narratives about the nation and race—that of America being a "colorless" society, yet one that thrives and principles itself upon a concept of a harmonious, multicolored society—which together function as a particular discourse on diversity (see plate 7). Although this discourse is operationalized through two competing "truths" about race that are, on one level, contradictory, they ironically function together to strengthen and reinforce a universal norm of white femininity. Williams's story provides us with an occasion to see precisely how these strategies work to construct and reconstruct not only a particular representation of black womanhood but, equally as important, the illusion of the perfectibility of whiteness. Focusing first on the unusually large body of media coverage on Williams's crowning, we can see how the media is a key factor in constructing American womanhood.

One headline reads, "Vanessa Williams: A New Voice for Miss America," and the first line of the article is simple and clear: "She is the new black woman."[26] The article continues by illustrating that the "new black woman" shies away from overt identity claims of blackness and instead adopts age-old tropes in American nationalism that recall Horatio Alger and liberal individualism. As Williams claims in the article, "I think I would be doing the same thing if I were Spanish or white or Chinese. I am still a person, I still feel the same way about being crowned. I don't think they chose me because I was black and it was time for a black Miss America. They chose me because they thought I could do the job."[27] Williams's focus on her individual merits constructs the "job" of Miss America as a specific and important one. It also uses the language of anti-affirmative action discourse—that of "doing the job"—in a historical moment when affirmative action policies and hires were under attack for tokenism and reverse racism. Williams's move here is to deny a racially specific identity and instead claim that she is "still a person." Bringing personhood into the picture maintains the structure of liberalism that frames the pageant and reaffirms the pageant as a site for constructing the autonomous, individual, white subject. Claiming that everyone is a "person" serves only to further the successes of those who construct the concept of personhood as an identity claim, a construction that celebrates the invisible power of whiteness at the expense of all other ethnic groups.

Indeed, the liberal concept of "personhood," divorced from being racially distinct, is one of the most powerful mechanisms at work not only in the liberal framework of the Miss America pageant, but also in U.S. culture at large. The invisible or unmarked category of whiteness is translated into a neutral and universal category of "personhood," a category that purportedly "transcends" differences of race, gender, and sexual orientation. Public concerns about the prevalence and power of recent identity politics movements—where the politics of various ethnic and racial groups are mobilized in terms of individual connections with racial and ethnic identities—are partly fueled by the knowledge that what identity politics do is expose the racialized nature of liberal categories of personhood.[28] This is one reason why there is such public outcry from predominantly white populations—from the news media to talk show audiences to university classes—about nonwhites and other groups who identify in terms of ethnicity and feel a need to identify themselves as "different," or as marked. The public wonderment about why nonwhites can't just "act like people" fails to appreciate that "acting like people" in the United States has historically meant to act like *white* people.

This kind of argument produces a normative standard of "just people" without interrogating the racial or white specificity of that norm. The prevalence of comments such as "Why do *they* have to wear their hair that way," or "Why can't *they* just get a job like everyone else, instead of relying on governmental support," or "Why can't *they* just learn English" reflects the threat posed by those members of society who choose, whether as a conscious political statement or as part of cultural representation, not to make an effort to assimilate into white society. In the case of Vanessa Williams, at least at the beginning of her reign, she both assuaged and legitimized white fears about personhood through her constant denials that her crowning had anything to do with race. The *Washington Post* reported that Williams "seemed to be getting testy about the racial symbolism," and Williams herself had this to say: "At times I get annoyed because people and the press aren't focusing on me as a person and are focusing on my being black. . . . I've made some waves and I'm ready to handle that. People aren't used to dealing with change, but I think it has to happen."[29] Williams's selection as Miss America functioned as many cases of exceptionalism do: as "proof" that extreme racial segregation and discrimination in all areas of U.S. life exist because people of color have failed to "live up to the bargain"—in other words, blacks who succeed do so because of their merits, and those who fail do so because of a lack of personal motivation, intelligence, or some other private problem.[30] In fact, the judges for the 1984 Miss America pageant were quoted constantly as claiming that Williams won based "on her own merits." Albert Marks, the pageant's chief executive officer, said that Williams's crowning as Miss America "should prove that you can be tops in America without regard to your color, as it should be. . . . I can assure you that this young lady got there on her merits."[31]

Williams's selection as Miss America worked to deflect charges that the pageant was a "lily-white" affair at the same time as it "confirmed America's liberal promise of do-it-yourself political improvement."[32] As feminist Jackie Goldsby points out, Williams's crowning was situated at a particularly important moment in the history of U.S. race relations and answered questions such as "How could anyone complain that the contest's outcome was anything but 'progress'? Didn't the nation have another racial 'first' to add to the mythic melting pot of American achievement? Wasn't this a fulfillment of the Civil Rights dream state of affairs—a black woman representing the ideal of American femininity?"[33] In fact, Williams's victory was often framed in the rhetoric of the "Civil Rights dream state of affairs," where specific definitions of diversity—definitions that privileged circumscribed and limited permutations of difference— were applauded and celebrated.

In press conferences, Williams continued to address the issue of race and continued to deny that race was significant in her success. This dual strategy of focusing on difference, only to insist that "difference" doesn't make a difference, served to reassure the Miss America pageant and most of America that selecting a woman of color was not going to disrupt dominant notions of (white) womanhood but would give the definition of womanhood a new twist, spice it up, and make it more accessible to all young American women. One article read, "From the first moments of her tenure as Miss America, Williams . . . seemed to accept the inevitable controversy and even crave the distinction of being different. That is one mark of her generation, born in the throes of the civil rights movement, immune from the physical strife of direct racial bias—and taught that a colorless world is the reward the last generation has bequeathed."[34] The obvious contradiction in this statement, that of "craving the distinction of being different" based on color and then reveling in the reward of a "colorless world," frames all of the media coverage of Williams's crowning.[35] This contradiction precisely captures the tensions characteristic of diversity in general and representations of black female subjectivity in particular within the pageant: the strategies of assimilation (the "colorless world") and eroticizing difference ("craving distinction") are mutually constitutive processes. Black contestants have no choice but to attempt to employ both of these strategies even while it is evident that this is an impossible task.

This use of diversity is successful because it sells products: many black scholars have called our public attention to the fact that when African Americans—and particularly African American women—are portrayed favorably in mainstream representation, they usually look the most "white." Not surprisingly, in terms of advertising, the logic behind this is rooted in an economic argument:

> When it comes to promoting everyday products, light-skinned models like Shari Belafonte and Kara Young are still the rule. A model like Belafonte can work both in high fashion and, because of her light skin and all-American looks, in the lucrative commercial market. But someone like Grace Jones is unlikely to be chosen to sell Fords or even Calvin Klein jeans, and many advertisers doubt that any dark-skinned Black woman, no matter how beautiful, can effectively sell their products.[36]

Insofar as American culture is organized according to a gendered and raced division of labor, the fact that only certain "types" of black women are considered to have an appropriate exchange value needs to be examined when investigating the construction of American feminine subjects. In the entertainment business—in mass media, film, television, and beauty pageants—the practice of hiring only light-skinned blacks, or those who have European features such as straight hair and light colored eyes, is not only highly encouraged but understood to be economically necessary.[37] For many African Americans, this was clearly the case with Vanessa Williams, who possessed European features and straight hair. Even if she herself denied representing a femininity historically associated with whiteness—"I've never felt like a beauty queen, and I don't think I ever will, because that's a stereotype I don't agree with"—others saw her as a perfect match with a stereotypical image of a (white) beauty queen: "She has all the stunning qualifications, with wide, green eyes and a full mouth boldly branded on a sunny, oblong face. Her brown shoulder-length hair falls in loose waves highlighted with gold. . . . And some blacks will probably use her looks, which fit the old Miss America standard of fair skin and straight hair, as a criticism of her victory."[38] Williams apparently received angry letters after newspaper articles mentioned that the man she dates steadily is a white man, and many criticisms emerging from the African American community focused on her fair coloring.[39]

Black women who are in this position clearly inhabit the contradictory subject that popular culture is so expert in producing. On the one hand, the embrace of blackness is necessary to flaunt "difference" and perpetuate the insistence that American culture is not about racist representation but about the playfulness of diversity. On the other hand, black women who are expected to represent and maintain this ideological practice are supposed to do it by not "being" black. Williams's reign was, for the most part, an exercise in playing and worrying this discourse of marketing diversity and difference. The tension endemic within these social practices was clearly present in constructing Williams's subjectivity as Miss America and was orchestrated brilliantly by Williams. Comforted by the aura the title brings, Williams was able to talk about race in a way that was not referencing *her* construction as a raced subject; indeed, she insisted that "color makes no difference."[40] Although this claim rendered her a frequent target of criticism from the black community, it was characteristic of her style; she distanced herself from any overt identification with black subjectivity and described herself as an "individualist": "Just because I'm black doesn't mean I'm going to support every black position."[41] Clearly, though, the questions asked of the first black Miss America were vastly different from the questions asked of all previous title holders. The American public was ready to both make her a hero and decry her crowning as political maneuvering. This kind of positioning is symptomatic of dominant social narratives that produce and situate African Americans within U.S. culture—whether in beauty pageants or as affirmative action hires. The charge for those African Americans who are represented in beauty pageants is to deny that racism exists simply by virtue of their representation in mainstream culture, while simultaneously constructing this representation in accordance with feminine disciplinary practices that translate into a white body. This conflicting subjectivity was frequently expressed by Williams: "I was chosen because I was qualified for the position. . . . The fact that I was black was not a factor. I've always had to try harder in my life to achieve things, so this is regular."[42] What is left unquestioned in this statement—by both the media and Williams— is the clear irony of claiming that race was not a factor while also acknowledging that she has had to work harder for everything, something she characterizes as "regular."[43]

As I mentioned earlier in this chapter, in another statement Williams claimed that "[h]er most vivid memory of the pageant . . . is of lining up with the three other black contestants for endless photo sessions and answering endless questions about what it felt like to have a chance to become the first black woman to win the crown."[44] If, as she so consistently claimed, her race was not a factor in her selection, why was it considered newsworthy to line up all the black contestants for press photos? Clearly, other contestants were not singled out because of their whiteness. Just as clearly, the only choice Williams had was to construct herself within the political boundaries of that historical moment, as someone dedicated to American liberalism and as a contestant who won based solely on her merits. The pageant functions as a site for managing these contradictions and, in so doing, keeps in check the tensions that are characterized by these contradictions.

SEX AND MISS AMERICA: VANESSA THE UNDRESSA

What should be clear is that in order to navigate the tensions of being the first black Miss America, Vanessa Williams needed to diminish if not make invisible the historical tropes and social meanings of blackness that provided the context for her reign. Perhaps the most forceful theme of this context was the unpredictable—indeed, the unknowable—trajectory of black female sexuality. As many scholars have pointed out, the set of narratives that signal black womanhood in the United States are persistent and dangerous: ranging from stories of teenage promiscuity and welfare dependence to tales of indiscriminate and irresponsible "breeding" by what has been called the "cognitive underclass," all centralize and focus on the body—or, more specifically, the use of the body—of the black woman.[45] In 1983, the year Vanessa Williams was crowned Miss America, these narratives had reached a heightened frenzy that had as its logical center a focus on welfare. As Herman Gray points out, "Welfare and the liberal permissiveness that created and nurtured it produced an underclass distinguished by sedation and satisfaction of bodily pleasures, dependency, immorality, hostility, erosion of standards, loss of civic responsibility, and lack of respect for traditional values."[46] Given this context, the Miss America pageant needed strategies to contain Williams's blackness, to make it familiar, and to envision it as respectable. Thus, in a forum that was conceived upon and continues to uphold a rigorous ideology of respectable sexuality, black contestants who succeed in moving up in the pageant ranks are women who have shown that they can operate within these dominant narratives. However, the threat (or perhaps anticipation) of failing to uphold the morality of the pageant is a specter that haunts all black contestants, especially since the "fall" of Vanessa Williams. What happens when a person, in this case Vanessa Williams, attempts to occupy conflicting discourses of representation? Neither the pageant nor the American public had at their disposal a dominant narrative that could accommodate Williams' position as both Miss America and apparent porn star.

As I have argued, the mere visibility of black contestants does not erase the ideology of whiteness that defines the pageant; on the contrary, the presence of black contestants foregrounds whiteness as the only appropriate field of representational power. In this regard, the beauty pageant shares political space with progressive cultural activists, who work to increase the visibility of racial, ethnic, and sexual "others." As Peggy Phelan argues about this kind of political positioning, "It is assumed that disenfranchised communities who see their members within the representational field will feel greater pride in being part of such a community *and* those who are not in such a community will increase their understanding of the diversity and strength of such communities."[47] She continues, "[Each] presumption reflects the ideology of the visible, an ideology which erases the power of the unmarked, unspoken, and unseen."[48] This is precisely the tactic beauty pageants employ regarding black contestants. Unlike pageants such as Miss Black America, or other pageants dedicated to a specific ethnic or racial group, the fact that white and nonwhite contestants compete together in the Miss America pageant functions to disrupt any presumption that the pageant is an all-white production. Pageant viewers supposedly read the physical resemblance a black contestant has with the African American community as a marker of inclusion, as foolproof evidence that the pageants are not racist. But, as Phelan reminds us, the visible has an inextricable connection with the invisible, and placing political focus only on the visible body erases the meanings that the invisible signifies. Phelan remarks, "Race-identity involves recognizing something other than skin and physical inscriptions. One cannot simply 'read' race as skin-color."[49] The impulse to do exactly this in beauty pageants results in a confusion when it comes to black contestants. For example, Deborah Johnson, Miss Compton 1985, discusses the confusion that arose from participating as a black contestant in the Miss California pageant:

> I think they [pageant officials] have an idea of what a Miss California is supposed to be, and black women, or women of color, or minority women, don't fit into that mold. And I never went in thinking, "Oh I'm not going to win because I'm black," I never had that attitude, until becoming a part of it—and then you start to think, "Oh, so that's what's happening here." . . . What you do feel is that they look at you more as a threat, instead of just another contestant. And especially if you were good—you got the feeling that no matter how good you were, you weren't going to win. . . . And I don't mean to say that everyone in Miss California is a racist—there are beautiful people in that pageant—but this is an American problem, and Miss California is part of that problem.[50]

Johnson points to an important distinction in the way racial politics work in U.S. society: the fact that she was viewed differently from the other contestants because she was black did not automatically signify that the entire pageant was racist. Rather, the construction of Johnson as a "threat" is symptomatic of the way that race relations are organized in the United States according to the terms and limitations of institutionalized racism. Johnson points out the subtlety of these disciplinary practices: black contestants are included as particular representational types within a broadening field of white womanhood—*included* within the field, not disruptive of the field. This social practice leads to statements like the following, from a pageant director for the Miss California pageant. When asked about the scarcity of African American contestants, she replied,

> We have many different cultures in this country and many different ethnic groups and religions, and we have the black girl versus the white girl and how her [the "black girl's"] body is formed, and there for a while you saw a lot of black girls who had . . . the contour if you were looking at it from the side would stick out more in back [gestures toward her buttocks]. We had to recognize that that was a part of their culture.[51]

This is a complicated statement, and its complexity is reflective of the way racialized subjects are organized in contemporary U.S. society. On the one hand, it could be read as testimony to the ways in which pageants have recognized and overcome their racism. On the other hand, it can be read as an example of how the black female body is fetishized in particular ways; their bodies (or, more specifically, their butts) *become* their culture. This pageant director is articulating precisely the pageant ideology of the direct correspondence between the visible body and invisible inner qualities: black women's butts directly and transparently communicate "their" culture. And "their" culture, the culture of black women, is reduced to a purely sexual representation; as bell hooks points out, "In the sexual iconography of the traditional black pornographic imagination, the protruding butt is seen as an indication of a heightened sexuality."[52] By accommodating the "black girls who . . . stick out more in back" within the pageant definition of womanhood, the racial anxieties of pageants are not reduced to racism in its conventional sense but constitute a racism that invokes integrationism as its driving power: people of color are members of the "common culture" of America, but members who have a place and know that place.[53] That place is always constructed through and by its relation to whiteness and sexuality, which through its normalization becomes the standard by which all other races are measured and constructed as "other" than white.[54]

We might ask at this point, how is the social practice of eroticizing difference used in the cultural marketplace? How does the "sexiness" of difference function not only to maintain a racial hierarchy but also to preserve the ideology that equates the category of "black woman" with aggressive and uncontrollable sexuality? The sexualizing of the black female body, the construction of this body *as* sex, displaces white anxieties concerning female sexuality and maintains the social practices and ideologies that make whiteness coextensive with sexual respectability and morality. We have seen how this functioned during slavery: the category of black woman as jezebel became the repository for fears and fantasies about female sexuality and constructed black women as sexually aggressive while simultaneously producing white women as chaste and moral.[55] In contemporary times, eroticizing difference works in a similar way, where the black female body becomes symbol, metaphor, and battleground for the anxiety and anticipation that defines sexuality. Thus the white female body maintains itself and is maintained as the more moral, the more pure, and the more respectable. In hooks's words, "Undesirable in the conventional sense, which defines beauty and sexuality as desirable only to the extent that it is idealized and unattainable, the black female body gains attention only when it is synonymous with accessibility, availability, when it is sexually deviant."[56]

There are few more illustrative tales of this cultural practice than Vanessa Williams's "fall from grace." In July 1984, *Penthouse* ran an issue that featured Vanessa Williams engaged in sexual acts with a white woman. These photographs, taken three years before the pageant, were the reason the Miss America pageant commission asked Williams to relinquish her crown and title. Although Williams denied signing a release form for the photos and claimed that they were intended for "private use only," she did not sue the magazine or its editor-publisher Robert Guccione; instead, she tearfully handed her crown to her first runner up, Suzette Charles, also a black woman.

The publication of these photographs is precisely the kind of event that reinvigorates anxieties and tensions about black female sexuality. We can read the photos' publication and the relinquishing of the Miss

America crown that resulted as a discursive move in which Williams eroticized difference—and failed to convincingly pass as chaste and respectable. Although Williams played the tension between these modes of experience skillfully, it became clear when she attempted to occupy them both fully and simultaneously that she could not be both pure and sexual, both straight and playfully lesbian.[57] As columnist Richard Cohen argues,

> [As Miss America,] you cannot have more than just a vague sexuality— maybe one that will ripen only after marriage and then, knock on wood, only in a modest undemanding way. . . . Vanessa Williams has sullied that myth. Her body, not to mention her simulated sexuality, is available on the newsstands to the enrichment of male fantasies and the coffers of Guccione. He sells one kind of myth; the Miss America pageant sells another. Williams has made the mistake of merging the two—madonna and tart in one woman, although like most woman she is neither one.[58]

Although Cohen insightfully points out the contradictions characterizing female sexuality for all women, he doesn't extend his point to insist that nonwhite female sexuality, although subject to some of the same cultural constraints as white female sexuality, is nonetheless played out differently and has distinct stakes and consequences. Williams's story cannot be told without considering the ways in which race and sexuality are mutually constitutive; to attempt to do so is to tell only half of the story. As Jackie Goldsby asks, "How does race condition the terms on which representation occurs? How does race effect (and affect) one's agency within the marketplace of sex?"[59]

One way that race, or in this specific case, blackness, conditions "the terms on which representation occurs" is seen in the manner that Vanessa Williams, as a representation in a pornographic magazine, became symbolic of all black women. Contrary to her efforts at the beginning of her reign to construct herself as simply "an individual"—a woman who was selected because of her unique merits and who could perform the "job" of Miss America just as skillfully if she were "Spanish or white or Chinese"—after the publication of the porn photos, she was vilified by both the black and white communities as a "bad example" of and for her race.[60] Her race conditioned the terms of her representation by foregrounding and recalling dominant social narratives of the black female as the "oversexed black Jezebel," who not only signifies sex but also initiates it. Just as she was granted individual personhood when she won the Miss America crown, she was summarily denied this same category when the photographs were published: she became all black women in U.S. society, and she affirmed mass-mediated representations of this identity.

And so, although there were outcries from the black community, most notably the NAACP, concerning the racism motivating the scandal, there was also an expressed sense of shame, of "letting us down." This sentiment reflects how whiteness "figures the normative center of political and theoretical debate about sexuality and identity."[61] For example, in an editorial in *The Washington Post* titled "A Sad Lesson," the author writes, "That [Williams] had been hailed as a particularly 'exemplary' queen, one who injected new life into the homogeneously bland pageant, only makes her fall more keenly felt by black women who are trying hard to exert a sense of self."[62] Of course, the ways in which nude photos might also "inject new life" into the pageant are, not surprisingly, ignored by this writer. And, in addition, this "sense of self" does not, presumably, include a sense of sexual self, or sexuality. Instead, a woman's "sense of self" here indicates the self defined by the liberal individual, where sexuality is relegated to the private sphere. Thus this reprimand for "letting down" the black community can be read as failing to successfully construct oneself as a liberal subject, one whose public persona does not include expressions of sexuality.

But perhaps more important, this subject is racially specific. When Williams was first crowned, her success at crossing the historically all-white barrier of the Miss America pageant was read as evidence that black women could be included within the parameters of white femininity.[63] Former congressmember Shirley Chisholm said at the time of Williams's crowning, "My first reaction is that the inherent racism in America must be diluting itself. . . . I would say, thank God I have lived long enough that this nation has been able to select the beautiful young woman of color to be Miss America." Chisholm continued by emphasizing the significance of Williams's victory for black communities in the United States, claiming that "because it didn't 'put bread on the table' people might say 'So what?' when considering the importance to the civil rights movement of a black woman's winning of the crown. . . . [But the event was] not trivial because it shows in a sense that the country, for whatever the motivation might be, seems to be trying desperately to move toward a more equalitarian set of circumstances."[64]

Thus it makes sense that, after the photographs were published,

> people have asked her, whereas she once was a credit, she now had become a "disgrace to her race." She replied that she didn't think so and felt black people wouldn't abandon her. It was an ironic answer since Williams herself has played down any racial symbolism when she was first crowned, and some blacks complained that her mulatto looks didn't represent them in a pageant already controversial and slipping in prestige. Now, some of her detractors are embracing Williams as a sister in trouble.[65]

Racial solidarity worked both for and against Williams during her reign; on the one hand, members of the black community did "embrace [her] as a sister in trouble," a gesture made specifically on behalf of her entire race. On the other hand, her downfall was seen (primarily by the white community, but also by some within the black community) as symbolic of—again—the entire black race. That is, the sexually explicit photographs brought up "old ghosts" about the oversexed black woman—not about the oversexed Vanessa Williams.[66] As Goldsby comments, Williams could not "revise the racial symbolism of film and the acts depicted in the images, precisely because the historical construction of black sexuality is always already pornographic, if by pornography I mean the writing or technological representation and mass marketing of the body as explicitly sexual."[67] Of course, the question we can put forward at this point is: What would have happened if a white Miss America had posed for *Penthouse?*[68] I would submit that because white female sexuality plays itself out differently in the cultural and social imagination, a white Miss America would have also been asked to relinquish her crown—but her act would have been publicly condemned as an *individual* moral failing. The act of posing in sexually explicit positions would not have been conditioned by and interpreted in terms of the whiteness of a white Miss America. But with Williams, her race was immediately implicated by her representation in *Penthouse;* dominant social narratives about black female sexuality were reinvigorated and resurfaced publicly. As journalist Dorothy Gilliam commented, Williams's decrowning "hurts because it raises the fear that the old images might again rise from the ashes—before they had been totally put to rest."[69]

But despite a few editorials by black writers, the media presented an account of these events that categorically denied any racist intention. William Safire, writing in *The New York Times*, claimed about Robert Guccione, editor-publisher of *Penthouse*: "The charge that he is deliberately harming the first black Miss America misses the point. . . . If *Penthouse* had an erotic photo of Geraldine Ferraro or Nancy Reagan—or of George Bush, for that matter—they would go with it. The editors discriminate only against clothes."[70] However, as history has shown, the black female body is almost always constructed as sexual, or as "pornographic"—in relation to the chaste, respectable, white female body—so Safire's hypothetical scenario with Ferraro and Reagan simply does not wash. The *Penthouse* spread is not an option open to the Ferraros and Reagans of the world, whose whiteness and class status make the erotic photo an unlikely place for them to go in an attempt to construct a "sense of self."

In addition, the fact that Williams's first runner-up, and therefore the de facto next Miss America, was also black was considered even more evidence that the exposure of the nude photos was not racially motivated. Suzette Charles, only the fourth black woman to ever make it to the finals in the Miss America pageant, was immediately cast as the "remedy" for the ills Williams brought to the pageant's reputation. According to one news article, "Suzette Charles, the new Miss America, also black, acknowledged the wound she saw and promised to try to heal it. 'The initial shock was heartbreaking to all black women who are achievers,' said Charles. 'But now I want to uplift that.'"[71] The quiet crowning of Charles, in combination with her efforts to "heal the wound," can be read as a triumph of liberalism; her crowning serves as evidence not only that the forced resignation of Williams was not motivated by a racist Miss America commission, but also (and more obliquely) that black women can in fact be white.[72]

However, if Williams's downfall was read, by the public and the pageant alike, as an event that was not about race, it was, of course, an incident that had everything to do with sex. When the Miss America commission asked Williams to resign, the executive director remarked that "the pageant celebrates the whole woman, and its spirit is intrinsically inconsistent with calculated sexual exploitation."[73] The pageant's suggestion that the "wholeness" of a woman is distinct from her sexual identity or performance is again part of constructing liberal subjects within the pageant. The pageant woman is whole in the sense that the public, liberal individual is whole—they leave their sexuality at the door, so to speak. The clear hypocrisy of an event that is dedicated and indebted to an ideology that constructs women through the discourses of sexual exploitation did not go unremarked in the media. In other words, the focus on sex was not limited to the pageant officials (and others) who condemned Williams's act as "repulsive," "shocking," or otherwise "indefensible." Advocates of Williams—feminist critics of the pageant's treatment of her—also singularly located the incident within a discourse of sex. The feminist group Women Against Pornography was quoted as saying that they "deplore the hypocrisy of the Miss America pageant officials for criticizing Miss Williams. The Miss America pageant differs from Penthouse in degree, not in kind. Like *Penthouse*, the pageant judges women on the basis of their conformity to a sexist ideal."[74] An editorial in *The Washington Post* claimed that "the insipid Miss America pageant went stereotypically Sicilian and denounced Williams—at least in a photographic sense—as no virgin."[75]

The intense focus on Williams as a victim of sexual exploitation, or, conversely, on Williams as an active agent of sex, denies the ways in which her identity is raced in an intersectional way.[76] In the story of Vanessa Williams, the only narrative that both pageant officials and feminists could rely upon was a trope of sexual, not racial, exploitation. Writing with respect to the Clarence Thomas-Anita Hill hearings, Kimberlé Crenshaw argued that the (white) feminist advocacy of Hill as a victim of "sexual domination" could only account for part of the context in which Anita Hill was positioned. Crenshaw claims, "The particular intersectional identity of Hill, as both a woman and an African-American, lent dimensions to her ideological placement in the economy of American culture that could not be translated through the dominant feminist analysis."[77] In a similar way, many feminists' reaction to the pageant's treatment of Williams ignored the ways that race conditioned both Williams's actions and the pageant's request for her dismissal. As Goldsby comments, "The publication of Vanessa Williams's split images as the beauty-cum-porn queen marked a crucial moment wherein lesbian feminists could—and should—have theorized about the historic workings of race in relation to sexuality because it, and not racism, explains most critically why Williams met the infamous end she did."[78] Like Goldsby, I am concerned with "locating race in a historical context in order to understand the effective silence which greeted and so defined Williams's fall, to consider why public discourse about colored sexuality remains conventional in its outlook on and response to boundary-shattering incidents such as this."[79] Goldsby argues that the telling and retelling of Vanessa Williams's impressive victory and equally impressive downfall provided an opportunity—a lost opportunity, in her opinion—to engage in public conversation about the various ways in which race conditions and intersects sexuality. Without interrogating the racial specificity of the context in which Williams was positioned, her story could not be told—indeed, there was no available social narrative for the telling. Like the feminist reaction to Anita Hill, the relative silence that greeted the events precipitating Williams's downfall was a result of America "[stumbling] into the place where African-American women live, a political vacuum of erasure and contradiction maintained by the almost routine polarization of 'blacks and women' into separate and competing political camps."[80]

And so, the social narrative that framed the public telling of Vanessa Williams's story is a conventional one about white female sexuality. Shaping every part of this discourse was a sometimes implicit but more often explicit theme of homophobia. The *Penthouse* photographs' depiction of Williams engaged in simulated sexual activity with another woman not only disrupted the heavily regulated moral boundary of femininity, but also dismantled the even more institutionalized framework of heterosexuality that defines the Miss America pageant. Despite the pageant's chief executive officer, Albert Marks's, statement about the pageant celebrating the "whole woman" with a spirit that is "intrinsically inconsistent with calculated sexual exploitation," many people in the community and in the mass media called Marks to task by implicitly questioning his use of the term *"calculated* sexual exploitation." In other words, many questioned the difference between the pageant and *Penthouse*: were they simply, as Women Against Pornography claimed, a difference in "degree, not in kind?" As Goldsby commented,

> [Guccione] leveled a body blow against the concept of the pageant itself: the photos framed the Miss America contest as simply another for(u)m for sex work. *Penthouse*'s publication of the images implicated the pageant in its cultural practice of making a commodity out of sex. . . . [In] presenting Williams for his readers' consumption as a centerfold treat, Guccione dealt back the pageant's card of respectability, for the pageant, no less than *Penthouse*, exploited Williams as an object of appeal.[81]

Why, many such as Goldsby asked, should the photographs of Williams be seen as anything different from parading down a runway in a swimsuit in front of a panel of judges?

The answer to this question was found in the photographs themselves. Apparently unwilling—or perhaps unable—to engage in a debate about whether the pageant was sexual exploitation, the pageant commission focused on the content of the photographs: the representation of sexual acts between two women. The specter of lesbianism hangs above almost all of the mass-mediated coverage of Williams's resignation, from claims about the "repulsive" nature of the photographs to reports about billboards erected at a shopping area in her hometown, Milltown, New York, with the spray-painted message "Vanessa is a lesbian nudie."[82] Journalists seemed unable to restrain their homophobia when describing the photos; as one writer from *The Washington Post* commented, "We tell ourselves that, in this day of nude scenes in PG-rated movies, nudity really isn't that big a deal. I might have been tempted to make that argument myself, but then I saw the *Penthouse* photos. I can tell you that nudity is the least of the problems. The thing is indefensible, and we ought to stop confusing our children by suggesting otherwise."[83]

Not surprisingly, Miss America officials shared this journalist's opinion that sexually explicit images involving two women were "indefensible." The pageant commission called attention to the fact that they only made the decision about Williams after "looking at those pictures." The executive director was quoted as saying, in response to the public support of Williams, "Now they're supplications. . . . 'Please don't do this to that girl,' they say. When I talk to them, I tell them to please withhold

judgment until they see the pictures."[84] The photographs were the turn-
ing point, the moment when the tensions intrinsic to Williams's mass-
mediated identity completely broke down. Apparently it did not matter
that these photographs, as all straight pornographic representations that
depict same-sex sex, were created for male heterosexual desire. As Susan
Sontag comments, "Photographs furnish evidence. . . . A photograph
passes for incontrovertible proof that a given thing happened."[85] The
"given thing that happened" for Vanessa Williams was sexual interaction
with a woman, and the social and cultural stigma of lesbianism in homo-
phobic society provided justification for Williams's downfall. The beauty
pageant always assumes the heterosexual contract, an unspoken but om-
nipresent commitment. When Williams posed nude with a woman, she
broke this crucial contract and thus became the site for crisis within the
pageant—a crisis that could only be controlled through her resignation.

Williams attempted to "set the record *straight*" in her press conference
following the exposure, claiming that "[Photographer Tom Chaipel] said
he wanted to try a new concept of silhouettes with two models. I had no
idea what he was talking about. He said it would just be two models, he
would tell us how to pose and that you wouldn't be able to recognize us,
only shapes and forms. It was not spontaneous. Everything was orchestrated by him."[86] In exempting herself from any connection with lesbian
desire, Williams powerfully reminds us of the patriarchal grid upon
which straight pornography rests. The photography session, she insistently claimed, was a "mistake," a bad judgment call blamed on youth
and inexperience: "I was enraged and I felt a deep sense of personal embarrassment. It is one thing to face up to a mistake one makes in youth,
but it is almost totally devastating to have to share it with the American
public and the world at large."[87] And, as Goldsby points out, it is clear that
Williams's unawareness—"I had no idea what he was talking about"—
was offset by the photos themselves:

> Once the photos hit the newsstands . . . their value and meaning trans-
> formed not around the fact of her ignorance, but around the *represen-
> tation* of her knowledge. . . . The question of whether Williams knew
> what she was doing is reflected by what it *looked* like she knew: how
> to eat snatch, how to please herself. It becomes impossible to classify
> and so withdraw the images as stock stereotypes from straight porno-

graphy precisely because Williams was the paragon of American prenuptial chastity; the beauty queen became, irrevocably, the derivative deviant that is the dyke.[88]

AFTER THE FALL

However, Williams's fall from virgin to whore is not irrevocably culturally signified as the "derivative deviant that is the dyke." After Williams relinquished her crown, she found a more tenable position in popular culture, a position where she could more successfully occupy the discourses of assimilation and eroticizing difference simultaneously. Williams chose the "soft" eroticization of the sexy pop-star, where her subjectivity is constituted as both safely white and sexily black.

But it is clear that within the pageant, black women are presented with few options in terms of constructing self-identity. The "exposure" of Vanessa Williams recalled and foregrounded historically powerful narratives about black women and sexuality, and it confirmed racist beliefs embedded within beauty pageants concerning the "questionable morals" purportedly held by all black women. It also can be seen as an instance of a broader discourse about race and difference, and we should consider the story of Williams a particularly instructive instance of the ways the discourse of diversity works in U.S. culture.

This story tells us much about racism, politics, and the nation. It is true that the *Penthouse* photographs functioned to recall to the public's collective memory "old ghosts" about insatiable—and "indefensible"—black female sexuality, but this recollection took place within the context of liberal tales of individual achievement, tolerance, and personhood. The strategies I have identified as assimilation and eroticizing difference, necessary to "appropriately" position Williams on the pageant stage, resonate with the processes and regulatory practices of popular culture that situate black women on the landscape of U.S. political and cultural life. In an increasingly diverse configuration of the nation, accompanied by an increasing absence of the notion of a universal citizen, popular cultural forms in the United States uniquely respond to a moral panic over the current state of national identity. The beauty pageant offers a performance of feminine subjectivity that functions as a national assurance that, despite the threats posed to dominant culture by fluctuating racial and gender codes, the pageant successfully manages and disciplines the construction of national identity, femininity, and racial identity.

This kind of management emerges in pageants through the forced confrontation between a history of celebrating universal whiteness and contemporary demands that pageants reflect racial and ethnic diversity. In the 1990s, pageants assuage nationwide fears and anxieties about multiculturalism and "political correctness" through both a reinvention of this hysteria and a simultaneous retrenchment of racist "moral" values. Appropriating the terms and language of diversity, the beauty pageant valiantly fights in what has been called the "Battle for America's Future."[89] It accommodates diversity, performs and exercises toleration, and simultaneously manages to efface any obvious signs of particular ethnicities or races. This strategy relies on representation or recognition of diversity— achieved through the presence of nonwhite bodies—where the physical representation of the few black and brown women on the pageant stage testifies to the pageant's claim that it does indeed represent all American womanhood. The nationwide political crisis concerning diversity, which is situated centrally in fears about identity politics, is reinvented in the beauty pageant as a classic liberal tale about individual achievement in a land of opportunity.

Within this "land of opportunity," social narratives of individual difference work alongside other classic liberal tales of achievement and assimilation in a broader political context that affirms the basic logic of competition between white people and people of color. Just as competition for points and glory on the playing fields of the baseball diamond, the job market, or the educational system is understood as the "natural" quest of an individual for self-fulfillment and success, contestants in the beauty pageant are presumed to compete on a level playing field of beauty. However, this status of the liberal female subject—as equal participants and as "unmarked"—excludes black women who are doubly burdened by the markers of race and gender. Within liberal society, the self-representation of black women thus takes place in a context of double exclusion. However, as Crenshaw argues, "The problems of exclusion cannot be solved simply by including Black women within an already established analytical structure."[90] Feminists have called our attention to the theoretical in-adequacy of "gender by addition," which merely inserts gender as a fac-tor in an existing theoretical structure that is not intended to truly and richly account for gender as an analytical category.[91] In a similar way, Cren-shaw's theory of intersectionality allows us to account for the various ways in which gender and race interact and intersect. It is only through such an intersectional framework that the complexities of Vanessa Williams's story become clear, so that we can better understand how the Miss Amer-ica pageant was an ideal site for simultaneously domesticating her dif-ference and exploiting dominant narratives about black female sexuality. As Miss America, Vanessa Williams may have been the "new black woman," but the cultural and political forces that shaped her "downfall" were all too familiar.

CHAPTER 5 # THE REPRESENTATIONAL POLITICS OF WHITENESS AND THE NATIONAL BODY

BESS MYERSON, MISS AMERICA 1945, AND
HEATHER WHITESTONE, MISS AMERICA 1995

In the last three chapters, we have seen various ways in which difference is contained and consolidated in and through the Miss America pageant. Examination of the swimsuit, talent, and interview competitions and of the racial politics that structured the reign of Vanessa Williams has deepened our understanding of various instances that threaten to expose these politics, or more specifically, to reveal as political the pageant's structure of whiteness. This chapter takes a closer look at how these strategies are successful at containing and controlling the politics of whiteness that are a determining factor in the pageant's production. I shift the perspective slightly to discuss in more detail the underlying structure for this containment and consolidation. In its vision of American national identity, the Miss America pageant attempts to construct, as Lauren Berlant has suggested, a simple, privacy-based vision of normal America, where both personal and civic duties are constituted and understood as a crucial element

in realizing the individual contestant's goal to be part of a "normal" white
heterosexual family. The pageant attempts to set itself apart from other
sites within the mass media as a unique place where ordinariness, typicality, and authenticity are not constantly under threat or in the throes of
critique, but instead are both desired and celebrated.[1] To maintain this particular imagined community, the Miss America pageant deploys various
strategies of containment, but all are fueled by constructions of whiteness,
an explicitly racialized category that has historically maintained dominance precisely by erasing its racial distinctiveness.

As I discuss in the introduction to this book, it is necessary to examine
the oppressive optimism in what Berlant calls "normal national culture"—
part of which is the Miss America pageant—in order to see, among other
things, "what kinds of domination are being imagined as forms of social
good."[2] How, for instance, are the often stultifying and always conservative conventions of femininity and family represented by the Miss America pageant transformed through the pageant as values and standards that
are liberating, modern, and even feminist? How is the position of each contestant as a spokesperson for charitable work (articulated in and through
the "issue platform" to which each contestant must demonstrate a commitment) translated as the pageant's attention and commitment to reme-
dying social ills and problems? Berlant asks, "What kinds of utopian desires are being tapped and translated into conservative worldviews?"[3] In
other words, what kind of citizen is imagined through the apparent multicultural stage of the Miss America pageant—a multiculturalism that disciplines and domesticates racial difference in a way that offers evidence of
equal opportunity as it simultaneously normalizes and naturalizes whiteness? The Miss America pageant is about utopian fantasies for women—
fantasies that follow the rhetoric of liberal feminism, where women are
free and equal beings, where equal opportunity reigns, and where the
imagined community is one in which liberal pluralism and tolerance disciplines rather than liberates nonwhite identities.

Situating the Miss America pageant as a site for both the constitution
and the realization of particular utopian fantasies about national community encourages a more complicated reading of this cultural form. To
be sure, the pageant, and especially the heightened politics of whiteness
that constitute and legitimate the entire event, is an example of mass culture that is overly accessible and available for reading, in the sense that

the dominant rhetoric of the event is fairly transparent and the results and consequences of the pageant typically predictable. Yet the pageant's extreme formulaic style does not necessarily mean that complicated cultural work is not also being performed. Indeed, its very accessibility and availability is that which urges us to do this kind of cultural reading; its apparent simplicity tells us something about how complicated cultural work is performed.

One of the ways that the Miss America pageant makes itself accessible to a mass-mediated audience is through the rhetorical strategy involving equal opportunity: we appeal to everyone, we threaten no one, and anyone can be Miss America. The representation of America that is performed on the beauty pageant stage is one in which cultural hopes and desires, anxieties, and fears about whiteness and national identity are crystallized. This reflects contemporary ideological musings and concerns about identity; concerns through which the pageant sustains its position on whiteness by projecting a national utopic vision of "typicality" and the ordinary. The "typical" American woman, as represented by the Miss America pageant, is marked by absence of identity markers—we are all "persons," after all. The Miss America pageant thus becomes a universal space defined in negative relation to all contours of differentiated and political identity. Within this space, traditional markers of identity—race, class, and ethnicity—are diffused and flattened out so that they better accommodate the politics of whiteness that structure the entire event. Indeed, the pageant contains and subverts the dynamic production of whiteness—the way in which this racial structure and institutional practice shifts and changes and is historically contingent—even as the pageant, as well as other U.S. cultural formations, fixes whiteness as the universally relevant category.

The questions that inform this chapter focus on the pageant's political and rhetorical strategies that support structures of whiteness: Whose body occupies the position of the "national" body? How, for example, does Bess Myerson, crowned in 1945 as the first Jewish Miss America, become a certain kind of national body for America, one that is never again symbolically needed? What other bodies disappear through this positioning? What qualifications does one need to be appropriately and properly national? How does Heather Whitestone, Miss America 1995, who is deaf, position her difference as something that can be successfully assimilated into a proper national identity? And more specifically, how do beauty pageants produce definitions of the national body? That is, how can we read the history of the pageant in relation to social and political contexts of American national identity?

These questions focus on how whiteness, as both a discursive and material politics, becomes a fantasy about national identity; in true melting-pot fashion, the pageant strategizes to dissolve identity and difference in order to sustain a national representation of womanhood. Through the stories of two individual Miss Americas—Bess Myerson, Miss America 1945, and Heather Whitestone, Miss America 1995—we witness how this utopian fantasy of national identity is produced in two very different historical moments. In highlighting these two moments, fifty years apart in the history of the pageant, I do not intend to conduct a historical investigation of the Miss America pageant as an entire institution. Rather, I focus on what I regard as two different formative moments—both within the pageant and within the nation as a whole—in order to see what they can tell us about the kinds of representative bodies that are produced and how they are produced, within different historical contexts. To the extent that the Miss America pageant sees itself as a litmus test for American womanhood, we can read it as a measure of what is happening in the nation politically, culturally, and economically. The pageant sees itself as moving with the times even as it simultaneously promotes an eternal feminine code; it understands itself to be a forum for the "typical" American woman—a woman living in a nation that prides itself on the coherence of its internal differences—even as it defines typicality according to white, middle-class norms, and even as these norms change. The pageant, then, is a cultural site in which we can witness what it means to be white and middle class in the United States (how whiteness and middle-class status signifies on a cultural scale) at various moments in history.

BESS MYERSON, MISS AMERICA 1945:
"YOU CAN'T BE BEAUTIFUL AND HATE"

In 1945, the Miss America pageant underwent significant transformations. Most notably, this was the first year that the pageant offered academic

scholarships as prizes (it now is the largest scholarship organization ex-
clusively for women in the United States). With a scholarship firmly in
place, the vision of the Miss America board of directors concerning who
Miss America ideally should be became less of an abstraction and more
of a real possibility. The women who entered the 1945 Miss America
pageant were quite different from those first contenders for the crown who
entered "bathing beauty" contests on the beaches of Atlantic City; they
were beautiful, and they were feminine, but they were also active agents
in a volatile political culture.[1]

The 1945 Miss America contestants experienced their adult lives in the
midst of a world war. The femininity performed on the stage of the pageant
was constructed in explicitly nationalist terms; with Rosie the Riveter as
their symbol, and "We Can Do It" as their motto, the 1945 contestants were
both acutely aware of and participants within this political context. Bess
Myerson, the first and only Jewish Miss America, was crowned in 1945.
In her memoirs, she recalls this moment: "Thousands and thousands of
[panorama pictures of the contestants] were produced. . . . A fellow I
knew from camp wrote to me that he saw one in Okinawa. Another fellow saw one in Berlin. We couldn't have realized it, standing on the bleach-
ers, sucking in our bellies, fixing our smiles, but we were at that moment
becoming the cheesecake that followed the flag."[5] Although Myerson
claims that she and the other contestants "couldn't have realized" what
they were doing, it is clear that these women were at least acutely aware
of their bodies as representations (as well as being aware of the disciplinary practices required to conform to this representation). "Becoming the
cheesecake that followed the flag" is both a statement and an action laden
with meaning about what the American flag represents. Myerson's remark
situates female bodies as specific embodiments of the abstract meaning
of the flag and clearly calls our attention to the way in which icons of femininity are constitutive of national meaning and sentiment.

Through a relentless focus on the body—sucking in bellies and fixing
smiles—the production of the contestants' identity circulated far beyond
the intentions of the contestants; the gaze at that moment wasn't just the
judges' but encompassed all U.S. soldiers. And the gaze was focused most
intensely on Myerson. Explicitly acknowledged as a Jewish woman, she
performed her identity around a series of narratives circulating in the na-

tion in 1945: she represented the thousands of people for whom American soldiers were fighting. Beautiful, talented, the daughter of immigrants, she was living proof of or testimony for the reliability of the American Dream. Her body, identified publicly as Jewish, situated Myerson as a specific site for displacing a nation's troubles, anxieties, and guilt (see plate 8).[6] The question is, how—through what social and cultural discourses and practices—did Myerson, during that particular moment, reassure the nation that there was, in fact, coherence to its identity?

Shifting our attention to the strategies involved in positioning a woman as a representative of the nation indicates a significant shift in scholarly focus. The bulk of the literature on nationalism and national identities has tended to focus on the male, or the masculine as the ideal representative of the nation. Recently, however, feminist scholarship on nationalism and postcolonial investigations about national identity and national bodies have profoundly disrupted traditional scholarship on nationalism. They call attention to the fact that there are usually two dominant tropes for figuring women as nationalist bodies: first, women are positioned according to the logics of heterosexuality, as the literal "bearers" of the nation, who, through their reproductive capacities, continue the national lineage. In this trope, women are seen as mothers of the nation. A second major trope is women as iconic figures, feminine bodies that are memorialized in their representation of the nation—the Statue of Liberty, German's Germania, and France's Marianne.[7] In either case, women are situated peripherally to masculine national identity—in the former case, as figures in a predictable scene, where the nation is imagined in terms of a familial metaphor and women are placed within a traditional heterosexual configuration, and in the latter case, as a spectacle that is decorative and symbolic (but not exactly an animated citizen).

Many feminists have called our attention to the fact that although there is an "astonishing absence" of the gendered dimensions and meanings of national discourse in most of the scholarly literature, women are not truly absent as crucial elements to the construction of national identities and sentiments. To see their presence, we need to investigate other realms that produce nationalist identities—realms outside the traditional purview of national discourse, in the spaces of the everyday: in the family and the household, in the education of children, and in all those places that, as

Berlant argues, "can be counterposed as 'the local' to the national frame of abstracted citizenship and power."[8]

The beauty pageant is one such place. In a domain that is defined as unpolitical, it remains a highly political practice.[9] The nationalist sentiment of the beauty pageant does not necessarily take into account dynamic social and historical contexts of national struggles, nor does it account for the formation of nation states; rather, it produces the formation and operation of what Berlant calls the "National Symbolic."[10] The pageant spectacularly performs every element of Berlant's National Symbolic for a collective national subjectivity: it is a site that constitutes icons and heroes, it functions as a metaphor for the collective nation, and it offers a classic liberal narrative as the appropriate life trajectory. In this sense, the pageant represents what might be called the *"political space of the nation,"* representing a shift from the conventional national realm of law and citizenship to a relation that links "regulation to desire, harnessing affect to political life through the production of 'national fantasy.'"[11] It is within this realm, the space of representation, desire, and fantasy—the space of the beauty pageant—where "the idea of the nation works, figuring a landscape of complacency and promise, inciting memories of citizenship, but bringing its claims and demands into the intimate and quotidian places of ordinary life."[12] The Miss America pageant produces images and narratives that articulate dominant expectations about who and what "American" women are (and should be) at the same time as it narrates who and what the nation itself should be through promises of citizenship, fantasies of agency, and tolerant pluralism. Therefore the beauty pageant provides us with a site to witness the gendered construction of national identity— and I mean this in its doubled sense, as both a statement of the *gendered* nation and the feminine body as *nationalist*.

Reading the feminine body as a national(ist) body requires us to recognize the interconnectedness of discourses of the nation and discourses of citizenship. On the one hand, the body of a beauty pageant contestant is constituted metaphorically— as symbolic articulation of the social body, or as testimony for what Lisa Lowe calls "the mutable coherence of the national body."[13] But on the other hand, the construction of this metaphor makes a statement about the individual citizen, where the array of bodies on a beauty pageant stage serve as visual testimony for ascribing political subjectivity: each woman "represents" the abstract characteristics of membership in the national imaginary of the United States, and all are positioned as regional identities that then function to "map the nation."

The pageant contestants thus "prove" the diversity of the American public, representing both the promise and the fantasy of citizenship. The curious focus on the dialectic between the public and the private—a public liberal identity embodied within individual, "private" contestants—fleshes out the mutually constitutive character of the feminine body, female liberal citizenship, and the national body. The pageant invites a reading of the body both as a symbol of the national social body and as the individual liberal citizen.

The 1945 Miss America pageant, where the contestants were situated (and situated themselves) explicitly as not merely beautiful bodies but patriotic subjects in the midst of a world war, was precisely the setting for this kind of reading. Shifting to popular cultural forms such as beauty pageants from the conventional realm of law as a site in which citizenship is produced does not deny that the language of the law profoundly informs the national fantasy that is constructed on the Miss America stage. Indeed, the pageant is deeply entrenched in what George Lipsitz calls the possessive investment of whiteness, in which a dominant definition of Americanness is formulated.[14] Locating whiteness as an ideology rather than solely upon a rigid racial hierarchy pries open how whiteness is an organizing principle of cultural life in the United States.[15] Charting FHA housing policies, urban renewal projects, and federal home loan policies, among other factors of suburbanization, Lipsitz convincingly argues that whiteness is an inextricable foundation of the language of liberal individualism, and as such it ideologically encourages the American public to think in individualistic terms rather than to understand "the disciplined, systemic, and collective group activity that has structured white identities in American history."[16]

Whiteness is an identity marker that, at least in part, centers on America's trust in and commitment to fetishizing the visible. The beauty pageant is situated within popular culture as the exemplary site for realizing this commitment—the stage is "equalized" by the apparent diversity of individual women who perform their femininity there. This move

toward representational integration confirms a nationalist desire for coherent resolution through visual—and visible—forms. So given that this
is the context for the beauty pageant, questioning why the nation "needs"
a certain body at a particular historical moment means that we must recognize that pageants take account of bodies of difference—and by this I
mean bodies that somehow register differently on an idealized scale of
femininity, whether it be in terms of race, class, ethnicity, sexuality, or
other markers of identity—as a way to account for national historical moments. The question in this specific context thus becomes, how do different bodies—or bodies of difference—become validations of the availability of the norm for everyone? For example, how is it that the selection
of a Jewish woman as Miss America functions as evidence that any Jewish woman can occupy that position if she tries hard enough?

MANAGING AMERICANNESS:
BESS MYERSON AND ETHNIC ASSIMILATION

In the 1930s and 1940s, the gendered definition of national identity was
culturally inscribed in many realms of American society. One significant
realm centered on the ideological efforts to assimilate new immigrants as
newly American—at the same time as racial "others" were marginalized
and situated outside the norm ever more vigorously. As Michael Rogin
has argued, during the 1930s and 1940s, the trope of Americanization and
the melting pot strongly resonated with vaudeville and film audiences.
The Miss America pageant was part of a process, along with movies and
vaudeville performances, that "turned immigrants into Americans." Re-
pudiating the nativism of the 1920s, the decades of the 1930s and 1940s
celebrated the melting pot of America, and entertainment culture effectively performed and articulated this version of national discourse.

    However, as many contemporary critics have astutely documented,
melting pot ideology moves ethnic persons from a "racially liminal position to a white identity."[17] In other words, those persons who could be
considered "racially liminal" are precisely those who, through their visually white skin, can become white morally and emotionally. This group
included (at different moments during this general era) Irish Americans,

Italian Americans, German Americans, and Jewish Americans. The Jewish identity of Bess Myerson can only be seen as an appropriate representative of the nation in the context of various cultural discourses and practices that functioned as part of a transformation that resulted in the "whitening of Jews." World War II was a transformative moment for solidifying the ethnic, rather than racial, identity of Jewish Americans. Jewish assimilation in the United States was about transforming immigrants into Americans while at the same time retrenching African American identity and other nonwhite ethnic groups as those that could not be assimilated. The role that popular entertainment such as vaudeville, minstrelsy, movies, and the Miss America pageant played in terms of Americanizing immigrants was one that could only function against the backdrop of blackness. Especially after World War II, the United States witnessed a refiguring of Jewish identity that focused on the successful assimilation of Jews into American society. This transformation confirmed the rhetoric of melting pot ideology and reinforced the promise of assimilation. As Rogin argues, in the United States, "African-Americans substituted for Jews as the dominant targets of racial nationalism," whereby legal and historical group distinctions begin to dissolve and biological racism finds legitimacy.[18]

Newly considered white, with a specific unique cultural heritage, immigrant Jews in the United States "were Americanizing themselves through their place in popular entertainment."[19] And it is *because* Jewish identity can assimilate in its white ethnicity that the pageant comes to produce a Jewish, white, female body as the representative of the nation—as the pageant also functions to rewrite U.S. history in terms of its morality. At the particular historical moment in which Myerson was crowned—1945—and in light of the racial genocide of World War II, Myerson as Miss America reaffirms the logic of assimilationist discourse: she does not threaten or disrupt, but instead represents the pluralist nation as well as American universalism. Her ethnic identity confirms the logic of the melting pot, where different races and ethnic groups supposedly coexist in productive harmony; her difference is precisely the kind needed to sustain the promise of American pluralism, because this difference ironically serves as a point of entry for successful assimilation. Through her commitment to disciplinary practices that constituted white femininity, through her education at

Julliard, through her success as a talented pianist, and through her immigrant history, Myerson was produced as an appropriate representative of the national body. Her white ethnicity did not threaten the nationalist hold that whiteness commands, and her Jewish identity justified and legitimated the presence of U.S. soldiers overseas.

In this sense, Myerson's reign was about consolidation; even given the fact that, at least for some, World War II was seen as a race war, it remained very clear that we couldn't have U.S. soldiers—"our boys"—dying for the Other, or for a raced body. Myerson as an iconic national figure contains this fear and transforms a shifted definition of the Other into a normative body. Perhaps as a response to these fears, during her reign Myerson not only went on the usual vaudeville and modeling tours, but was also a participant in the Brotherhood Campaigns with the Anti-Defamation League (ADL). She gave speeches for the ADL during the entire year of her reign, drawing on her identity as both Jewish and Miss America.

Her motto, "You can't be beautiful and hate," was offered to high school students, housing project residents, and others on the tour of the Brotherhood Campaigns. In her first speech for the ADL, she said, "Miss America represents all America. It makes no difference who she is, or who her parents are. Side by side, Catholic, Protestant, and Jew stand together . . . and we would have it no other way. . . . And all those things are important in Atlantic City—or anywhere else where real Americans take your measure and pass judgment." Myerson explicitly uses her body or her status as a national feminine representative as a means through which evidence of the success of assimilation can be—and is—realized. Her rhetorical strategy of "You can't be beautiful and hate" forces her audiences to conceptualize femininity, nationhood, and tolerance as mutually constitutive categories of identity.

Nonetheless, the fact that Myerson represented what was considered an "appropriate" Jewish identity, and that the national confusions and contestations about the war were displaced and "resolved" through her representational form, does not mean that this resolution or this displacement was felt by every U.S. citizen. Some of those "real Americans" Myerson mentions so glowingly in her ADL speech denied her entry into country clubs, reneged on traditional Miss America sponsorships, and refused to allow her to visit their sons in veteran's hospitals. Despite her whitened ethnicity and despite her commitment to the conventional understandings of what it meant to be "American," there were experiences that could not be contained within her representational form—there were things that she could *not* do that other Miss Americas could. In other words, there was clearly an excess to her meaning as Miss America; positioned as a symbol for a nation that was so clearly fraught with racial and ethnic tension guaranteed that some of these tensions would be negotiated and contested around and within her iconic status. Indeed, one reason why she could not "resolve" these tensions is that she was part of the shifting discourse on Jewish identity, producing it even as she was being produced by it. She represented the nation at that particular moment, and she both constructed and maintained the conflicts and complications inherent within that representation.

SHIFTING VISUAL REGIMES:
THE ADVENT OF TELEVISION

Bess Myerson marks the end of one visual regime in U.S. popular culture and the beginning of another; in 1945, her body was positioned as a visual reminder of the triumph of a specifically American liberal individualism, culminating in an apparently seamless melting pot, even as her selection as "queen of America" worked to solidify a racial hierarchy that ensured the supremacy of whiteness. After 1945, however, the pageant was on its way to a different kind of stage: a nationally televised one. The advent of television shifted the culture of the visual to one in which the camera provided what seemed to be iron-clad evidence of diverse womanhood; indeed, the image of the taxonomic array of feminine bodies that is now the most recognizable sign of the Miss America pageant is possible only through the technology of television. Clearly, the politics of whiteness that structured the crowning and reign of Bess Myerson remain evident and powerful, but they shifted with the commodity and entertainment cultures of late-twentieth-century American society.

The national fantasies motivated by the figure of Bess Myerson are created primarily around the political context of 1945, the ideological power of assimilation and Americanization, and the role that women were expected to play in assisting these processes. Although assimilationist rhetoric remains powerful in the later part of the twentieth century, the positioning of the mass media as a national public sphere has changed what we, as Americans, can and do fantasize about. The televised nation (which is, after all, perhaps the most readily available relationship with the "nation" that most Americans have) changes what can be visualized as crucial components of national identity. The American national public sphere is, as Berlant has argued, an intimate public sphere, where citizenship is rendered "as a condition of social membership produced by personal acts and values, especially acts originating in or directed toward the family sphere. No longer valuing personhood as something directed toward public life, contemporary nationalist ideology recognizes a public good only in a particularly constricted nation of simultaneously lived private worlds."[20] This tells us what is to be included in a national fantasy about the American way of life: "In the new, utopian America, mass-mediated political identifications can only be rooted in traditional notions of home, family and community."[21]

Television becomes the site for enacting this kind of utopian national fantasy. The scopic regimes that structured the crowning and reign of beauty queens such as Bess Myerson shifted with the advent of television and the mass-mediated public sphere, and television itself is now situated as the place for negotiating cultural contests over who gets to count as part of the nation. In other words, what changed from the time of Bess Myerson's reign to contemporary conceptualizations of feminine national identity were the social practices of vision themselves; the fetishization of the visual that legitimates television's ubiquitous presence in the lives of contemporary Americans does not necessarily take place in the *imagined* community so much as in the *embodied* community—which, in turn, is structured and legitimated in the national imaginary. The imagined community theorized by Benedict Anderson goes beyond the point of merely being imagined; it is a community that is embodied through televised performances. Through particular "economies of visibility," television democratizes both accessibility to and availability of national identity; positioning representational politics—as opposed to political representation—as the heart of national identity becomes more possible and more necessary in the late-twentieth-century mass-mediated public sphere.[22]

In 1945, the figure of Bess Myerson as the feminine representative of the nation was visualized through pinup photographs; she was, as she herself articulated, "the cheesecake that followed the flag." In the 1990s, the representational politics of national identity have reinvented themselves within the terms and boundaries of a postindustrial, highly massmediated political context, and symbols of the nation are embedded in the utopic fantasies of television. What are these utopic fantasies? In a decade characterized by continually shifting demographics about the ethnic and racial makeup of U.S. society, these fantasies focus on difference and diversity as the vitality and vibrancy of American national identity.[23] It is a diversity and difference, however, that must be disciplined and domesticated to ensure national "coherence," and television provides this kind of management in "realist" clarity. It is to this American nation, one characterized by a different set of scopic regimes that allowed for the crowning of Bess Myerson, that we now turn. Heather Whitestone, Miss America 1995, is the first deaf Miss America and an exemplary model for a new face of America; through her innocence (gained apparently through her inability to hear), she is positioned in the place of civic virtue and situated by the pageant and the pageant's audience as special evidence that testifies to the success of a liberal America, uniquely marked by difference even as the myth of meritocracy is ever more invigorated.

THE DIFFERENCE THAT MAKES NO DIFFERENCE, OR WHY CAN'T WE ALL JUST GET ALONG?: HEATHER WHITESTONE, MISS AMERICA 1995

> Heather's becoming Miss America has enabled her to pursue an even more worthy dream—to be a bridge between two worlds, so that hearing and deaf people throughout our country and around the earth will have a better understanding and appreciation for each other and for what we can learn from one another.
>
> DAPHNE GRAY,
> *Mother of Heather Whitestone,*
> *Miss America 1995*

The Miss America pageant clearly prides itself on its commitment to liberal ideology—especially the theme of equal opportunity. The statement "Anyone can do it if they try" continues to be the rhetorical driving force of the pageant, even as the standardized practices of femininity required to enter the event—slim body, "good," long hair, European facial features—are ever more vigorously and viciously regulated. In 1995, the Miss America pageant "proved" once again to the American public—as it did with Bess Myerson and Vanessa Williams—that the pageant was committed to equality and the ideals of meritocracy: in that year, the pageant selected as queen the first contestant with a physical disability. Deaf since she was eighteen months old, Heather Whitestone, Miss Alabama 1994, wowed the pageant's audience with her ballet routine and her response to the on-stage interview questions.

What interests me about the Whitestone crowning is not so much her deafness itself, but what her deafness signified to the American audience about the kind of woman—and the kind of identity—that was symbolically needed for the American nation in 1995. What sorts of strategies were deployed through her "difference," a physical disability, to consolidate dominant conventions and conceptions of national identity in that particular historical moment? Moreover, what kind of citizenship is imagined in and through the 1995 Miss America pageant, where both the material stage of the event and the virtual stage of the nation are characterized by a multicultural vision and conservative pluralist politics? And finally, how does the technology and apparatus of television assist this vision?

Whitestone's deafness—contracted through illness at a tender age—was very clearly an issue of anxiety and confusion during her participation in pageants. Her family was determined to raise her as an active participant in the oral-centric world, and therefore Whitestone interacted only sporadically in the deaf community (she attended a school for the deaf between the ages of eleven and fourteen). She did not learn sign language until she was an adult, because her mother, Daphne Gray, wanted her to practice speech and not rely on sign until her oral speech was perfected.[24] She once participated in a Miss Deaf Alabama pageant but apparently felt alienated and confused when she was given the cold shoulder because of her inability (interpreted as unwillingness) to sign. As her mother tells it, sign language was understood by the Whitestone family as a second language, one intended to bolster—not replace—her primary language of spoken English. For the Whitestones, the deaf community was situated as many minority communities are: as subcultures, conceptualized only in terms of the distance of their relationship from the norm, or from hegemonic, and in this case, oral-centric, culture. Whitestone's mother commented that if and when Whitestone learned sign language, she "figured she'd [Whitestone] then have the best possible chance to access both worlds—the hearing world *all of us live in* and the smaller deaf world with its own rich and unique heritage."[25] As many if not most in the deaf community will argue, "all of us" do not live in the hearing world. This construction of a larger world all of us live in as encompassing a smaller one, exotic (and often erotic) in its "rich and unique" heritage, is a familiar strategy of reducing the threat that a subculture or a minority culture poses to the dominant culture. The disabled community, like communities of people of color, is thus situated on the periphery of the dominant culture.[26] Because Whitestone has some hearing and thus is physically capable of speaking, her family believed that the "best choice" for her was the choice to live in the hearing world. As her mother commented, "I see it as an advantage if deaf people can speak. Then you can communicate in both worlds." Whitestone herself said, "Maybe God wants me to be a bridge between the two worlds."[27] For the Miss America pageant, Whitestone is an exemplary spokesperson for those people who are marked by "difference": she accommodates the dominant world by subsuming or obscuring her own difference. Her difference indeed makes no difference; she, like Rodney King, asks all of us, "Why can't we all just get along?"[28] In fact, she not only asks us to "get along," but she, as the bridge between two worlds, will facilitate our friendship.

The pageant is just the site for this negotiating between different worlds. After several years during which the pageant vehemently insisted that it was not a racist production, Whitestone was crowned as a final testimony to the notion that the pageant encourages difference (see plate 9). Her whiteness, of course, underscores and legitimates her disability; it also represents the triumph of a reactionary "multicultural" U.S. society in the mid 1990s. The complicated negotiations between dominant and marginal cultures are perhaps most seamlessly and satisfyingly resolved in popular culture. The visual supremacy of popular culture makes it an ideal site to fetishize the visual body as "difference," even as it erases the social and political structures and practices that both facilitate and diminish this very same difference. In 1993, for example, *Time* magazine published a special issue on immigration and multicultural society. The cover featured a computer-morphed woman who was the technologically generated offspring

of "seven men and seven women of various ethnic and racial backgrounds"; this image was proudly represented as "the new face of America."[29] This "new face," argues Michael Prince, offers a resolution to any
threat of ethnic or racial crisis: "Her name is reassurance: mixture obey-
ing an inner rule, disproving all the feared consequences of miscegena-
tion. Her truth is beauty: a placid sensuality whose immediate appeal sus-
pends all doubts about her questionable origin."[30] The editors of the
magazine, commenting about doing the research on what the future
United States would look like given the realities of a multicultural society, assured their public that any conflicts or potential crises were again
subverted through feminine representation: "The highlight of this exercise in cybergenesis was the creation of the woman on our cover, selected
as a symbol of the future, multi-ethnic face of America. . . . Little did we
know what we had wrought. As onlookers watched the image of our new
Eve begin to appear on the computer screen, several staff members
promptly fell in love."[31] Although beauty pageant contestants can hardly
be compared to computer-morphed representations, the idea that newly
crowned Miss Americas are also conceptualized as "new Eves" is one that
deserves critical reflection. The inclusion of racially diverse contestants
over the past ten years has increasingly posed the problem of constructing representations of a unified and singular national identity while acknowledging difference. Popular discourse and the pageants themselves
attempt to resolve this contradiction by relying on classic liberal stories
about individual achievement and pluralist tolerance. Heather Whitestone
is perhaps the most logical new Eve; her significant achievement and successes are attributed to her commitment to liberal ideology and the overcoming of obstacles (the primary one rooted in her own body).

By making invisible the social technologies that produce difference,
these liberal stories result in the retrenchment of a national identity
defined by white middle-class norms. For Heather Whitestone, the pageant's privilege of the rhetoric of "personhood" proved to be an entry into
an event that previously dismissed women with disabilities as too weak
to represent the nation. Her statement to the interview judges focused on
this point; she said at the interview, "I want to be Miss America, and I want
to graduate from college. But I know each of you has a question in mind,
and I want to answer it for you right now: Can a profoundly deaf woman

fulfill the duties of Miss Alabama and Miss America? To this I say, yes. I can do it! Because I realize that everything is possible with God's help. I don't see my deafness as an obstacle, but as an opportunity for creative thinking."[32] Translating difference into "an opportunity for creative thinking" relies on a liberal ideology that suggests that eradicating racism and other prejudices is as simple as an attitude adjustment, or a mere tinkering with already established ideological frameworks.

This rhetoric colludes perfectly with the dominant ideology of the Miss America pageant, where it is expressed either through liberal agency—"I'm a person, I can do what I want"—or through success stories in a meritocracy—"I just kept telling myself: you can do it, and here I am!"—or even through appropriated feminist language—"No, I don't feel exploited, I feel like a winner."[33] In the 1995 Miss America pageant, Whitestone spoke the right rhetoric to bridge difference. The language of abstract personhood seems to have an entirely new level of currency given the recent cultural climate of multiculturalism and diversity. Neoconservatives such as syndicated columnist George Will hysterically claim that "multiculturalism attacks individualism by defining people as mere manifestations of groups (racial, ethnic, sexual) rather than as self-defining participants in a free society"—without, of course, ever scrutinizing his and others' use of the term *people* as a category that is always racially coded as white, middle-class, and able-bodied.[34] Or consider an episode of Oprah Winfrey's show that discussed the so-called problem of identity labels. The guests on the program represented various ethnic groups and were called upon to defend claims to identity that differed from those imposed by hegemonic white supremacist society. In the midst of the discussion, a white woman from the audience stood up and very sincerely asked the guests why they felt a need to identify themselves as "different," or as marked, and wondered why they couldn't just "act like people." What this audience member fails to appreciate is that "acting like people," in the case of the Oprah Winfrey show, not to mention the larger U.S. culture, has historically meant to act like white people—as Richard Dyer, Cheryl Harris, George Lipsitz, and others have argued, it is precisely the privilege of whiteness to be both everywhere and nowhere.[35]

A contestant in the 1992 Miss America pageant perhaps best expressed how successful the deployment of the powerful liberal discourse of personhood can be. The only African American finalist in the pageant, she responded to a question about multicultural society in the United States:

> It is so important that if we want to stop the problem of racism that is so prevalent in our country we all have to view ourselves as Americans. Not as Hispanic Americans or Afro Americans—we have to look at ourselves as one nation because our ethnicity makes us special, and we need to understand each other instead of beating down each other and acting superior. We're one people and we have to start acting like one people: Americans![36]

Not surprisingly, this contestant shifts the problem of racism from a social, institutionalized problem to one involving the efforts of the individual: if we would all just adjust our attitudes and think of ourselves as Americans, racism would presumably be eradicated. In this way, she echoes conservatives who argue that if we would merely stop obsessing about our racial and sexual identity and remember that the best sources of individuality and social cohesion are a "shared history, a common culture and unifying values," we could return to the golden age of liberal personhood and erase identity politics from our social and political landscape. Heather Whitestone also joins this camp, but is perhaps even more effective in her call for an end to identity politics because, as is so often the case, even while she denies that her difference limits her (thus reinforcing the dominance of the speaking world), it is precisely her deafness that marks her as extraordinary. She situates herself—and is situated by the pageant—as an inspiration because she overcomes obstacles as a classic liberal heroine should. But simultaneously, she is only able to be recognized as a liberal heroine through her active erasure of identity characteristics that mark her as different. She does not sign, and she does not use an interpreter. She went to a deaf school only to learn what was absolutely essential for her to "pass" in the hearing world. By embedding her deafness in liberal doctrine—as an obstacle to overcome—she accommodates the pageant's construction of universalized femininity even as her body is testimony to its diversity.

TELEVISING FEMININITY

One of the major differences between the stories of Bess Myerson and Heather Whitestone is that of technology: the Miss America pageant was first televised in 1954, nine years after Bess Myerson was crowned. Both stories are about accommodating difference, and both demonstrate the effectiveness and efficiency of the beauty pageant stage for these strategies of accommodation. But the technology of television allows the pageant and the pageant audience to indulge in the utopian fantasies offered by the spectacle in a directly visual manner; indeed, if the commodity and entertainment cultures of twentieth-century America provide the setting for asking questions about national identities, then it is through a regime of the visual that these questions are both posed and answered. It is precisely within the visuality of the beauty pageant, or what Robyn Wiegman calls "the economies of visibility," that the national body is constituted. More specifically, mass-mediated entertainment culture—the culture of the Miss America pageant—provides the venue for a national identification with the Miss America contestant, as she simultaneously embodies national desire.[37]

In the late 1990s, it is precisely within this venue of popular entertainment culture that we witness the construction and articulation of political subjects. Wiegman goes on to wonder, "What does it mean . . . that the visual apparatuses of photography, film, television, and video . . . serve as our primary public domain, our main shared context for the contestations of contemporary, cultural politics? And perhaps more important, what does it mean that within these technologies the body is figured as the primary locus of representation, mediation, and/or interpretation?"[38] In the context of beauty pageants, Wiegman's query points to the notion that pageants provide a public domain for demonstrating America's cultural trust in the objectivity of observation and the collapse of identity with representation. This, in turn, translates into an interpretation of the individual contestants both as representations of the nation and as examples of single moments of individual transcendence neatly represented by particular bodies.

Heather Whitestone performed individual transcendence on the beauty pageant stage; she chose as her ballet routine "Via Delarosa" (the story of the Crucifixion of Christ), and she initially wore a yellow dress tinged with red to symbolize Christ's blood (she later changed her costume to an all-white dress). But more than the choice of the song and its symbolism, or the actual outfit she chose, her ballet routine demonstrated her commitment to liberalism and individual transcendence. She performed a dance where the music was the most important element, yet she could not hear; she triumphed over convention by becoming purely somatic, feeling the beats through her feet and interpreting the music through her faith. Not surprisingly, the hosts Kathie Lee Gifford and Regis Philbin made much of her amazing ability to feel the beats through her feet, and the focus of the pageant's attention on Whitestone centered on the fact that she was able to dance in the first place, unlike the other contestants, where the focus was placed on the method and skill demonstrated through the dance, song, or other routine.

Her talent, and the dual performance of self and culture embodied in and through the talent competition, was intensely centered on her deafness, but with a particular focus: deafness was an obstacle Whitestone had overcome, and her ballet routine was the required evidence of that triumph. Accommodating the dominant liberal narrative of the United States functioned in turn to situate Whitestone as a clearly capable representative of that nation. But this self-construction can only take place in the realm of the visual; only through the televised pageant can Whitestone convince the audience—and by extension, the American public—that she is an exceptional Miss America.

Indeed, what is instructive about the various strategies employed by the Miss America Corporation to adapt their production to television is the recognition that what was happening onstage was the equivalent of a "news event"; identities were being crowned up there in front of the judges, and part of the self-production of the pageant was that it was, at its heart, a serious event. The pageant represented the "broad terrain of 'America,'" and the contestants embodied all this America had to offer. This cultural construction was not occurring on the battlefields, or in a conventional understanding of the public sphere, it was happening in commodity and mass entertainment culture—and it was happening through and upon the bodies of the contestants.

In fact, who and what can be appropriately named "American" always relies on some notion of the body (both male and female) and its public and private configurations. The beauty pageant constructs and maintains a particular configuration of the female citizen through the imagined promise of citizenship, the fantasy of female agency, and the deferral of inequalities in the public realm to the apparently level playing field of culture. In that sense, the pageant is about the coherence of a national body, but because pageants are about real as well as imagined bodies, about visual and cultural representation, they "erupt in culture," as Lisa Lowe has pointed out. Lowe continues, "Because culture is the contemporary repository of memory, of history, it is through culture, rather than government, that alternative forms of subjectivity, collectivity, and public life are imagined."[39]

Because they both situate and are situated by popular and national culture, pageants are crucial sites to consider when figuring the national body within the imaginary that is created and sustained by this culture. Lowe comments:

> Although the law is perhaps the discourse that most literally governs citizenship, U.S. national culture—the collectively forged images, histories, and narratives that place, displace, and replace individuals in relation to the national polity—powerfully shapes who the citizenry is, where they dwell, what they remember, and what they forgot. . . .
> It is through the terrain of national culture that the individual subject is politically formed as the American citizen: a terrain introduced by the Statue of Liberty, discovered by the immigrant, dreamed in a common language, and defended in battle by the independent, self-made man.[40]

Although it is through this notion of national culture that citizens are constituted, the beauty pageant specifically characterizes national culture through television, the medium in which the pageant is produced and viewed. Television serves as the main representational domain in late-twentieth-century U.S. culture; it not only provides the context of producing and performing a nationalist identity, but also functions accessibly and visually as a display of the nationalist body. It is through this medium that dominant understandings and definitions of who can become, who can act, and who can commodify themselves as "Americans" are formed.[41] It is also the site for tension, disruption, and remembering collective and individual struggles—simply, television is one element of mass entertainment culture that constitutes subjects. As Marita Sturken has argued, "In watching national television events, viewers engage with, whether in agreement or resistance, a concept of nationhood and national meaning."[42]

The subjectivities produced within the context of the beauty pageant are firmly and squarely situated within the logics of television structure: commodity culture. In fact, the women who participate in beauty pageants pose as particular commodities; they position their bodies and their personalities to "sell" an idealized version of American citizenship and American life. Television, and the way it both produces and commodifies differences, similarities, conflicts, and affiliations, allows us to ascribe meaning and substance based on an interpretation of the visual.

This process of ascribing meaning and substance is particularly effective in terms of strategizing and organizing what "multicultural" society should look like. As Wiegman points out, "In the Bush-Reagan era in particular, we witnessed a deft appropriation of the liberationist demand to make 'visible' the subjectivities and histories of the cultural margins, as consumer culture harnessed ethnic, racial and national specificities for its expanding global purposes."[43] The beauty pageant proves to be a remarkably effective domain to market ethnicity and commodify diversity. The sort of integration that occurs through visual representation is perhaps the primary means by which Americans constitute themselves as diverse citizens, or as members of a diverse civic body.

"ANYTHING IS POSSIBLE"

Whitestone's official issue platform, "Anything Is Possible," focuses on her deafness as a way to insist that difference is truly what one makes of it—one can strategically use it to "get ahead," which is the familiar argument against federal programs such as affirmative action and other civil rights initiatives that intend to rectify a historical and social structure of discrimination. Or one can, as Whitestone did, develop a program detailing how to succeed against the odds: named the STARS program, for Success Through Action and Realization of your dreamS, her program has five points (like a star):

1. Have a positive attitude.
2. Believe in your dreams.
3. Be willing to work very hard.

4. Be honest with yourself; face your weaknesses and obstacles.

5. Build a support team you can depend on.[44]

Her mother comments about Whitestone's development of this program: "The entire program was a summary of the strategy our whole family used to help her overcome her obstacles to achieve success in life against incredible odds."[45] Whitestone tells her success story according to these five points as a way to demonstrate their innovation and unique features. But is this program a new narrative? Hardly. Whitestone's STARS program is a recitation of the principles of liberalism combined with a good dose of Horatio Alger stories; it does not present any new (or effective, for most of us) strategies for succeeding in American life. But although her story and her platform are hardly novel, they are situated in an important way in the late 1990s' U.S. social and cultural politics. Her crowning as Miss America occurs within the context of increasing national anxiety about marginalized communities, an anxiety that is fueled by the potential threat these communities pose to dominant society and culture. Her STARS program enthusiastically performs this ideology: the narrative of good attitude and hard work that will bring success references apparently faulty and politically wayward federal programs such as affirmative action.

The reason that Whitestone's STARS program carries such contemporary weight is because the cultural climate of the late 1990s' United States is one in which there is a great deal of theoretical and cultural attention to questions of identity. In fact, the decade of the 1990s is one in which identity, and the problems and practices that constitute identity, continually emerge front and center in all realms of U.S. political and popular culture.[46] The beauty pageant in particular provides an especially rich and accommodating site for disrupting, recouping, and retrenching our cultural understandings about who and how "we" are and should be, simply because part of its self-production is its unique ability to recognize the ideal American woman. The Miss America pageant is the setting for a contemporary public debate over the meanings and practices of identity, and the performances of the contestants clearly contribute to shaping how Americans formulate and make sense of their own identities through various modes of self-representation.[47]

One consequence of these very public struggles over personal meaning is the conservative reading of them: in this reading, identity markings such as race and gender are clearly unproductive and only create cultural, political, and individual dilemmas. Rather than focus on these marks of difference, we should all merely conduct ourselves as "persons." The question, however, becomes, if contemporary desires to do away with the dilemmas of race and gender are culturally sanctioned, what racial and gender apparatuses of power underwrite such strategies? This desire is represented as a particular social need—the need not only to address problems of difference differently, but also to, in fact, evade these problems altogether.

Heather Whitestone is the Miss America pageant's answer to this dilemma. The strategies she used for self-representation not only were a way of constructing personal identity, but were also tailor-made for television. Television was a particularly appropriate medium for the demonstration of Whitestone's identity because it functions so well as an equalizer; difference is obscured, and at the very least, flattened out and made to seem insignificant. Again, I do not mean to suggest that Whitestone's disability was not a "true difference," or that she should not be admired for her accomplishments. I do mean to suggest that at her particular moment in U.S. cultural history, Whitestone functioned as an exemplary spokesperson on the dangers of identity politics precisely because she had the ability to "closet" her own identity. Whitestone truly followed a utopic fantasy about the liberal, postindustrial, multicultural world: she presented her identity as a deaf person as one that could be tried on and taken off almost at whim, and it is this ability (or perhaps it is merely the belief or the hope that all marginalized peoples have this ability, regardless of their markers of difference) that transforms accommodation into inspiration, or assimilationist into liberal heroine. In this way, her deafness functioned much as race does in the rhetoric of the "color-blind" society, which, as Neil Gotanda has argued, relies upon the ability of the law to initially recognize the racial identity of a person and then promptly forget it. This process of recognizing only to then erase works to create all of us as "persons," equal before the law, and thus dismisses any overt identity claims of individuals outside of this basic characterization.[48]

Indeed, Whitestone was an especially interesting celebrity for the press because of this complicated self-presentation. Of course, the fact that she was the first Miss America with a disability meant that the press focused intensely on Whitestone, although in a very different register than the attention they placed on Vanessa Williams. For example, columnist Barbara Lippert wrote about Whitestone's selection by the judges as an exemplary choice but also queried the judges' motivation in selecting a deaf contestant. Lippert wrote, "What does it mean that at a time of identity crisis for both genders, we seem able to reclaim the standards of American purity, innocence and fairness only by focusing on people with disabilities?"[49] What I find especially interesting about her comment is her recognition of the Miss America pageant as an apparently unique site in which to "reclaim the standards of American purity, innocence and fairness" in a time of what Lippert calls a gender identity crisis. Part of the cultural climate of 1995, as I have mentioned, was a conservative desire to eliminate difference as a viable category for identity—at least when it came to employment, education, and politics. Nineteen-ninety-five was a banner year for reclaiming American purity.

This was the year that *Forrest Gump* won the Oscar. At its heart, this film was about the disavowal of history—especially the disavowal of the history of racial formations and social protests as they structure U.S. society. Forrest Gump becomes a national icon through this disavowal, through his vulnerability, his purity, and his innocence. He wipes the slate clean, and as Wiegman has pointed out, the film argues that through the embrace of his injured body we are healed—we can each disavow our own injuries and heal our own injured body. In other words, it is the guilt of dominant white America, our intolerance, that gets healed. Forrest Gump provides a way for dominant America to heal ourselves by seeing ourselves as *innocent*. He is, as Berlant (and others) have argued, simply "too stupid to be racist, sexist, and exploitative; this is his genius and it is meant to be his virtue."[50]

We can see how Heather Whitestone occupies a similar position—and as Miss America, she symbolizes the ideal American woman, the corollary to the ideal American man that is Forrest Gump. Unlike Gump, she is not stupid, but she represents an ideal of purity at a time where the national imaginary, or the imagined community of the nation, is one of whiteness and injury. This national imaginary of whiteness and injury—and in particular the injury that comes from being white—produces Heather

Whitestone as Miss America, who denies domination by representing a kind of purity through her nonhearing body—and in fact is purely somatic as she dances her ballet routine, hearing no music but instead feeling the beats through the vibrations in the floor. At this historical moment, Whitestone's purity and innocence trumps identity politics.[51]

Her deafness is explicitly constructed as a sort of innocence by her family, a shield by which she was protected from the cruelties of the world, including the deaf world. Her inability to hear shielded her from the cruel gossip and speculation of the pageant world and enabled her not only to avoid answering questions about her capabilities as a national representative, but also to determine the site and audience for that question. So, her lack of hearing allowed her to experience the world as one without overt, personal cruelty. As her mother comments, "She doesn't pick up on nuances and innuendoes. Her hearing impairment actually proved an advantage, a natural cocoon, sheltering Heather from the air of tension and conflict."[52] Although the focus of this comment is on gossip, representing a disability as a cocoon gives credence to Whitestone's representation as pure, someone, like Forrest Gump, who simply does not see (or hear) negativity or cruelty in the world. Through this self-representation, Whitestone renders identity politics invisible. Her marked body becomes the universal body, precisely because she transcends difference through assimilation. She extends inclusion as she dissociates herself from adversity, and in doing so, neatly represents the 1995 American nation.

THERE SHE IS

The Miss America contestant's body—through her disciplined physique, her commitment to virtue, and her testimony to stability—"codes the tantalizing ideal" of a well-managed collective American body. Through the display of female bodies and the performance of a particular version of female subjectivity, the beauty pageant transforms a culture's anxiety about itself—its stability as a coherent nation—into a spectacular reenactment and overcoming of that very anxiety.

It is through the performance of the local and the national, and navigating how these categories are mutually constitutive, that those women crowned Miss America also perform the abstract character of liberal political membership within a particular national imaginary. This chapter's focus on Bess Myerson and Heather Whitestone characterizes and represents particular spectacular moments of this performance, but all Miss Americas are produced and produce themselves as national bodies.

The particularization of each queen—her race, ethnicity, culture, and commitment—functions in tangent with her universality as a visual representation of eternal femininity. This, in turn, constitutes what Frank Deford, a journalist and former Miss America judge, called "good old Miss America," who "still talks like Huckleberry Finn, looks like Patti, LaVerne, and Maxine, and towers over the land like the Ozarks. She really is the body of the state, and the country is in her eyes."[53]

CHAPTER 6 INTERNATIONAL SPECTACLES, NATIONAL BORDERS

MISS UNIVERSE AND THE "FAMILY OF NATIONS"

As we have seen, the Miss America pageant is a place where cultural meanings about the local, the national, the typical, and the ideal are produced, negotiated, and circulated. In this chapter, I examine these meanings and their circulation in an international context and focus on pageants produced outside of North American borders. In the Miss America pageant, the formation of national identity depends upon the political structure of whiteness and representation for its articulation. The complex interplay between the local and the national is clearly modeled upon an even broader, international plane, where the national and the international are mutually constitutive in the field of representational politics. Like the Miss America pageant, national pageants such as Miss India or Miss Italy and international pageants such as Miss World or Miss Universe engage issues of nationalism, ethnicity, and localism in what are often somewhat trivial—but nonetheless vital—aspects.

There was little that was trivial about the 1993 Miss Sarajevo under Siege Competition, held in the former Yugoslavian capital of Sarajevo at the height of one of the most brutal civil wars in European history. This pageant was unlike any other in the history of the city; certainly the fanfare that usually surrounds beauty pageants was subdued, there weren't as many contestants as in other years, and at its climax, the contestants unfurled a banner pleading, "Don't Let Them Kill Us." While "shells crashed into the streets outside as the city suffered one of its heaviest weeks of fighting," the contestants performed the typical beauty pageant routine: they competed in sportswear outfits and swimsuits and paraded in front of a panel of judges. Atypically, one of these judges was a Bosnian general, who apparently held tightly to his AK-47 throughout the entire process. If she followed the traditional pattern, the winner of the pageant, seventeen-year-old Imela Nogic, would enter the Miss World competition the following year. When asked, however, about her plans, she replied, "Plans? I have no plans. I may not even be alive tomorrow."[1]

Three years later, in Italy, the Miss Italy pageant also generated national introspection. On September 9, 1996, Denny Mendez, a black Caribbean immigrant, was crowned Miss Italy amid much controversy and questions concerning national identity. Commentaries in newspapers all over the country used Mendez's victory "to analyze racial tolerance in Italy, the relative nature of beauty, and, above all, what it means to be Italian."[2] The pageant stimulated national questions and concerns over Italy's seeming transition from a "homogenous" nation (apparently meaning a nation with very few foreigners) to a nation with a growing population of non-European immigrants. The controversy over Mendez's crowning began several days before the pageant, when two pageant judges were suspended "for saying that Mendez, as a black woman, could not represent Italian beauty." One of the judges defended her actions by citing other examples of national identity, questioning whether "China would accept a Miss China without almond-shaped eyes, or if a non-black African could become Miss Senegal."[3]

And in yet another controversial beauty pageant, the Miss World pageant held in Bangalore, India, in November of that same year, India had internationally known news anchor Peter Jennings claiming that beauty pageants "had a nation in an uproar" when feminist and nationalist protesters picketed the pageant and threatened mass suicide.[4] The reason for the protest was formulated on both feminist and nationalist grounds: not only did the Miss World pageant demean women, claimed the protesters, it also threatened India's two-thousand-year history through corrupt Western standards and values.

What can the Miss Sarajevo Under Siege Competition, Miss Italy, and Miss World (as well as other international pageants) tell us about the ways in which women come to represent the nation politically, culturally, and morally? It is evident from these three stories that struggles over both national and international gender identity take place on beauty pageant stages. As Richard Wilk has argued, pageants are places "where local values and imported foreign ones collid[e] on stage."[5] Pageants are often situated as sites where contradictions, conflicts, and claims of diversity are simultaneously constructed and maintained; as Wilk says, "Pageants as an institution can serve the state's goals of 'domesticating difference,' of channeling potentially dangerous social divisions into the realm of aesthetics and taste. But they can also fail in getting this message across, and can end up emphasizing and exacerbating the very divisions they are meant to minimize and control."[6] Such was the case with all three of the pageants just mentioned. Sarajevo's political crisis in 1993 was not only represented by the pageant's title, "Miss Sarajevo Under Siege," nor was this crisis merely reinvented on the actual stage through the unconventionally explicit gestures toward political struggle. The contestants themselves collapsed the distinction between womanhood and the nation; pleading to whatever audience they could garner, they asked, in the name of their beauty, their sexuality, and their nation, "Don't Let Them Kill Us." In India, at least for some, death was the promised price for compromising an independently negotiated identity and nationhood. And in Italy, the long asserted pageant-enforced illusion that gender and beauty are universal categories was disrupted, and femininity emerged as what it has always been: race- and class-specific.

As the protesters of the 1996 Miss World pageant in Bangalore so dramatically claimed, the (largely U.S.-produced) international pageants have frequently depicted the events as global showcases for American products and understood the women who participate in these events as being constructed according to American norms and standards: commodities and women alike are revered and celebrated in this forum long conceptualized as good publicity for tourism. This critique of pageants, which equates the selling of women with the selling of products in an international market, is legitimate to a degree: broadcast to more than eighty different countries, the Miss Universe pageant alone has a viewership of six hundred million people and is clearly a transnational showcase in many ways.[7] However, critical assessments of international pageants have been far too narrowly focused on the organizing structure of Western imperialism and so have not paid enough attention to the complicated nature of pageants or how these events become a showcase for the formation of national identity. In the context of the world cultural economy, "resolving" nationalist tensions through the representation of the female body is about securing a place in the "family of nations" that comprises an international community.[8] For many of the national pageants—Miss India or Miss Lebanon, for example—that international community is not solely defined by the West. Not only does *nation* have vastly different meanings depending on the political, cultural, and geographical context, but, as many Third World and postcolonial feminists have incisively pointed out, categories such as femininity, womanhood, or sexuality resonate differently on different bodies.

According to Andrew Parker, Mary Russo, Doris Sommer, and Patricia Yaeger, the editors of the volume *Nationalisms and Sexualities*, the categories of nationalism and sexuality are "volatile sites for condensing and displacing the ecstasies and terrors of political life."[9] Indeed, the editors stress, "It is the lived crises endured by national and sexual bodies that form our most urgent priorities"—in other words, the crises of a given nation, ranging from civil unrest to political tyranny to limited economic resources, are displaced and diffused onto "national and sexual bodies."[10] In this chapter, I take a closer look at these "lived crises" by focusing on a small sampling of international pageants that simultaneously complicate and further my claims about U.S. beauty pageants. Specifically, I situate pageants such as Miss World and Miss Universe within the global cultural economy by examining competing sets of truths about these spectacles, focusing on stories that are told by the producers and participants of these pageants as well as those told by persons who live out their daily existence as members of this "global cultural economy." My question is, within the context of these competing sets of truths, how are nationalist and internationalist claims formulated, legitimated, and performed?

Securing a place within an imagined community for any nation or national identity entails efficient and successful management on an international stage.[11] Guaranteeing a place in the family of nations involves the self-conscious construction of a nation as a moral community that deserves to be "adopted" into a culturally constructed version of an international family. Given this requirement, it makes sense, when examining individual nations and nationhoods, to situate nationalism within an international context, because it is within the context of the global, or the international, that the local or the national is both naturalized and legitimized. If, as Lisa Malkki has argued, underlying "all the competing nationalisms of the modern era lies a fundamental vision of global order itself, a vision of the international," then pageants such as Miss World and Miss Universe are celebratory embodiments of that vision.[12] Malkki and others have directed our attention to the places in which this vision is imagined in idealized form, such as Disneyworld (the ride "It's a Small World" perhaps demonstrates the most irritatingly palpable display of romantic internationalism) or the Olympic Games, with its own set of interesting cultural meanings and regulations concerning what it means to belong to an international family. These kinds of ceremonial arenas provide the opportunity "for national, categorical individuals to take their place at the table (or on the playing fields) of the family of nations."[13]

Like the Olympic Games, international beauty pageants categorize individuals into competing yet mutually affirming representations of what could be called the global "feminine." The romance of the international family, where difference is domesticated through the constructed diversity of nations, correlates with the romance of the pageant, where feminine symbols of the nation perform as well as domesticate their different femininities into one harmonious, unitary "feminine." The diversity of the various participating nations is arrayed in bodily form in the Miss World or Miss Universe pageant, and through this arrangement, unequal relations of power "are actively erased in the romance of internationalism."[14] This array of "feminized diversity" that the Miss Universe pageant both celebrates and creates is evaluated by the judges and the audience of the Miss Universe pageant, who are cast as the neutral and objective spokespersons, authorized to select a heroine in this international romance.

Key to the success of this romantic vision of the local and the global is the active reliance on rhetorics of liberalism, where the construction of the Miss Universe stage is one of a level playing field on which a variety of feminine representations compete in what Malkki calls an arena for the "taxonomic . . . representation of national selves." In this way, the Miss Universe or Miss World pageants operate in a fashion similar to the Miss America pageant, where an idealized concept of equality is invoked through the discourse of diversity that frames these events. Unlike U.S. pageants, however, diversity on a global stage gestures toward an imagined international community: each contestant represents a particular nation and that nation's commitment to joining the family of nations. The international pageants' version of diversity is one produced within a structure and organization that encompasses and constitutes a general "humanity."[15]

MONOPOLY ON BEAUTY:
MISS WORLD AND MISS UNIVERSE 1994

International beauty pageants represent what Malkki calls a "ritualized and institutionalized evocation of a common humanity."[16] For example, the pageants held in India in 1994 situate India within the family of nations by simultaneously imagining difference among women and neutralizing precisely this difference. Both the Miss World and the Miss Universe titles were won by representatives from India in 1994. A *Los Angeles Times* article detailing the successes of the two women led with this query:

> If China boasts the world's fleetest female swimmers, France the most select of vintages and Ukraine the greatest pole vaulter, where do the world's most comely women come from?
> From India, of course. It's as official as these kinds of things ever get. This year, anyway.[17]

The popular press explicitly situates India as a nation that can boast the "best" women of all—and femininity (or beauty) is considered a commodity, similar to sports ability and wine in the world cultural market. As such, femininity is seen as subject to mercurial fluctuations in the market (evidenced by the comment, "this year, anyway"). Positioning "India's women" in popular discourse gains the nation a respectable place in the global economy, where the value of the nation is measured, at least in part, in terms of sexuality, and specifically feminine sexuality. The article continues:

> Some [citizens of India] felt as jubilant as if the country had received an armful of Nobel Prizes or Olympic medals. The unexpected honors paid to two young Indian women were also debated for what they signaled about India—its international image, the place of women in its society and its attitudes toward sex.
>
> "It's a victory for the nation. The Indian subcontinent has come into the limelight," said a happy Deepa Bhatia, an executive in the advertising section of *Femina*, a woman's magazine.[18]

Selecting Indian women as Miss World and Miss Universe signals an international (at least as far as the pageant defines the "international") acceptance of India's "notions of womanhood and style as the country increasingly opens up to the outside world."[19] In other words, because of its newly acquired monopoly on international beauty pageant titles, India successfully performs femininity to a larger international community. This performance is predicated on what George Mosse calls "the proper attitude toward sexuality," by which he means an attitude constituted and enacted according to the terms of "respectability."[20] If nationalism and sexuality are mutually constitutive categories of experience, then securing an international identity as a member of the family of nations indicates, among other things, an unproblematic collapse between womanhood and nationhood. Not surprisingly, this relationship is usually constructed against the backdrop of the West: one Indian woman commented, "Time has come for the women of the West to stop and look back at India, that Indian women are not lagging behind in any manner. They have both talent and beauty."[21] This comment sets the West up as the leader in representations of womanhood and suggests that now that Indian women have been selected to uphold the international marker for womanhood, they are no longer "lagging behind."

However, the success of the two title holders was not unanimously received as a "victory for the nation." International beauty pageants can be seen as colonizing arenas, and success in such an arena means accepting the colonizer's values: as many postcolonial feminists have pointed out, the tension that surrounds definitions of femininity and sexuality creates this kind of colonizing move. In other words, what sort of victory was the selection of two Indian women as Miss Universe and Miss World? As many saw it, it was a victory for the nation precisely because it successfully situated India within a political and cultural context determined and legitimated by Western norms and standards. Thus the selection of Indian women as Miss Universe and Miss World represented a victory for the nation because it "proved" that Indian women could successfully enact Western disciplinary practices of femininity. The victories in the two most well-known international beauty pageants signified to a global community that Indian women now have "currency" and can circulate in world markets.

Colonizing moves of this sort are not only deployed by events such as the Miss Universe pageant, but often also by Western feminists and scholars of nationalism. The invocation of terms such as *women* or *nation* as stable categories of analysis, defined and represented by Western practices and cultural discourses, assumes a unity between and within women and nations based on a generalized notion of their subordination, or upon their status as victimized.[22] The reliance on these supposedly universal terms eclipses a range of distinct social experiences of different nations and denies any historical specificity to various agents—including beauty pageant contestants—operating within the borders of these nations. This Western arrogance is precisely what Partha Chatterjee finds objectionable in his work on Western concepts of the nation and on Indian nationalism. The imagined community, he argues, is not that which is conjured up in a specifically Western (and thus typically thought to be the universal) imagination, but exists in the projects various nations undertake to "fashion a 'modern' national culture that is nevertheless not Western."[23] Non-Western beauty pageant contestants are not mere puppets of Western imperialist values and standards regarding femininity, but are symbols of various national traditions—and therefore would be different from the Western woman.

Perhaps one of the more volatile examples of fashioning a modern national culture "that is nevertheless not Western" is the Miss Tibet beauty contest. In Carole McGranahan's discussion of the struggles over the various nationalist claims on the Miss Tibet title, she writes that "the *Tibetan nation debuted* on stage December 1991 at the Lhasa Holiday Inn as twenty five women in 'traditional' Tibetan costume competed for the title of 'Miss Tibet.'"[24] This contest was no mere commercial gimmick for Holiday Inn (although it was that, too), nor was it part of the usual cultural festivities celebrated in Tibet that year. It was the debut of the entire "Tibetan nation," the definition of which was the subject of intense debate and struggle on many different fronts: the Chinese Communist Party ordered workplaces to enter their most beautiful employees, the Lhasa Holiday Inn (a Western enterprise) staff organized and sponsored the pageant, and Tibetan women vied for entry so that they could represent "their" nation. McGranahan argues that "[i]n negotiating readings of the pageant, it is clear that while Tibetan Woman is the object upon which our gaze is focused, she is not the subject of the pageant. Instead, the Tibetan nation and the Tibetan state are the subjects under contention."[25] I argue that while the contestants may not be the *only* subject of the pageant, or indeed, even a primary one, they are subjects nonetheless, negotiating identities in a complex crossfire of nationalist tensions between the West, China, and Tibet. The Western (or Western-style) beauty pageant is, as McGranahan argues, a well-established framework for the promotion of specific agendas through the trope of "Woman-as-Nation," but this framework is not seamless, nor is it without room for negotiating and even challenging Western notions of femininity. As Chatterjee insists, local, ethnic, or nationalist identities can be formulated within the context of hegemonic structure, and the beauty pageant can be that kind of space where women can articulate subject positions, positions linked inextricably to national identity, that are constituted within and through the pageant itself.

Indeed, although international beauty pageants incite a different feminist response than say, male violence or familial systems, they nonetheless function as sites for crucial conversations about the definition of femininity, sexuality, and national identity. In 1994, after Sushmita Sen was crowned Miss Universe, a New Delhi social scientist observed, "Anything that promotes India and brings it recognition is something great, and if these ladies have managed to make a dent in the Western mind that India is not a mythical place with tigers running in the streets, it's a great thing. . . . But their lives are completely divorced from what is happening with most Indian women."[26] This is a complicated statement. On the one hand, it legitimates Western norms as representative of all womanhood, because the selection of Indian women as Miss Universe and Miss World functions above all else to "make a dent in the Western mind" that Indian women are beautiful and womanly precisely in Western terms. On the other hand, the statement recognizes a disjuncture in this construction of womanhood: the lives of Miss Universe and Miss World are not in fact representative of all Indian women. The pageant victories inspired debate not only about the material conditions of most Indian women, thus throwing into question the "representative" status of Miss India, but also about the definition of sexuality and femininity. Although the pageant works to actively erase issues and concerns about various gender constraints within India in the name of internationalism, it also exposes—even if briefly and superficially—issues of national identity and representative status.

PERFORMING RESPECTABILITY ON AN INTERNATIONAL STAGE

An international family of nations is structured according to specific terms and intended goals, even though these terms and goals may shift in different historical moments. The 1994 victories for India in the Miss Universe and Miss World pageants, and the even more recent protests surrounding the Miss World pageant in Bangalore, suggest that any discussion of international beauty pageants must be situated within a context of Western cultural imperialism. In the context of a world system of images and commodities, the United States has historically occupied a pivotal position in the distribution and management of resources. And yet, as Arjun Appadurai has argued, the United States now is "only one node of a complex transnational construction of imaginary landscapes."[27] In other words, international and other non-U.S. national pageants that are dedicated to the celebration of a specific ethnic, national, and global identity are situated within, yet distinct from, a context of mainstream U.S. beauty pageants such as Miss America and Miss USA.

In order to make this argument, we must first explain how pageants become what Appadurai has called "indigenized," an argument that complicates a more reductive position of cultural homogenization. When viewing the Miss Universe or Miss World pageant, there is a sense that these spectacles are unambiguously defined by their Americanization: the program's format is identical to mainstream pageants in the United States; English is the dominant language spoken (other languages are used only by those contestants who cannot speak English, and a translator is provided to translate her words into English); U.S.-based transnational corporations sponsor the program; and, perhaps most telling, the Miss Universe pageant is owned by an American entertainment entrepreneur, Donald Trump. But there are different, more complicated cultural practices at work within international pageants, and these practices distinguish them as "indigenized forces" that challenge a simplistic portrayal of the United States as "the puppeteer of a world system of images."[28] What is the character of these practices? How do they function to make particular kinds of nationalist claims, and what are these claims? How do international and non-U.S. national pageants define womanhood and sexuality? And finally, how do the categories of nationalism and sexuality function in turn as a dialectical process of crisis and containment?

The discourses of tourism and development are powerful forces in both producing indigenized forces and in organizing the Miss Universe pageant. Tourism and tourist revenue motivate countries such as Thailand, the Philippines, and Peru to operate a "franchise" of the Miss Universe pageant, because the pageant promotes tourism. The televised production of the pageant always includes publicity vignettes about the host country, highlighting popular tourist and recreation sites. These segments explicitly intend to attract tourist dollars: usually narrated by the previous year's Miss Universe, they almost always end with an invitation to come and visit. The host country, regardless of where it is actually located, is represented in the pageant as an exotic locale, meant to provide both adventure and safety for the tourist, a place for escape and where one may submit to desire. Yet at the same time as the host country is presented as an exotic "virgin land," uncorrupted by industry and commerce, it is also represented as sophisticated in terms of Western entertainment and culture. Many of the publicity vignettes during the Miss Universe broadcast are shots of ancient traditions and unspoiled lands juxtaposed with scenes at a Western disco, or shots of the contestants eating hamburgers or other familiar foods. In this way, tourism—especially in Third World countries—functions to showcase development while at the same time demonstrating an unspoiled beauty.

The contestants in the Miss Universe pageant are represented in a similar way. The array of diversified and categorized women offers the audience a variety of exotic "locales"—each woman represents a unique site to "come and visit." Like the tourism locale, each contestant is constructed as a site of both adventure and safety, and each woman represents an opportunity to succumb to desire. Yet, as with the host countries, the desire embodied and performed by contestants must also be disciplined, regulated, and contained; the women are represented as exotic but respectable.

Indeed, this negotiation between the unknown and the known—the exotic and the ordinary—is precisely what is needed to discipline desire. The potential for transgression that characterizes public displays of the female body within the Miss Universe pageant (as well as any other public display of female bodies), and the construction of pageant contestants as particular kinds of exotic locales, is subverted, contained, and made accessible through the inculcation of tropes of respectability, stability, and the typical. Laura Mulvey noted the importance of respectability early on in a short essay detailing her experience protesting the 1970 Miss World pageant. Here, she focuses her critique on what she calls the "ordinariness" of the spectacle: "The atmosphere was emphatically respectable, enlivened by a contrived attempt at 'glamour.' The conventionality of the girls' lives and the ordinariness of their aspirations—Miss Granada (Miss World): 'Now I'm looking for the ideal man to marry'—was the keynote of all the pre- and post competition publicity."[29] Beauty pageants and their contestants, Mulvey argues, are invested in the production of a femininity and a heterosexuality that is grounded in the ordinary, or the typical. Through situating their identities—as representatives of various nations—they, in turn, situate the nation itself as ordinary, or, at the very least, familiar. It is important to note that the status of being ordinary does not necessarily erase the exclusionary foundation of pageants; rather, the standards that structure beauty pageants are firmly based on a particular feminine ideal that is then constructed as the "ordinary." But what then does a femininity defined in terms of the ordinary mean? Beauty pageants, despite all their gestures toward the spectacular, are not about perpetuating the erotic fantasies that, say, high fashion models represent. Rather than fashioning themselves after traditional runway models, pageant contestants constitute themselves as role models for the community, as tourist attractions, and as "goodwill ambassadors."[30] To construct this identity, beauty pageant contestants distance themselves from fashion models in the same way that Miss America pageant contestants distance themselves from bikini contest participants—in other words, this identity involves obscuring the commercial structure of the pageant. For Miss America contestants, this means an intense focus on education; for Miss Universe and Miss World contestants, the assignation of goodwill ambassador explicitly signifies mediating between particular communities and playing an active role as diplomat. Although part of this role includes recognizing the host country as a worthy tourist site, international pageant contestants do not usually mention revenue earned by tourism. In identifying the contestants as ambassadors rather than as objects who attract tourist dollars, the pageants domesticate and make respectable the display of the female body—and it is only by avoiding mention of tourist revenue that a self-construction of Miss Universe contestants as respectable goodwill ambassadors is possible.[31]

Mulvey ends her critique about the "ordinariness" of beauty pageants by quoting the 1970 master of ceremonies, Bob Hope. She assumes that the quote is self-explanatory to the reader: Hope, commenting about the pageant protesters, says: "They said we were 'using' women. I always thought we were using them right. I don't want to change position with them. Why do they want to change position with me? I don't want to have babies. I'm too busy."[32] There *is*, of course, something self-explanatory about this quote. Hope's cavalier shrugging-off of a feminist protest and his unproblematic relegation of women as things that men use is powerful in its simplicity. But Mulvey's focus on Hope's construction of women as playthings and helpmates for men eclipses the way this sexist quote can be mobilized as a point of departure for examining the various ways in which women *are* "used" as national figures and for asking what it means, in an (inter)national sense, to be "using women right." Both Mulvey and Hope recognize the high quotient of "respectability" structuring the pageant (although clearly they assign different values to this quotient). Women are constructed in this context in terms of respectability and domesticity. Both in the sense of devotion to home and family life and in terms of the domestication of both self and sexuality, the woman is defined by her moderation and her tameness. How do respectability and sexuality work symbiotically together, so that nationalist claims are made on the surface of the female body? The female body domesticates nationalism and national difference, constructing a vision of sexuality that is successful on the beauty pageant stage despite its uneven histories in terms of constructing feminine identity in other parts of the world.

In his two pathbreaking studies of European nationalism, Mosse offers a compelling account of the ways that citizenship and nationalism have come to be defined in cultural and moral terms rather than political terms. In *Nationalism and Sexuality*, Mosse traces the relationship between nationalism and respectability, "a term indicating 'decent and correct' manners and morals, as well as the proper attitude toward sexuality."[33] In an argument similar to that in Foucault's genealogy of discipline and punishment, Mosse asserts that in order to establish controls and impose restraint as well as moderation, modern European society needed to utilize various technologies of surveillance, characterized primarily by physicians, educators, and police. However, as Mosse points out, "their methods had to be informed by an ideal if they were to be effective, to support normality and contain sexual passions. In most timely fashion, nationalism came to the rescue. It absorbed and sanctioned middle-class manners and morals and played a crucial part in spreading respectability to all classes of the population, however much these classes hated and despised one another."[34] In late-twentieth-century postindustrial societies, the various technologies and discourses involved in the production and surveillance of individuals need a similar ideal of nationalism. In this context, beauty pageants come to the rescue, not only by spreading respectability, but also by institutionalizing respectability as a key element in the production of femininity.

BEAUTY AS A PASSPORT TO PRISON:
DISRUPTING THE RESPECTABLE

Institutionalizing respectability through the use of women's bodies as nationalist icons is part of a social practice that institutionalizes, in turn, the position of an individual nation in the family of nations. And yet, however useful Mosse's study is in pointing out the inseparable connection between nationalism and sexuality, it is formulated within a context of Western Europe. His argument about the normalizing practices of respectability that characterize nationalism and sexuality fundamentally broadens discussions on nationalism—even as it also functions to homogenize and essentialize the uneven definitions of sexuality and femininity across cultures. A Western construction of sexuality is not a universally recognized or available category. Non-Western definitions of both sexuality and nationalism—and the ways in which they are mutually constitutive categories—complicate Mosse's argument about "spreading respectability." In those beauty pageants that challenge Western norms and conventions by their political, economic, and cultural context, conversations over the definition of sexuality and nationalism disrupt the supposedly seamless performances on stage.

The tension that characterizes the relationship between woman and nation is not always articulated in terms of Western imperialism. Domesticating difference among nations on and through the bodies of women does not only or always mean conforming to U.S.-based, hegemonic conventions of femininity, but also can indicate a strategy of taming volatile contests and controversies among different nations. For example, in the 1994 Miss World pageant, Miss Lebanon, Ghada Turk, posed for a photograph with Miss Israel, Tamara Porat. Historically, posing with other contestants is an important tradition in beauty pageants, because it reflects—in immortalized form—the "natural" competition between and among women. Contestants are usually posed with their geographic neighbor; however, with this particular pair the problem was both immediate and obvious: "As distant as Lebanon and Israel are ideologically and politically, they are close geographically and alphabetically, and there lay the makings of a scandal."[35] Though to some this story has an almost absurd plot-line—after all, the two women merely posed for a photograph for thirty seconds—the reality of the situation for Turk (Miss Lebanon) had serious consequences: upon her return to Lebanon, she was interrogated for two and a half hours by a judge at the military tribunal, and military prosecutor general Nasri Lahoud charged her with violating Lebanon's boycott of Israel, a crime that is punishable by three to fifteen years in jail.[36]

Although Turk "never imagined that beauty was a passport to prison," the complicated way in which Lebanon positioned their representative demonstrates how women's bodies, in international beauty competitions, not only *become* the nation, but also represent crisis within the nation. In other words, the festival nature of the pageant is charged with political and moral choices; through the fusing of womanhood and nation, the event becomes simultaneously a constructed ideal of "one" world and a spectacle of implicit social and cultural conflict.[37] As is clear by the intensity and significance of Lebanon's reaction to the "scandal," the Miss World pageant tells a tale—at least to Lebanon and Israel—about crises in meaning, identity, and politics.

And this tale has its share of villains and heroines: Miss Lebanon and her supporters accused Miss Israel of "pulling a stunt" when she posed with Miss Lebanon. Constructing Ghada Turk as a pawn as opposed to an agent in the alleged crime was paramount: Turk's lawyer in Lebanon called her at the pageant and "counseled her to declare that it was all an unintentional error and to publicly announce that her country was still at war with Israel." Turk refused, stating that she "had not gone there for politics but as an ambassadress of felicity and beauty." Still, the constructed quality of her position becomes clearer when we note that she added, "If I had done as he said, how do you think the jury and organizers would have reacted to me?"[38] Although her statement asserts her position as an "ambassadress of felicity and beauty," it simultaneously exposes her use of this position as a strategy for the judges. In so doing, it also exposes the problem of how to stage the *visibility of nationhood*. In other words, is representing "beauty" and "felicity" the same thing as representing the nation? In the case of Ghada Turk, it is clearly the same. Her concern about the reaction of the jury and organizers of the Miss Universe pageant was not merely personal but also national: if she positioned herself as anything other than an ambassadress of respectability, the reaction of the judges and pageant organizers would be reflective of not only Turk's but Lebanon's status within the family of nations. The clear irony in her forced separation of womanhood and nationhood (or beauty and politics) is demonstrated by her enforced exile from Lebanon, the charge that she collaborated with the enemy, and her willingness to place the blame (thus implicitly conceding that the photo event was in fact a crime, albeit one not committed by her) on Tamara Porat, Miss Israel. Constructing oneself as an "ambassadress," whether of beauty or of good-will, is explicitly placing oneself in a political arena; to be an ambassador is to represent one's country in all dimensions—culturally, morally, and politically.[39]

The position of goodwill ambassadress automatically placed Miss Lebanon in a perilous position—she was expected to simultaneously forget and remember the hundreds of years of war with Israel. This expectation was not only imposed by the government and citizens of her own country, but also by the other pageant participants, who seemed to relentlessly remind Turk of exactly what and who she was representing. Writing about the competition and her participation in it, she had this to say:

> The experience was saddening for me when I saw that my place was not here [at an international beauty contest in South Africa] and that Lebanon was not among those great countries. For its name abroad is tinged with terrorism, destruction, and war. They don't even know where Lebanon is located. One man asked me: "Where is your pistol?" But I know the truth about Lebanon and its history of thousands of years.[40]

At the very same moment that global harmony is performed on the stage of the Miss Universe pageant, conflict and crisis erupt from outside and within. The nation of Lebanon is allegorically inscribed upon Ghada Turk's body, and it is her body that is then left to perform the labor of containing and converting this crisis.

Miss Lebanon and Miss India are only two examples of the various ways in which the trope of woman-as-nation is representationally powerful in international beauty pageants. Palesa Jacqui Mofokeng, who became the first black Miss South Africa in 1993, is another example of how women—embodying the mutually constitutive categories of nationalism and sexuality—are sites "for condensing and displacing the ecstasies and terrors of political life."[41] In a country structured by apartheid, and where pageants are taken quite seriously, the selection of a black woman for a national beauty pageant title is no trivial matter. Indeed, as the *New York*

Times claimed, Mofokeng's selection was considered by many in the African National Congress as "a major breakthrough for the oppressed masses of our people."[42] Within the first few weeks of Mofokeng's reign as Miss South Africa, she was apparently determined to connect both her own politics and the conflict-ridden politics of South Africa with her representational status: she publicly stated her opinion in favor of reproductive and abortion rights and in opposition to the African tradition of paying for brides, and she "led a peace march through the battle-weary black township of Katlehong."[43] The crises of apartheid and of tenuous rights for women were raised as a specter simply by Mofokeng's attention to these issues; she then effectively both reinvented and contained these crises by occupying the position of woman-as-nation—the first time a black body ever occupied this position for South Africa.

"NO EYESORES, PLEASE": SECURING A PLACE WITHIN THE FAMILY OF NATIONS

Political and moral crises are reflected and reinvented not only on the stage of international beauty pageants, but also in the interplay between the performances of femininity onstage and similar performances in a much less glamorous setting—the material realities of lives offstage. Because the pageant is widely recognized as a lucrative venue for tourism, countries bid to host the pageant each year (much like the Olympics). The globally projected image of the host country is a constructed representation of a desirable place to visit and spend money. Consequently, the imagined community that is constantly reinvented on the pageant stage becomes representative for the host country as well, complete with a set of social practices and invented traditions that establish and advertise each particular country as worthy of a place within the family of nations—and each particular contestant as worthy of a place within dominant, Western conventions of femininity.

In 1982, a Peruvian filmmakers union, Grupo Chaski, produced a documentary video called *Miss Universe in Peru*. This video juxtaposes the production of the Miss Universe pageant, held in Lima that year, and the material, cultural, and political lives of women in Peru. Rhetorically, the video takes critical aim at U.S. cultural imperialism. A typical cinematic technique juxtaposes billboards advertising U.S. products such as Coca-Cola with civil unrest in union lines and peasant women and children panhandling on the streets of Lima. The pageant contestants are overtly compared with "other" U.S. products. As one pageant demonstrator commented, "Transnationals have a worldwide forum to advertise their products—all under the pretext of selecting the most beautiful woman in the world."[44]

But more than selling products, the Miss Universe pageant functions as a powerful and specific nationalist message to the rest of the world. Statements made by pageant producers and directors in Peru—statements such as "Peru feels proud to send its love to all countries of the world through this beauty contest"—may appear overly opaque or purely bombastic, but the notion that the "beauty" of Peru is demonstrated through the beauty of the contestants powerfully and practically collapses woman with the nation. Just as the contestants offer the audience a taxonomic display of various femininities, Peru offers the tourist a spectacular array of diversified femininity—each woman and each nation are different, yet displaying them together manages to stress their sameness. Peru, as the capable host of the Miss Universe pageant, renders visible the exchangeability of the different beauty contestants. Firmly embedded in the display of stable sexuality, of respectable femininity, and of a moderate sort of glamour is the message that the host country is itself both stable and respectable.

This notion—that if a city is selected to host the Miss Universe pageant, the beauty and desirability of the contestants somehow reflects the beauty and desirability of the city—is a dominant theme in many of the stories about international pageants. The lead paragraph in a *New York Times* article titled "Where Beauty Queens Preen, No Eyesores, Please" reads: "The World Bank and Miss Universe are coming to town, and for that reason some of Bangkok's struggling poor have been told to move out."[45] Included within the two-hour-long 1992 Miss Universe pageant program were several publicity vignettes on the beauty of Thailand. But, as this article revealed, the practices that were enforced in order to produce these segments included the uprooting of thousands of poor Thai residents so as not to offend a group of Western bankers and potential future visitors to Bangkok. These practices are reminiscent of a similar "beautification" program organized by Imelda Marcos in the Philippines for the 1976 Miss

Universe pageant, where families were evicted from slums in order to make a more visually pleasing nationalist claim to the rest of the world. In order to make the Philippines visible as both a "respectable" and "developing" nation, something else—the poor, the unsightly, or the morally corrupt—must be obscured and put out of sight. Beauty pageants, then, function as an important element in the practice of aestheticizing and depoliticizing "development" for an international audience.

Manila, also the site of the 1994 Miss Universe pageant, again created controversy when, according to the *Washington Post*, the "Manila police rounded up more than 270 street children in late April and early May, prompting an investigation by the Philippine Commission on Human Rights. The urchins commonly beg at intersections, weaving among traffic-blocked motorists."[46] There was further controversy and conflict surrounding this Miss Universe pageant: Senate President Edgardo Angara, apparently upset over the amount of money the Philippines had allotted to the pageant, claimed, "This Miss Universe contest is a misuse and abuse of our women that panders to the most ignoble instincts of our people." Tourism Secretary Vicente Carlos responded, "Beauty contests are part of Philippine culture. They say if you want anything to succeed in the Philippines, hold a beauty pageant or a cockfight."[47] What is instructive about these remarks is that they explicitly comment on the discourses of nationalism and sexuality as they are performed within the pageant, and thus they establish the spectacle as an important nationalist event. A Filipino feminist organization, Makibaka, also responded to the pageant in explicitly nationalist terms: "There is nothing redeeming that the country can gain from this flesh festival. As the regime basks in the splendor of a world beauty pageant, the violence and degradation of Filipino women are swept under the rug."[48]

Even events such as photographing the contestants while they were sunbathing (which apparently increases a risk of taking "unwholesome" pictures), or the controversy that surrounded a particular contestant, Miss Israel Ravit Yarkoni, when she wore a Philippine-designed dress with a transparent hoop skirt, were interpreted as direct commentary about the Philippine nation. Miss Israel's skirt prompted two congresswomen to bring the issue to the Philippine House of Representatives, where they then proceeded to "denounce the outfit as an 'insult' to Philippine womanhood and religion, especially since it was worn during a procession commemorating the Virgin Mary."[49] Nationalism comes to the rescue in this potential disaster, as it, in Mosse's words, "absorbed and sanctioned middle-class manners and morals and played a crucial part in spreading respectability to all classes of the population, however much these classes hated and despised one another."[50] Pageants create the context that *needs* rescuing, only to then gloriously and efficiently *do* the rescuing. The tension that surrounded the pageant was framed in terms of an instability: as demonstrated by the various contestants, the Philippine nation is potentially teetering on precarious ground in terms of respectable womanhood. This instability, however, becomes stable and the tension is resolved by the inclusion of the Philippines in the family of nations, demonstrated by the televisual performance of an imagined global community on the pageant stage.

International pageants, like their U.S. counterparts, do the cultural work of crisis and containment, but on a scale that involves the global capitalist economy. Pageants such as Miss Universe attempt to resolve national tensions of stability and instability through the presentation and representation of stable women, stable sexuality, and stable femininity. As explicit discourses about nationalism, pageants come to the rescue and manage global crisis on an international stage. Part of the way global crises perform what Christopher Newfield calls "managerial democracy" is through the familiar but still very powerful discourse of Western cultural imperialism.[51]

And yet pageants such as Miss Universe do more than merely reflect images of Western norms of femininity and nationhood; as we have seen, international pageants manage crises regarding the display of female bodies—bodies that function simultaneously as a potential site of transgression and a site of stability. Although the Miss Universe pageant unproblematically subsumes the faces of pageant contestants with the "face" of its host country, this union is not a seamless one; rather, the potential for disruption is represented clearly by those women who perform a different version of femininity off and on the Miss Universe stage. Both the contestant and the nation are rendered visible on the "world stage"—a stage that is also a television studio and monitor. Those bodies that can disrupt the discourses of cultural imperialism and tourism with their color, their ethnicity, and their politics manage to send a different message—albeit just as nationalist—to the "family of nations."

CONCLUSION

In 1997, American entrepreneur Donald Trump purchased the Miss Universe pageant from Madison Square Gardens, Inc. After the purchase, he promised to "give a new face" to Miss Universe, indicating that the pageant was in need of a "face-lift," a more contemporary visage, a hipper image.[52] The ownership of the pageant by an individual—especially an individual so invested in U.S. capitalist success—puts a new spin on my argument about the elaborate kinds of national and international claims made by beauty pageants and about the "imagined community" that pageants such as the Miss Universe pageant construct. If nationalism is a discourse that mediates constructions of femininity and diversity or difference and, in so doing, produces a particularly gendered and raced notion of citizenship, how does the imagined community of the pageant manage and control different styles and practices of citizenship?

The Miss Universe pageant is a performance of diversified femininity, where each contestant simultaneously becomes her ethnic neighbor and maintains her sovereignty as a unique, attractive nation. This move to harmonize is an opportunistic appropriation typical of a cultural production dedicated to a vision of a harmonious yet diversified family of nations. And although each contestant (and each nation represented) is informed and constructed by a deep social and cultural logic, and each carries its specific weight of historical association and affiliation, these characteristics of both individual and national identity are obscured in what could be called the "hybridization" of femininity. The resulting configuration of representative femininity is not unlike the "ethnic mergers" that take place in American film; in discussing such mergers, Ella Shohat and Robert Stam argue, "These metamorphoses render palpable the constant process of synchresis that occurs when ethnicities brush against and rub off on one another in a crowded ambivalent space of cultural interaction."[53] The Miss Universe pageant is one such "crowded ambivalent space of cultural interaction," where, although non-European nations and heritages are clearly supported in terms of their presence on stage, the structural and ideological basis of the pageant remains firmly embedded in U.S. and Western European values and histories. The domesticating of a nation (and, by virtue of representation, a contestant) is clearly about domesticating ethnic and racial traditions and backgrounds.

In 1985, Laura Martinez-Herring became the first Latina to win the Miss USA pageant. As part of her duties as Miss USA, she was asked to be the featured speaker at a naturalization ceremony where her mother, among others, was becoming a U.S. citizen. In her speech, Martinez-Herring had this to say: "Becoming a U.S. citizen does not mean you may not take pride in your culture or be proud of your roots or love your people. . . . It simply means that you are now loyal to this wonderful country that is full of opportunities and you will support the Constitution."[54] Martinez-Herring's vision eschews the problem of maintaining a particular ethnic heritage while participating in a culture that systematically erases and denies that heritage. Her statement also belies her own experience with pageants: in an interview after she won the title of Miss USA, she expressed her gratitude to her pageant directors for sending her to voice classes to "soften her Spanish accent."[55]

This statement can be read as an example of Newfield's "well-governed integration"—whereby racial anxieties of pageants cannot be reduced to racism in its conventional sense but instead constitute a racism that invokes integrationism as its driving power: people of color are members of the "common culture" of America, but the common culture itself is predetermined by dominant power relations. As Newfield comments, "Integrationism partially replaces exclusion from membership as a mechanism of producing cultural unity, but exclusion from *power* remain[s] the common effect."[56] Whiteness remains intact as the norm, whereas Latino Americans, African Americans, Asian Americans, and other "minorities" are relegated to an assigned place on the racial hierarchy.[57]

As Martinez-Herring reminds us, voice lessons and becoming bilingual were requisite steps in her process of representing the United States. Although bilingualism (one of the two languages must be English) is not yet a requirement for the Miss Universe pageant, it may as well be: the pageant is performed entirely in English (with some help from translators in isolated instances), and, as I have mentioned, the winner of the pageant is expected to perform the duties of a "goodwill ambassador." In part, the term *goodwill ambassador* refers to cultural exchange: the contestants, as tokens of exchange, represent their own culture but strive to become (or at the very least, learn about) other cultures. Indeed, it is a "small world after all."

All in all, contestants in pageants such as Miss Universe and Miss World, as well as in national pageants, formulate their feminine identities within a context of representation and self-representation. It is precisely this dialectical process that situates pageants in what Foucault calls the "matrix of modern power relations." The ambivalence of the contestants— the tension between being the same and being different—identifies national and international pageants as ideal spaces to witness liberal constructions of citizenship formation.

Performing in pageants liberates the contestants even as it also disciplines them according to racially and sexually hierarchized standards. Contestants in the Miss Universe pageant demonstrate a commitment to both the national and the international and are called upon to construct themselves as "different" yet deserving of a place within the family of nations. In the context of the world cultural economy, pageants provide a site to resolve nationalist tensions through the representation of the female body. This resolution is ultimately organized around *securing a place*—whether that place be within the family of nations or within U.S. capitalism. In this way, international pageants are cultural productions that, through the ambivalent articulation of both dominance and resistance, circulate power in a capitalist world. The international pageant is a site of negotiation between ethnic cultures and hegemonic culture, implying the borrowing, taking, appropriating, and sharing of distinct historical, cultural, and political discursive practices between and within different kinds of pageants. Pageants such as Miss Universe or Miss Tibet or Miss India function as both hegemonic contexts for the formation of national identity *and* as openings for contesting such hegemonic formations. Contestants of these pageants spectacularly perform the relationship between the national and the international through a discourse of cultural diversity arrayed in and through the bodies of women. They are rich sites for mapping the complex interplay constitutive of sameness and difference, femininity and feminism, and ethnic identity and nationalism.

CONCLUSION

The 1998 Miss America has adopted AIDS awareness as her issue platform. In one of her early appearances, she was chided by the Miss America Corporation for advocating the use of a condom during sex as one
means of preventing AIDS transmission. Apparently, the only way of promoting AIDS awareness as Miss America is to promote abstinence; anything that encourages sexual activity (even if indirectly) is inappropriate
and not in keeping with Miss America's respectable image. This is merely
one example among many that demonstrate that, despite all of the Miss
America Corporation's efforts to offer the American public a seamless and
harmonious vision of femininity, the conditions on which gender is represented within and through the pageant are constantly and vehemently
negotiated.

The Miss America pageant, despite all of the public lore, makes a statement about gender ambivalence as much as it makes a claim to universal

femininity. Columnist Barbara Lippert identifies the Miss America pageant as being a particularly exaggerated articulation of an "identity crisis for both genders" in 1990s American society:

> Miss America is not the only one feeling conflicted about image and identity, about what to shed and what to add, about who a woman is these days and how she should be represented. But a beauty pageant reveals this ambivalence in Technicolor glory. The finalists [in the 1995 Miss America pageant] were like a bunch of raised-on-*Star Search,* pre-Hillary, would-be first ladies, each with a catchily named "cause."[1]

It is interesting that *Glamour*—a magazine that produces what could only be described as a dominant narrative about ideal femininity and womanhood—would provide a forum for exploring the ambivalence that characterizes being engendered female in a postindustrial, postfeminist, "diverse" U.S. culture.[2] It is perhaps even more interesting that this particular columnist would identify the Miss America pageant as a site for negotiating such gender ambivalence—indeed, would identify it as an apparently unique site in which to "reclaim the standards of American purity, innocence and fairness" in a time of a gender identity crisis. Yes, the pageant may be anachronistic in its style and format, and yes, perhaps the pageant officials overstate the significance of the talent portion of the spectacle. However, notwithstanding the pageant's kitschy format and carnivalesque style, the Miss America contestants represent a femininity that characterizes the current cultural and political climate in the United States in terms of conflict over both gender and racial identity (see plate 10).[3] Lippert calls this gender identity "anomalous" and insists that "[t]he contestants seemed interchangeable in sensibility . . . [embodied by the identity of] good girl/future tycoon/competitive beauty queen/I'm-not-a-feminist-but."[4] In contrast to Lippert, I find nothing anomalous about this identity; as I read it, the Miss America pageant remains both a popular televisual event and a recognizable American icon precisely because this identity captures the ambivalent definition and structure of American femininity and racially specific identities.

In fact, it seems to me that this study itself can be characterized by a similar ambivalence. Although on the one hand it makes no sense to consider the beauty pageant as only a fundamentally conservative articulation of masculine discourse, on the other hand the pageant is not exactly an oppositional space. The indistinctness of this cultural form makes it clear that a study that focused solely on a single aspect of the pageant—the objectified female body or its status as "low" culture, for example—would be wholly inadequate in exploring the cultural work that both produces and is produced by the Miss America pageant. Specifically, such a singular, comprehensive reading of a fixed and unified feminine subject cannot account for the full complexity of the subjectivities produced in and through the cultural form and practice called the beauty pageant. In fact, though pageants are important sites for the construction and maintenance of the white, middle-class American "ideal," they are also, and equally as powerfully, sites for the construction of female liberal subjects, and as such they have successfully appropriated liberal feminist discourse into their own self-definition and promotion.

In the 1990s, pageants have been forced to confront and respond to contemporary demands that they more fully reflect racial and ethnic diversity. And this they have done by assimilating difference through the enforcement and regulation of disciplinary practices of femininity that are racially coded as white. However, despite efforts to uphold a universal standard of beauty for all women, the representation of women who historically have been excluded from this standard renders "beauty" itself—which is otherwise treated as a fixed and self-evident category of experience—unstable and in flux. By this I mean, following feminist Teresa de Lauretis, that beauty, like gender, is "not only the effect of representation but also its excess, what remains outside discourse as a potential trauma which can rupture or destabilize, if not contain, any representation."[5] Although the instability of beauty as a category of experience may represent a "potential trauma," it also ironically serves as an opening for pageants to enthusiastically respond to the current political and cultural climate of diverse womanhood. Indeed, "diversity" is performed on the stage of the Miss America pageant in a way that invites women of color into the carefully guarded boundaries of white femininity even while the pageant denies and obscures opportunities for celebrating particular ethnic identities.

The inclusion of racially diverse contestants in the Miss America pageant has increasingly posed the problem of constructing icons or rep-

resentations of a unified and singular national identity while acknowledging difference. Popular media discourse and the pageants themselves
attempt to resolve this contradiction by relying on classic liberal stories
about individual achievement, pluralism, and tolerance. By making invisible the social and material conditions that produce difference, these
stories retrench a national identity defined by white middle-class norms,
but this is a retrenchment with a "twist"—what bell hooks has called the
"spice of ethnicity."⁶ In the current cultural climate of multiculturalism,
the language of abstract personhood and "hip diversity" work together
to produce a new definition of the American ideal.⁷

With this shift in focus, beauty pageants emerge as a particular cultural
form that accommodates a liberal feminist rhetoric that relies on particular fantasies of agency, voice, and citizenship as crucial components of
identity construction for most American women. The Miss America pageant offers a site for enacting—indeed, performing—a version of liberal
agency that both draws from and resists a mainstream feminist agenda.
Contemporary beauty pageants are not mere expressions of masculine
dominance, nor are they a setting for the construction of women who are,
in activist Ann Simonton's words, "thin, white Barbie Dolls [who are] usually religious."⁸ Rather, the Miss America pageant is a cultural form in
which a connection between subject formation and liberal agency is explicitly made; in other words, pageants are a site for the complicated nav-
igation between a particular version of liberal *feminist theory* and a specific way of *theorizing the feminine.*⁹

I am not suggesting that beauty pageant contestants, through their particular performance of femininity, are posing formidable challenges to the
dominant means in and through which women are engendered female in
late-twentieth-century U.S. culture. What I am suggesting is that the ways
in which beauty pageant contestants imagine agency should not be dismissed as either "false consciousness," or, worse, a bit of commercialized
fluff. Beauty pageant contestants are particular kinds of theorizing agents:
contestants perform liberal narratives about women's rights, individual
achievement, pluralism, self-determination, and voluntarism in a similar
way and on similar grounds as liberal feminists articulate these very same
narratives. And in an interesting—and surprising—twist, beauty pageant
contestants manage to parallel a liberal feminist agenda about the desir-

ability of escaping rigid gender identity. That is to say, although the pageant self-consciously claims to be the paragon of "American womanhood," the spectacle itself is organized around the efforts of each contestant to somehow distinguish herself from common cultural constructions of "womanhood" and construct herself rather as a "pure individual," as a person able to transcend conventional constraints of gender and race. A common feminist argument is that popular culture defines gender identity through the tension between Woman as representation and women as live, historical beings. This tension, or slippage, as de Lauretis has put it, is both motivated and sustained by real (and, de Lauretis claims, irreconcilable) contradictions within U.S. culture, where women are always situated within the bounds of representation even as they are systematically denied access to that very same represented image.[10] It is clearly true that gendered identity is always already characterized by particular tensions and contradictions, but I am not so sure that these contradictions are always irreconcilable—at least not within the heavily regulated borders of the Miss America pageant.

I do not mean to imply that the pageant is situated somehow outside of dominant narratives of gender and race; on the contrary, I argue throughout this book that the work enacted, exercised, and performed within beauty pageants is precisely that of constructing a gendered and raced identity. However, the process of identity construction as it occurs within the pageant is dedicated to the imagining of a particular kind of agency, one that paradoxically allows contestants to occupy a subject position that is considered outside of the *constraints* of gender and race. In other words, in a familiar liberal tradition, beauty pageant contestants assume an "unmarked" position, and this unmarked status is precisely what provides the conditions of possibility for agency (insofar as liberal agency promised by patriarchy is about being both marked and unmarked). Agency is possible because one is gendered and raced in particular ways, but the way to enact and perform agency is to convince oneself that you have done the work in spite of gender and race: "I *can* be a subject outside of gender and my race; I *can* be the pure individual and transcend my gender and race."

I initially began with a simple feminist question: Why *do* women participate in beauty pageants? During the course of my research, this question was both amended and complicated in order to more specifically theorize how, in this particular cultural and political climate, women wield (and yield) power. In other words, in liberal society, how are liberal narratives with respect to personhood and individual choice mobilized in such a way as to unproblematically produce those practices of femininity and racialized identity that have been historically invoked to *deny* personhood and individual choice? Or, more simply, what does agency look like for women in 1990s' postindustrial U.S. society? Agency is imagined by beauty pageant contestants in a way that is not so different from the way many (liberal) feminists imagine agency. True, there are clearly different goals, different agendas, and different stakes involved depending on whether one is a feminist or a beauty pageant contestant, but the processes of imagining female agency are similarly situated within this particular historical moment.

With a shift in focus like the one I make in this work, beauty pageants can be situated as part of a liberal feminist rhetoric that relies on particular fantasies of agency, voice, and citizenship. Pageant contestants are both representations and self-represented, they are both sexual and serious, and they are both smart and feminine. I would like to suggest, as a sort of conclusion, that the questions I asked in the introduction to this book—What are the historical processes that produce a definition of agency? How are subjectivity and agency linked? How is power configured and wielded in an era of "power femininity" and "hip diversity"?—might be explored in a more substantive fashion were feminists to look to popular cultural forms such as beauty pageants that have been long dismissed as simplistic and obvious. Pageants do not mark the beginning (or the middle, or the end) of the path to feminist social reform, but they do represent a site for contestants to challenge, through their particular performance of femininity, conventional constraints of gendered and raced identity. If we, as feminists, disregard the significance and the salience of this performance of identity, if we chalk it up to complicity or false consciousness or even arrogance, then we risk obfuscating the curious and often ironic ways that power works to produce and reproduce gendered and racialized subjects in what is being called a postmodern world.

NOTES

INTRODUCTION

1. Fran Lebowitz cited in Rick Marin, "Ms. America: Making Over an Icon Very, Very Carefully," *New York Times*, 13 September 1993.

2. Peter Jennings, *ABC World News*, November 1996.

3. "Beauty on Parade against Sarajevo's Agony," *The European*, 3–6 June 1993. The high point of the Miss Sarajevo Under Siege contest was the pageant's climax, when a banner was unveiled that read "Please Don't Let Them Kill Us." The Miss Italy pageant witnessed the selection of a Black Dominican immigrant as the queen, a selection that sparked national controversy over what a feminine national representative should look like. Celestine Bohlen, "Italians Contemplate Beauty in a Caribbean Brow," *New York Times*, 10 September 1996, A3. For more on both events, see chapter 7.

4. Alison Schapker, "Shifting 'Identity': Paul Gilroy's *The Black Atlantic* and Questions of Modern Subjectivity," unpublished paper, University of California, San Diego, 1996.

5. Clifford Geertz, *The Interpretation of Cultures* (New York: Basic Books, 1973).

6. Frank Deford, *There She Is: The Life and Times of Miss America* (New York: Penguin Books, 1978), 3.

7. Academics have suggested that this book be a "popular" one, not geared for an academic audience. I understand the need for a book about visual culture and gender representation that has crossover potential, but I also see these comments as suggestive of another critique: one that has to do with the problematic issue of women writing theory as well as an intellectual elitism about what counts as scholarly study.

8. Lauren Berlant, *The Queen of America Goes to Washington City: Essays on Sex and Citizenship* (Durham: Duke University Press, 1997), 12.

9. The dominant approach pioneered by Frankfurt School scholars Theodor Adorno, Max Horkheimer, and Leo Lowenstein argues that mass, or popular culture—as defined by what Adorno and Horkheimer call the "culture industry"— is in danger of achieving total ideological domination through the exploitation and construction of the unconscious desires of the masses. Popular cultural forms such as beauty pageants are constituted in terms of an "obsessively mimetic relationship between consumer and cultural commodities" and, as such, are monolithic and dangerous expressions of dominant ideology. Max Horkheimer and Theodor Adorno, *The Dialectic of Enlightenment*, translated by John Cummings (New York: Seabury Press, 1972); Leo Lowenstein, *Literature, Popular Culture, and Society* (New Jersey: Prentice-Hall, 1961).

10. George Lipsitz, "Popular Culture: This Ain't No Sideshow," in *Time Passages: Collective Memory and American Popular Culture* (Minneapolis: University of Minnesota Press, 1990), 13. See also Stuart Hall, "Notes on Deconstructing 'the Popular,'" in *People's History and Socialist Theory*, edited by Raphael Samuel (London: Routledge and Kegan Paul, 1981), and Stuart Hall, "Culture, Media, and the 'Ideological' Effect," in *Mass Communication and Society*, edited by James Curran, Michael Gurevitch, and Janet Woollacott, (Beverly Hills: Sage, 1979).

11. Stuart Hall has formulated pioneering studies on the various and complicated ways in which television news can be "read" as simultaneously dominant and oppositional. Stuart Hall, "Encoding and Decoding in the Television Discourse," paper for the Council of Europe Colloquy on "Training in the Critical Reading of Televisual Language," Leicester, England, September 1973. He has also provided invaluable insight with respect to the multiple ways in which cultural institutions and formations constitute ethnic identity. Stuart Hall, "New Ethnicities," paper for the ICA Conference, "Black Film/British Cinema," February 1988; *Policing the Crisis* (New York: Macmillan, 1979); and "What Is This 'Black' in Black Popular Culture," in *Black Popular Culture*, edited by Gina Dent (Seattle: Bay Press, 1992). Likewise, cultural theorist Janice Radway has challenged dominant arguments about why romantic fiction captivates millions of female readers by insisting that we interrogate the "complex social event of reading" rather than singularly focus on the content of the text itself. Janice A. Radway, *Reading the Romance: Women,*

Patriarchy, and Popular Literature (Chapel Hill: University of North Carolina Press, 1984). Historian Eric Lott has convincingly argued that scholars should take a second look at nineteenth-century blackface minstrelsy, claiming that the premise that minstrelsy was "simply" a tool of white supremacy takes us only so far. He complicates the picture of conventional studies by insisting that the "whiteness" of white audiences is an integral element in a complex set of racial and racializing practices—and specifically in the practice of minstrelsy, where there "were in fact contradictory racial impulses at work, impulses based in the everyday lives and racial negotiations of the minstrel show's working-class partisans." Eric Lott, *Love and Theft: Blackface Minstrelsy and the American Working Class* (New York: Oxford University Press, 1993), 4. There are also many new works on popular culture by people of color, including Michelle Wallace, Tricia Rose, Kobena Mercer, and Michael Dyson. See also Susan Davis's work on theme parks and corporate culture, and Marita Sturken and Lisa Cartwright's forthcoming work on visual culture. Michelle Wallace, *Invisibility Blues: From Pop to Theory* (London: Verso, 1990), and *"Boyz N the Hood* and *Jungle Fever,"* in Dent, *Black Popular Culture.* Marlon Riggs, "Unleash the Queen" in Dent, *Black Popular Culture.* These listed authors are merely a handful of scholars conducting research on popular culture.

12. For a further discussion of the cultural aspect of nationalism, see Benedict Richard O'G. Anderson, *Imagined Communities: Reflections on the Origin and Spread of Nationalism* (London: Verso, 1983), and Eric J. Hobsbawm, *Nations and Nationalism since 1780: Programme, Myth, Reality* (Cambridge: Cambridge University Press, 1990).

13. For more on the connections between nationalism and sexuality, see George L. Mosse, *Nationalism and Sexuality: Middle-Class Morality and Sexual Norms in Modern Europe* (Madison: University of Wisconsin Press, 1985). See also Andrew Parker, et al, eds. *Nationalisms and Sexualities* (New York: Routledge, 1992). The nation, Anderson argues, is *imagined* in the sense that, although members of a nation may never know each other, there exists a deep connection between them, because "in the minds of each lives the image of their communion." Anderson traces the origins of this kind of image to the fourteenth-century development of "print-capitalism," in which increasingly rapid communications and sophisticated forms of technology allowed for the "imaginings" of connected others in the context of new ideas of simultaneity. As Anderson argues, the nation is not only imagined but is also a community "because, regardless of the actual inequality and exploitation that may prevail in each, the nation is always conceived as a deep, horizontal comradeship" (12). Although what constitutes the "nation" in late-twentieth-century postindustrialist U.S. society is more or less determined on the basis of inequalities and exploitative practices, cultural events and rituals remain absolutely necessary to sustain the idea of a "deep, horizontal comradeship." There are few studies concerning the connection between nationalism and sexuality, and specifically female sexuality or the female body. Historian George Mosse's *Nationalism and Sexuality* exam-

ines how female symbols of the nation, such as France's Marianne or Germany's
Germania, demonstrate explicitly how the nation (or the state) uses sexuality for
its own promotion and preservation. As Mosse points out regarding the German
state, "Nationalism—and the society that identified with it—used the example of
the chaste and modest woman to demonstrate its own virtuous aims." Mosse,
Nationalism and Sexuality, 90.

14. Historian Eric Hobsbawm discusses nationalism and nations as phenomena
that demand analysis "in terms of political, technical, administrative, economic
and other conditions and requirements." However, he extends his definition to
the cultural realm, claiming that nations and nationalisms are "dual phenomena,
constructed essentially from above, but which cannot be understood unless also
analysed from below, that is in terms of the assumptions, hopes, needs, longings
and interests of ordinary people, which are not necessarily national and still less
nationalist." Hobsbawm, *Nations and Nationalisms since 1780*, 10. See also Bryan S.
Turner, *The Body and Society: Explorations in Social Theory* (Oxford: Basil Blackwell,
1984).

15. Alice Echols, "Nothing Distant about It: Women's Liberation and Sixties Rad-
icalism," in *Women Transforming Politics: An Alternative Reader*, edited by Cathy J.
Cohen, Kathleen B. Jones, and Joan C. Tronto (New York: New York University
Press, 1997), 456. For a discussion of this critique, see Naomi Wolf, *The Beauty Myth:
How Images of Beauty Are Used against Women* (New York: W. Morrow, 1991); Wendy
Chapkis, *Beauty Secrets: Women and the Politics of Appearance* (Boston: South End
Press, 1986); Kathryn Pauly Morgan, "Women and the Knife: Cosmetic Surgery
and the Colonization of Women's Bodies," *Hypatia* 6 (fall 1991): 25–53; Robin T.
Lakoff and Raquel L. Scherr, *Face Value: The Politics of Beauty* (Boston: Routledge
and Kegan Paul, 1984); and others.

16. Michel Foucault, *Discipline and Punish: The Birth of the Prison*, translated by Alan
Sheridan (New York: Pantheon Books, 1977), and Foucault, *The History of Sexuality*, vol. 1, translated by Robert Hurley (New York: Pantheon Books, 1978). See also
Teresa de Lauretis, *Technologies of Gender: Essays on Theory, Film, and Fiction* (Bloom-
ington: Indiana University Press, 1987); Sandra Lee Bartky, *Femininity and Domination: Studies in the Phenomenology of Oppression* (New York: Routledge, 1990); Hazel
V. Carby, *Reconstructing Womanhood: The Emergence of the Afro-American Woman Novelist* (New York: Oxford University Press, 1987); Kimberlé Crenshaw, "Whose Story
Is It, Anyway? Feminist and Antiracist Appropriations of Anita Hill," in *Race-ing
Justice, En-gendering Power: Essays on Anita Hill, Clarence Thomas, and the Construction
of Social Reality*, edited by Toni Morrison (New York: Pantheon Books, 1992); and
Kimberlé Crenshaw and Gary Peller, "Reel Time/Real Justice," in *Reading Rodney
King, Reading Urban Uprising*, edited by Robert Gooding-Williams (New York: Rout-
ledge, 1993).

17. Judith Butler, *Gender Trouble: Feminism and the Subversion of Identity* (New York:
Routledge, 1990), 140.

18. For an example of this kind of postfeminist thinking, see Camille Paglia, *Sexual Personae: Art and Decadence from Nefertiti to Emily Dickinson* (New Haven: Yale University Press, 1990); Katie Roiphe, *The Morning After: Sex, Fear, and Feminism on Campus* (Boston: Little, Brown, and Company, 1993); and Wolf, *The Beauty Myth*.

19. For more on the benefits and limitations of employing a specific feminist methodology, see Sandra Harding, ed., *Feminism and Methodology: Social Science Issues* (Bloomington: Indiana University Press, 1987); and Mary Margaret Fonow and Judith A. Cook, eds., *Beyond Methodology: Feminist Scholarship as Lived Research* (Bloomington: Indiana University Press, 1991).

20. For an enlightening discussion of utilizing one's involvement in dominant practices as a resource, rather than a limitation, see Kathy Davis, *Reshaping the Female Body: The Dilemma of Cosmetic Surgery* (New York: Routledge, 1995). I develop her argument later in the chapter.

21. These interviews were conducted in San Diego, California, with approximately fifty current or former beauty contestants over the years 1990–1993. All quotes attributed to a specific contestant in the chapter text are from these interviews.

22. Mary [pseud.], interview by author, San Diego, California, 26 September 1991. All names of interviewees have been changed to ensure confidentiality.

23. Following Foucault, I use the term *disciplinary practices* to mean the different discourses of power that we participate in to create ourselves as "subjects." Here specifically, I mean body configuration, ornamentation such as makeup and dress, and bodily movement. For more on disciplinary practices, see Foucault, *Discipline and Punish*.

24. Stuart Hall uses the term *cultural dupes* to make a similar criticism against Marxist cultural critique. See S. Hall, "Encoding and Decoding in the Television Discourse."

25. De Lauretis, *Technologies of Gender*, 3.

26. Ibid., 10.

27. When I refer to the "universal sex opposition," I am referencing the sex and gender binary of woman versus man. If the category of Woman is normalized as a natural category, then it logically follows that the relationship of Woman to Man would similarly be naturalized.

28. Joan Wallach Scott, "Experience," in *Feminists Theorize the Political*, edited by Judith Butler and Joan W. Scott (New York: Routledge, 1992) 25.

29. Ibid., 25.

30. Susan Bordo, *Unbearable Weight: Feminism, Western Culture, and the Body* (Berkeley: University of California Press, 1993), 253.

31. Alice [pseud.], interview by author, San Diego, California, 15 April 1991.

32. Ibid.

33. Spivak quoted in Scott, "Experience," 33.

34. The section epigraph is from Christopher Newfield, "What Was Political Correctness? Race, the Right, and Managerial Democracy in the Humanities," *Critical Inquiry* 19 (winter 1993): 320.

35. Hazel V. Carby, "The Multicultural Wars," in Dent, *Black Popular Culture*.

36. George F. Will, "A Kind of Compulsory Chapel: Multiculturalism Is a Campaign to Lower America's Moral Status," *Newsweek*, 14 November 1994, 84.

37. Newfield, "What Was Political Correctness?"

38. Carby, "The Multicultural Wars," 190.

39. On racism, diversity, and the Benetton Clothing Company, see Patricia Williams, *The Alchemy of Race and Rights: Diary of a Law Professor* (Cambridge: Harvard University Press, 1991).

40. Shirley Lord, "Everybody's All American," *Vogue* September 1986.

41. Carby, "The Multicultural Wars," 194.

42. Will, "A Kind of Compulsory Chapel," 84.

43. K. Davis, *Reshaping the Female Body*, 28.

44. Ibid., 160.

45. James Wolcott characterizes Noonan and Huffington and other neoconservative "feminists" as advocates of "power femininity." See James Wolcott, "Beyond the Values of the Supervixens," *New Yorker Magazine*, 13 February 1995.

46. Ibid., 178.

47. Ibid., 178.

48. Paglia, *Sexual Personae*.

49. K. Davis, *Reshaping the Female Body*, 180.

50. Samuel Gompers, cited in Lois Banner, *American Beauty* (New York: Knopf, 1983).

CHAPTER 1. "A CERTAIN CLASS OF GIRL"

1. The chapter epigraph is from Deford, *There She Is*, 3. The statistics are from Marin, "Ms. America."

2. For more on the myth "The Judgment of Paris," see A. R. Riverol, *Live from Atlantic City: The History of the Miss America Pageant before, after, and in Spite of Television* (Bowling Green: Bowling Green State University Popular Press, 1992), 4. Of course, the events that followed Paris's judgment resulted in the Trojan War, a hard lesson that seems not to affect the longevity or popularity of more contemporary beauty pageants.

3. Despite the "republican principles" of the early American public, pageantry and monarchy held special appeal when performed in the context of community festivals.

4. Being crowned a "queen" in the United States was quite unlike any other distinction, and though it may seem trivial and overly romantic in the current political and cultural climate, the monarchical element of beauty pageants remains, albeit in diluted form.

5. Banner, *American Beauty*, 253.

6. Ibid., 254.

7. Ibid., 256–260.

8. Ibid., 260–261.

9. For more on commercial culture as authority, please see Richard Wightman Fox and T. J. Jackson Lears, eds., *The Culture of Consumption: Critical Essays in American History, 1880–1980* (New York: Pantheon Books, 1983). See especially the essay by Chris Wilson, "The Rhetoric of Consumption: Mass-Market Magazines and the Demise of the Gentle Reader, 1880–1920." See also Kathy Peiss, "Making Faces: The Cosmetics Industry and the Cultural Construction of Gender, 1890–1930," *Genders* 7 (spring 1990): 143–169.

10. For more on the conception of the Miss America pageant as a response to the popularity of Coney Island, see Riverol, *Live from Atlantic City*. Also see Deford, *There She Is*.

11. For more information about the changing position of professional women at the end of the nineteenth century and beginning of the twentieth, see Kathy Peiss, *Cheap Amusements: Working Women and Leisure in Turn-of-the-Century New York* (Philadelphia: Temple University Press, 1986); Banner, *American Beauty*; and Robert C. Allen, *Horrible Prettiness: Burlesque and American Culture* (Chapel Hill: University of North Carolina Press, 1991).

12. Deford, *There She Is*.

13. Nancie S. Martin, *Miss America through the Looking Glass: The Story behind the Scenes* (New York: Messner Books, 1985), 39.

14. For a more detailed history of pageantry circa the beginning of the twentieth century, see Banner, *American Beauty*, Deford, *There She Is*, and Riverol, *Live from Atlantic City*.

15. Riverol, *Live from Atlantic City*, especially chapter 2.

16. It wasn't until later that the contestants in the Miss America pageant represented states; the early pageants saw not only state and city representatives, but also contestants from resorts and amusement parks, such as Miss Coney Island. For a further discussion of this topic, see Riverol, *Live from Atlantic City*, and Susan Dworkin, *Miss America, 1945: Bess Myerson's Own Story* (New York: Newmarket Press, 1987). Dworkin's study on the life of Bess Myerson provides a rich archive of historical material on the pageant. Throughout this work, I refer to her text and her citations.

17. Deford, *There She Is*, 113.

18. For a more detailed discussion of these preliminary eliminations, see Riverol, *Live from Atlantic City*.

19. Ibid., 24.

20. For a more general discussion of women in the early twentieth century, see Peiss, *Cheap Amusements*. See also Christine Stansell, *City of Women: Sex and Class in New York, 1789–1860* (Urbana: University of Illinois Press, 1987).

21. Riverol, *Live from Atlantic City*, 24. The pageant itself insists that the reason the

event was discontinued in 1927 was because of the Great Depression, "when the Bathing Beauty Contest was considered an extravagance that could no longer be afforded." However, the Depression did not begin until October 1929, after the great stock market crash, so this explanation seems unlikely. For a further discussion, see Deford, *There She Is*.

22. Unfortunately, the "new" Miss America got off to a dismal beginning; it was reinstituted in 1933, at the height of the Great Depression, and lack of funds severely diminished the event's festival atmosphere. The competitive prizes for the contestants were not monetary, sponsors could not afford to donate funds to an event with a precarious history, and the scholarship awards had not yet been instituted. The contestants were few, and those who showed up were subdued and wary. The producers and organizers of the pageant declared it a "financial fiasco," and the Miss America pageant was once again discontinued. Riverol, *Live from Atlantic City*, 26–33.

23. For a more detailed discussion of Slaughter, see S. Dworkin, *Miss America, 1945* and Riverol, *Live from Atlantic City*.

24. S. Dworkin, *Miss America, 1945*, 96.

25. Allen, *Horrible Prettiness*, 95.

26. Riverol, *Live from Atlantic City*, 33.

27. S. Dworkin, *Miss America, 1945*, 90.

28. Ibid.

29. Ibid., 106–107.

30. Riverol, *Live from Atlantic City*, 32–33. The 1935 pageant was the first to include a talent competition—although it was an optional event—and the judges did not take that competition into consideration in their final scoring.

31. Ibid., 33.

32. Deford, *There She Is*, 152.

33. Beverley Skeggs, *Formations of Class and Gender* (London: Sage Publications 1997), 1.

34. Riverol, *Live from Atlantic City*, 35.

35. For a further discussion of Jean Bartel's reign as Miss America and her tour selling war bonds, see Deford, *There She Is*.

36. Lenora Slaughter cited in S. Dworkin, *Miss America, 1945*, 98.

37. Deford, *There She Is*, 154.

38. S. Dworkin, *Miss America, 1945*, 98–102.

39. Deford, *There She Is*.

40. I discuss the feminist protest of the pageant in the introduction and in chapter 3.

41. The details of the particular issue platform, as well as evidence of the contestant's dedication, constitute most of the substance of the interview segment during the Miss America pageant.

42. For more on how early feminists in the United States were considered moral

custodians of society, see Stansell, *City of Women*; Katherine Kish Sklar, *Catharine Beecher: A Study in American Domesticity* (New Haven: Yale University Press, 1973); Peiss, *Cheap Amusements*; and Ellen Carol Dubois, *Feminism and Suffrage: The Emergence of the Independent Women's Movement in America, 1848–1869* (Ithaca: Cornell University Press, 1978). Contestants avoid the potentially "radical" edge to social issues, such as the connection between AIDS and homosexuality.

43. Frank Deford claims that the idea for the Miss Universe pageant was given to Stewart by a former Miss America, Jacque Mercer, who was at the time estranged from the Miss America pageant. Deford, *There She Is*, 181.

44. Ibid.

45. Riverol, *Live from Atlantic City*, 41.

46. *Miss San Diego Pageant 1994 Program.* In referring to the "pageant family," the program says that these directors, producers, and other volunteers are "civic leaders whose positions and business endeavors encompass all fields of activity."

47. *The 68th Annual Miss California Pageant Program*, 1991.

48. Alice, interview. For more on the decisions about entering pageants, see chapter 3.

49. Tina [pseud.], interview by author, San Diego, California, 12 August 1993. The contestant's status as either Miss America or Miss USA "material" is much more significant at the state and national level than at the local level. For example, many contestants "shop around" pageants at the local level, attempting victory in any pageant for which they qualify. At the state level, however, the Miss America franchised pageants become more self-conscious—and defensive—of their status as part of a scholarship program.

50. Interestingly, Madison Square Gardens tried to gain rights to the Miss America pageant during the years of the Great Depression. Rather than move the pageant from beloved Atlantic City and relinquish rights, Miss America officials produced it on a shoestring budget. For a further discussion, see Riverol, *Live from Atlantic City*, and Deford, *There She Is*.

51. Deford, *There She Is*, 11.

52. At the local level, sponsors are not multinational corporations like Clairol or Chevrolet. Rather, the companies and businesses that decide to sponsor particular contestants are usually members of local Jaycees or community businesses.

53. Discussions about selling tickets and soliciting local sponsorship emerged in all my personal interviews, San Diego, California, 1991–1993.

54. There is a different system that organizes the Miss USA pageant, where titles other than the official Miss USA franchised pageants can participate. Tina, interview.

55. I was listed as "pageant staff" when I conducted my fieldwork for nine weeks at a local city pageant.

56. Part of a beauty queen's duties during her reign is to appear in crown and banner at various pageants around the city.

57. *1989 Rules and Regulations of the Miss Fairest of the Fair/Miss San Diego County Pageant.*

58. I am grateful to Judith Gregory for her thoughts about cover stories and alibis.

59. Alice, interview.

60. See Deford for a further discussion of "state-hopping." Deford, *There She Is.*

61. Alice, interview.

62. The Miss USA and Miss Universe organization does not include a talent competition in their pageants, so the score for contestants in that pageant organization is distributed among the offstage and onstage interviews, the evening gown competition, and the swimsuit competition. The woman who garners the highest composite score in these categories is considered the representative of the area or event for which she is crowned and is thought to personify the values and attitudes of the state or nation.

63. Deford, *There She Is,* 41–60.

64. *Miss San Diego 1994 Pageant Program.*

65. Deford, *There She Is,* 45.

66. Remark heard at the Miss San Diego 1994 pageant.

67. Deford, *There She Is,* 58.

68. This "analysis" usually consists of Miss USA reiterating the scores for the audience, always exclaiming about the superlative performances of each of the contestants, as well as commenting on the difficult task the judges must have when faced with such beautiful contestants.

69. For more on the "invention of tradition" and how events become blends of different traditions, see Eric J. Hobsbawm and Terence Ranger, eds., *The Invention of Tradition* (Cambridge, England: Cambridge University Press, 1983), and Susan G. Davis, *Parades and Power: Street Theatre in Nineteenth-Century Philadelphia* (Berkeley: University of California Press, 1986).

70. For more on the disciplinary practices of femininity, see Bordo, *Unbearable Weight,* 187, and Sandra Lee Bartky, "Foucault, Femininity, and the Modernization of Patriarchal Power," in *Feminism and Foucault: Reflections on Resistance,* edited by Irene Diamond and Lee Quinby (Boston: Northeastern University Press, 1988).

71. Robert Goldman and Stephen Papson, *Sign Wars: The Cluttered Landscape of Advertising* (New York: Guilford Press, 1996), 218.

CHAPTER 2. ANATOMY OF A BEAUTY PAGEANT

1. The chapter epigraphs are from Diana [pseud.], interview by author, San Diego, California, 15 October 1991; and Foucault, *Discipline and Punish,* 152.

2. Genie Polo Sayles, *How to Win Pageants* (Plano, Tex.: Wordware Publishing, 1990). These swimsuits are expensive—the average price for a competition suit is

150 dollars. Labeling a swimsuit "competitive" is an automatic signifier that the purpose of the suit is for display, not swimming.

3. In national pageants such as the Miss America pageant, every contestant is remarkably close to this idealized feminine form. However, in the smaller, local pageants, there is a more disparate display of bodies. Because the idealized feminine form remains the norm for these pageants as well, a swimsuit parade is an especially humiliating experience for those with bodies that fall somewhere outside the norm.

4. In the widely publicized protests of the Miss California pageant, media activist Ann Simonton and others protested the sexualized bodies of contestants. In fact, most public protests of the pageant are concerned with the issue of the objectified female body, beginning with the first Miss America protest, held in 1968. See Chapkis, *Beauty Secrets*, and Wolf, *The Beauty Myth*. The first feminist protest of the Miss America pageant, in 1968, took particular aim at the spectacle's focus on the body. More recently, feminists have responded to the competition by dressing in swimsuits made entirely out of meat, dramatizing their view that the "true" purpose of the pageant—a large-scale meat market in which women are reduced to judgable body parts—is revealed in the swimsuit competition.

5. CBS Television Network, 15 September 1994.

6. As early as 1951, the newly crowned Miss America, Yolande Betbeze, responded to this contradiction by refusing to pose "for photographs in a swimsuit, saying that she was a singer, not a pinup." Despite the fact that her refusal had a price, leading to the withdrawal of a major sponsor (swimsuit manufacturer Catalina), Betbeze's decision was supported by the Miss America Corporation, who maintained strong interests in organizing the pageant as a legitimate, respectable event. N. Martin, *Miss America through the Looking Glass*, 53. Catalina left the Miss America pageant and started its own pageant, Miss Universe. Miss Universe is owned by the same company that owns Miss USA, a pageant that is often harshly criticized by participants in the Miss America program as only a beauty pageant, not a scholarship event.

7. Grace, [pseud.], interview by author, San Diego, California, 2 November 1992.

8. Miss Alpine 1990 contest, Alpine, San Diego, February 1990.

9. Miss San Diego contest, San Diego, California, 10 December 1994.

10. Jacqueline Urla and Alan C. Swedlund, "The Anthropometry of Barbie," in *Deviant Bodies: Critical Perspectives on Difference in Science and Popular Culture* (Bloomington: Indiana University Press, 1995), 282.

11. Susan Willis, *A Primer for Everyday Life* (New York: Routledge, 1991).

12. Urla and Swedlund, "The Anthropometry of Barbie," 282.

13. Sandra Lee Bartky, "Foucault, Femininity, and the Modernization of Power," in *Femininity and Domination*.

14. For example, Bartky points out that women's bodies, in congruence with current standards of femininity, must be small, compact, and thin to the point of ema-

ciation. Because adult women's bodies do not usually resemble those of adolescent boys, dieting and other disciplinary practices are often necessary to remake a female body into an ideal feminine one. As many scholars on beauty and femininity have shown, what is considered to be the ideal body size has changed historically. See, Banner, *American Beauty*.

15. N. Martin, *Miss America through the Looking Glass*, 27.

16. Sayles, *How to Win Pageants*, 219. We can also link the terms *self-care* and *self-respect* to the liberal facade. In other words, the body is equated with the "self," not with sex.

17. Lisa [pseud.], interview by author, San Diego, California, 10 December 1993; emphasis is in the original.

18. Sayles, *How to Win Pageants*, xvi.

19. Lisa, interview. The women involved in mainstream beauty pageants consistently call each other "girls," or possibly "ladies," but never "women."

20. Mary, interview.

21. Lisa, interview.

22. *Entertainment Tonight*, CBS Television Network, April 1990. Another disciplinary practice regarding weight is found in Arlie Hochschild's *Managed Heart*, where she details the weight restrictions of flight attendants. These restrictions parallel those of beauty queens. Arlie R. Hochschild, *The Managed Heart: Commercialization of Human Feeling* (Berkeley: University of California Press, 1983).

23. Donald Trump, who purchased the Miss Universe pageant in 1996, was one of the most vocal protesters against Machado's weight gain.

24. N. Martin, *Miss America through the Looking Glass*, 32.

25. "The Winning Edge," March 1993.

26. Bartky, *Femininity and Domination*, 72.

27. Diana, interview.

28. Bordo, *Unbearable Weight*, 189.

29. Ibid., 190.

30. Ibid., 188; *Miss USA Pageant 1992*, NBC Television Network, February 1992.

31. "Shape Up, Miss America!" *Woman's Day*, September 1, 1994.

32. As a measure of this vulnerability, in 1993, the Miss America pageant officially changed its name to the Miss America Scholarship Program. At one meeting I attended, the California representative of the Miss America Scholarship Program gave a schoolmarmish lecture to the contestants about getting the name right.

33. Diana, interview.

34. N. Martin, *Miss America through the Looking Glass*, 74.

35. For a further discussion of the connection between weight and self control, see Bordo, *Unbearable Weight*.

36. On how this connection between the inner and the outer selves is also a connection that is figured in racial terms, see chapter 4.

37. One such "do's and don'ts" seminar was part of a day-long pageant expo I

attended. Other seminars included a session on lighting and makeup for portrait photography, stage makeup, correct posture, and interview decorum.

38. The fact that there is a swimsuit shop that specializes in pageant gear signifies that pageant contestants represent a particular consumer group: they are a "market" and, as such, have a logic and momentum of their own.

39. Pageant Expo, San Diego, California, October 4, 1993.

40. Mary, Miss San Diego pageant, San Diego, California, December 10, 1993.

41. N. Martin, *Miss America through the Looking Glass*, 115–116.

42. Alice, interview.

43. Sayles, *How to Win Pageants*, 238.

44. Ibid., 238.

45. Pageant Expo, San Diego, California, October 4, 1993.

46. Bordo, *Unbearable Weight*, 166.

47. Miss San Diego pageant, San Diego, California, December, 1993.

48. Bernarr MacFadden, *The Power and Beauty of Superb Womanhood: How They Are Lost and How They May Be Regained and Developed to the Highest Degree of Attainable Perfection* (New York: Physical Culture Publishing, 1901), 15.

49. Alice, interview.

50. As I argue later, the swimsuit competition is much like the debased state of burlesque performers in the early twentieth century, when striptease artists, like beauty pageant contestants, were required to be silent and thus denied their power to "unsettle and subvert." See Allen, *Horrible Prettiness*.

51. Foucault, *Discipline and Punish*, 136. For more on Foucault's articulation of the two registers of the body in specific relation to the body, see Bordo, *Unbearable Weight*, 181.

52. Foucault, *Discipline and Punish*, 138.

53. Gayle Rubin, "The Traffic in Women: Notes on the 'Political Economy' of Sex," in *Toward an Anthropology of Woman*, edited by Rayna Reiter (New York: Monthly Review Press, 1975), 175. As I argue in other chapters, the swimsuit competition is only one element for the traffic in women in which the beauty pageant is engaged. In other components of the pageant, such as the talent and interview sections, pageant contestants present themselves as marriageable subjects through their commitment to heterosexuality, family, helping professions, and so forth. The fact that contestants must be single to enter the contest is directly related to their exchange value, as is their purported virgin status, which is signified by being both single and nonreproductive, because reproduction directly and forcefully evidences the sex act. As Rubin claims, "If women are exchanged, in whatever sense we take the term, marital debts are reckoned in female flesh" (182).

54. Willis, *A Primer for Daily Life*, 28.

55. Bordo, *Unbearable Weight*, 253.

56. Robyn Wiegman, *American Anatomies: Theorizing Race and Gender* (Durham: Duke University Press, 1995).

57. Academic scholarships form the bulk of the prizes given to winners in the Miss

America pageant organization, although the queen also receives money, clothing, and other prizes. In the Miss USA contest, the winner receives a cash prize (ostensibly to be used for education), a new car, and a fur coat.

58. Michelle [pseud.], interview by author, San Diego, California, 11 December 1993.

59. The emphasis on the "cheapness" of the woman in a bikini contest is important, because it signals that a woman's worth is dependent on how "expensive" she looks. For example, in their study of women and romance in college culture, Holland and Eisenhart comment that "attractiveness" works as a symbol of ranking in the student culture in terms of social worth and prestige: "[T]he model of romance also implies that attractive women will be well-treated—a sign of their attractiveness—and correspondingly, that unattractive women will be badly treated." Dorothy C. Holland and Margaret A. Eisenhart, *Educated in Romance: Women, Achievement, and College Culture* (Chicago: University of Chicago Press, 1990), 99. In other words, if a woman constructs herself in particular ways that signify "attractiveness," she looks like she would be, in the words of the marketplace, "bought" by a high-status man. This idea is legitimated in popular entertainment; for two relatively recent examples, see the films *Pretty Woman* and *Indecent Proposal*.

60. For the historical perspective, see Peiss, *Cheap Amusements*, and Stansell, *City of Women*.

61. This ideology is manifest in the legal system as well. It is a common defense to accuse women who are raped of having "asked for it" by the way they dress or act. For further discussion, see Catherine MacKinnon, *Feminism Unmodified: Discourses on Life and Law* (Cambridge: Harvard University Press, 1987).

62. Wiegman, *American Anatomies*, 45.

63. The exposed body in the swimsuit competition is incontrovertible evidence that the "appropriate" feminine body is the white body, with a very few (and quite necessary) exceptions.

64. Bordo, *Unbearable Weight*, 187.

CHAPTER 3. "IF YOU WERE A COLOR, WHAT COLOR WOULD YOU BE?"

1. Lynn [pseud.], interview by author, San Diego, California, 16 October 1994.

2. Butler, *Gender Trouble*, 140.

3. Riverol, *Live from Atlantic City*, 30–40.

4. Rochelle [pseud.], interview by author, San Diego, California, 10 December 1993.

5. The importance of public speaking skills was a theme that repeatedly emerged in conversations with pageant contestants.

6. By *political* here I mean a willingness to associate with certain prescribed social and cultural issues.

7. The question about which color one would be is especially interesting, because embedded within it is a notion of choice. Color is apparently something one can simply "put on" and then take off. What is also interesting to consider is whether this question is ever asked of a black contestant. Of course, the "color" referred to in the question is not overtly about race, answers usually being blue, or green, or orange. But this question inevitably calls race to mind, because it assumes whiteness as the neutral, starting point for all contestants.

8. Like the strategies employed by flight attendants, as Arlie Hochschild has astutely demonstrated, pageant contestants engage in "deep acting"—the process by which one convincingly offers spontaneous responses even after months of rehearsal devoted to such a response. Hochschild, *The Managed Heart*.

9. At the end of each question-and-answer period, the rest of the group (but mainly the producer and assistant producer) commented on and critiqued the contestant's performance. This was an especially informative element of my fieldwork, because I was able to participate in both questioning and critiquing, truly acting as a participant-observer. My own clear, "instinctive" sense of what constituted good versus wrong or inappropriate answers made clear my deep embeddedness in the liberal framework.

10. The way in which I was positioned during these rehearsals was interesting. Because all the contestants knew that I was a doctoral student conducting research, women approached me after each session and asked what I thought of their answers. They also looked to me for advice on political matters. For example, after I once mentioned that a newspaper article had detailed a political proposition about the education of Mexican immigrants, I became the "source" for current events.

11. This example reminds me of Miss America 1993, Leanza Cornett, whose platform involved AIDS awareness. She was censored by the Miss America Pageant Committee for using the word *condom*, as in "Use a condom." She thus pointed to the act of having sex, which is clearly inappropriate if one aspires to be Miss America. Cornett resolved this issue by renaming condoms "latex." The same issue came up again with the 1998 Miss America, who also embraced AIDS awareness as her "issue" and was also reprimanded by pageant officials for advocating the use of a condom to prevent HIV transmission.

12. For more on the concept of "role models," see Erving Goffman, *Frame Analysis: An Essay on the Organization of Experience* (Boston: Northeastern University Press, 1986).

13. *Miss USA 1993*, NBC.

14. *Miss America 1991*, CBS.

15. Sut Jhally and Justin Lewis make a similar argument in their work on the success of *The Cosby Show*. They write about a trend that *The Cosby Show* stimulated,

a trend toward the proliferation of middle- and upper-middle-class black characters on television. This trend is not the boost for positive race relations that it appears to be. Our evidence suggests, in fact, that the presence of these apparently benign images of black people on television constitutes, for African-Americans, a serious step backward. . . . Our argument is, in essence, a simple one: programs like *The Cosby Show* encourage the viewer to see the real world through rose-tinted spectacles. . . . The viewers' ability to distinguish the TV world from the real one does not prevent them from confusing the two. *The Cosby Show*, we discovered, helps to cultivate an impression, particularly among white people, that racism is no longer a problem in the United States.

Sut Jhally and Justin Lewis, *Enlightened Racism: The Cosby Show, Audiences, and the Myth of the American Dream* (Boulder, Colo.: Westview Press, 1992), 71. See also Herman Gray, "Television, Black Americans, and the American Dream," *Critical Studies in Mass Communication* 6 (1989): 376–386.

16. *Miss USA 1993*, NBC.

17. Ibid.

18. Pierre Bourdieu, *Distinction* (New York: Routledge and Kegan Paul, 1984).

19. Matthew Arnold cited in Joan Shelley Rubin, *The Making of Middlebrow Culture* (Chapel Hill: University of North Carolina Press, 1992), 14.

20. Janice Radway, "The Scandal of the Middlebrow, the Book-of-the-Month-Club, Class Fracture, and Cultural Authority," *South Atlantic Quarterly* 89, no. 4 (fall 1990): 726. See also Radway, "On the Gender of the Middlebrow Consumer and the Threat of the Culturally Fraudulent Female," *South Atlantic Quarterly* 93, no. 4 (fall 1994).

21. Radway, "Scandal of the Middlebrow," 727.

22. J. Rubin, *Making of Middlebrow Culture*; Radway, "Scandal of the Middlebrow."

23. Sayles, *How to Win Pageants*, 157.

24. Andrew Ross, *No Respect: Intellectuals and Popular Culture* (New York: Routledge, 1989), 59.

25. For more on women's role in civilizing the nation, see Sklar, *Catharine Beecher*; Stansell, *City of Women*; Peiss, *Cheap Amusements*; and Linda Kerber, *Women of the Republic: Intellect and Ideology in Revolutionary America* (Chapel Hill: University of North Carolina Press, 1980).

26. Ross, *No Respect*, 60.

27. The remaining three winners performed on the piano, played the marimba, or danced ballet.

28. Sayles, *How to Win Pageants*, 159.

29. Ibid.

30. Lynn, interview.

31. In fact, at the most recent Miss America pageant, a white contestant performed a Whitney Houston song. It is clear that in this arena, as in all others of popular culture, the constraints on black women are much more stringent and that black women who break those constraints suffer greater penalties.

32. George Lipsitz, *Dangerous Crossroads: Popular Music, Postmodernism, and the Poetics of Place*, (New York: Verso, 1994), 51.

33. Adolph Reed Jr., "The Fiction of Race: Skin Deep," *Village Voice*, 24 September 1996, 22.

34. Ibid.

35. Sayles, *How to Win Pageants*, 160.

36. Lott, *Love and Theft*.

37. This kind of argument about the natural also makes genetic links between black men and violence, and black people and low intelligence; see, for example, the "scientific" text by Richard Herrnstein and Charles Murray, *The Bell Curve* (New York: Free Press, 1994).

38. Denice Becker, "Secrets to a Polished Performance," from the Pageant Worldwide Marketplace website.

39. Richard Wightman Fox, "The Miss America Pageant: A Scholarship Organization," *Z Magazine* (December 1990).

CHAPTER 4. BODIES OF DIFFERENCE

1. Susan Chira, "To First Black Miss America, Victory Is a Means to an End," *New York Times*, 19 September 1983.

2. "Black Leaders Praise Choice of First Black Miss America," *New York Times*, 19 September 1983; Jacqueline Trescott, "Her Crowning Achievement. Vanessa Williams: A New Voice for Miss America," *Washington Post*, 20 September 1983.

3. Trescott, "Her Crowning Achievement."

4. Elizabeth Kastor, "Miss America Asked to Resign: Pageant Officials Act after Learning of Nude Photos," *Washington Post*, 21 July 1984; Esther B. Fein, "Miss America Gives Up Her Crown," *New York Times*, 24 July 1984.

5. Judy Mann, "Sleaze," *Washington Post*, 25 July 1984; William Raspberry, "Missed America," *Washington Post*, 23 July 1984; Richard Cohen, "Pageant of Hypocrisy," *New York Times*, 25 July 1984; William Safire, "There She Goes . . . ," *New York Times*, 23 July 1984.

6. Esther B. Fein, "Miss America Denies Giving Consent to Run Nude Photos," *New York Times*, 23 July 1984.

7. Fein, "Miss America Gives Up Her Crown."

8. For more on "types" of people, see Peiss, "Making Faces." See also Liisa Malkki, "Citizens of Humanity: Internationalism and the Imagined Community of Nations," *Diaspora* 3, no. 1 (1994): 41–68.

9. Karima A. Haynes, "Miss America from Vanessa Williams to Kimberly Aiken: Is the Crown a Stumbling Block or Steppingstone?" *Ebony* 3 (January 1994): 42.

10. For examples of such accusations, see the highly publicized protests of Miss California pageants from 1980 to 1990. Media activist and protest organizer Ann

Simonton informed me in a personal interview of these accusations and her response to them. Santa Cruz, Calif., December 1991. See also Deford, *There She Is.*

11. Herman Gray, *Watching Race: Television and the Struggle for "Blackness,"* (Minneapolis: University of Minnesota Press, 1995), 18.

12. Ibid.

13. For more on race-transcending icons, in the case of the marketing of Michael Jordon, see Michael Eric Dyson, *Reflecting Black: African-American Cultural Criticism* (Minneapolis: University of Minnesota Press, 1993). On the marketing of diverse Barbie Dolls, see Ann Ducille, "Dyes and Dolls: Multicultural Barbie and the Merchandising of Difference," *Differences: A Journal of Feminist Cultural Studies* 6, no. 1 (1994). See also the study of the O. J. Simpson trial, Toni Morrison and Claudia Brodsky Lacour, eds., *Birth of a Nation'hood: Gaze, Script, and Spectacle in the OJ Simpson Case* (New York: Pantheon Books, 1997).

14. Fox, "The Miss America Pageant," 66.

15. Deford, *There She Is.*

16. Mary, interview.

17. H. Gray, *Watching Race;* Ella Shohat and Robert Stam, *Unthinking Eurocentrism: Multiculturalism and the Media* (New York: Routledge, 1994).

18. *Newsweek,* February 1995. For more on the commodification of diversity within a climate of "political correctness," see "A Symposium on Popular Culture and Political Correctness," *Social Text* N36 (fall 1993).

19. Bebe Moore Campbell, writing in the *Los Angeles Times,* coins the term *The Firsts,* arguing that this distinguished group of blacks are revered by the black community: "We revere every champion among us who dared to venture into untried and even forbidden territory and triumphed, opening the door for others to follow. . . . The Firsts proved to the world that, given the same opportunities, blacks do as well as anyone. Or even better." Campbell, "A New Black Freedom: To Fail," *Los Angeles Times,* 29 April 1984.

20. See Wahneema Lubiano, "Black Ladies, Welfare Queens, and State Minstrels: Ideological War by Narrative Means," and Nell Painter Irvin, "Hill, Thomas, and the Use of Racial Stereotype," in *Race-ing Justice, En-gendering Power,* edited by Toni Morrison; Patricia Hill Collins, *Black Feminist Thought: Knowledge, Consciousness, and the Politics of Empowerment,* (New York: Routledge, 1991); and bell hooks, *Black Looks: Race and Representation* (Boston: South End Press, 1992).

21. Chira, "To First Black Miss America."

22. Alice, interview.

23. H. Gray, *Watching Race,* 19.

24. For more on the circulation of cultural narratives about the black body, see Lubiano, "Black Ladies, Welfare Queens, and State Minstrels"; Collins, *Black Feminist Thought*; Wiegman, *American Anatomies*; and H. Gray, *Watching Race.*

25. Lubiano defines cover stories as narratives that "cover or mask what they make invisible with an alternative presence; a presence that redirects our attention, that

covers or makes absent what has to remain unseen if the *seen* is to function as the *scene* for a different drama. One story provides a cover that allows another story (or stories) to slink out of sight." Lubiano, "Black Ladies, Welfare Queens, and State Minstrels," 324.

26. Trescott, "Her Crowning Achievement."

27. Ibid.

28. For more on these public concerns, see the discussion of diversity and multiculturalism in the introduction.

29. Jacqueline Trescott, "Miss America's Winning Ways: Vanessa Williams Breaks One Racial Barrier," *Washington Post*, 19 September 1983.

30. I'm thinking here of Herman Gray's discussion of *The Cosby Show* in *Watching Race*. Gray discusses *The Cosby Show* and the Bill Moyers piece on the "disappearing Black family" as instances that construct the exception as the norm—so that Bill Cosby is seen as having the same opportunities as any other black man, and the reason why he is successful is because he worked hard for his success.

31. Chira, "To First Black Miss America." Part of the elaborate cultural work to construct Vanessa Williams as "just a person" involved focusing on her family as a "normal," average, U.S. family. *Normal* in this context connotes a family unmarked by any of the standard racial codes such as poverty, inner-city housing, welfare dependence, or "broken" families (homes without fathers). Williams, along with her brother and her two married parents, "grew up in a quiet suburb of New York, free of social problems, boasting one of the most competitive, highly rated public school systems in the country. Both her parents teach. She and her mother describe the home as 'deeply religious.'" Trescott, "Her Crowning Achievement." Newspaper articles are riddled with examples of the discipline and commitment her parents required of her in terms of education and musical training, adding even more credibility to the testimony that Williams's success was possible because she tried hard, she worked hard, and she was disciplined. What this did more than anything else was to construct Williams as familiar, as "one of our own," as part of the white middle class.

32. Jackie Goldsby, "Queen for 307 Days: Looking B(l)ack at Vanessa Williams and the Sex Wars," in *Sisters, Sexperts, Queers: Beyond the Lesbian Nation*, edited by Arlene Stein (New York: Plume Books, 1993), 119.

33. Ibid.

34. Trescott, "Her Crowning Achievement."

35. The word *crave* is interesting, insofar as it suggests that her difference is a choice, something she wants or lusts after, rather than something that she is. Again, this notion of "choosing" identity emerges from liberal discourse and the idealized concept of meritocracy: one can be anything, as long as the desire (or craving) and effort is there.

36. Kathy Russell, Midge Wilson, and Ronald Hall, *The Color Complex: The Politics of Skin Color among African Americans* (New York: Doubleday, 1992), 154–155.

37. Ibid.

38. Trescott, "Miss America's Winning Ways."

39. Susan Chira, "First Black Miss America Finds Unforeseen Issues," *New York Times*, 3 April 1984.

40. Trescott, "Her Crowning Achievement."

41. Trescott, "Miss America's Winning Ways."

42. Chira, "First Black Miss America."

43. Class is not the reason she had to work harder; she comes from an upper-middle-class family in a elite suburb of New York.

44. Chira, "First Black Miss America."

45. For more on narratives that signal black womanhood, see Lubiano, "Black Ladies, Welfare Queens, and State Minstrels"; Collins, *Black Feminist Thought*; Morrison, *Race-ing Justice, En-gendering Power*; and Valerie Hartouni, *Cultural Conceptions: On Reproductive Technologies and the Remaking of Life* (Minneapolis: University of Minnesota Press, 1997). See also Painter, "Hill, Thomas, and the Use of Racial Stereotype," 210. The term *cognitive underclass* is coined by Richard Herrnstein and Charles Murray in their controversial volume on race and IQ, *The Bell Curve*.

46. H. Gray, *Watching Race*, 23.

47. Peggy Phelan, *Unmarked: The Politics of Performance* (London: Routledge, 1993), 58.

48. Ibid., 59. Phelan argues that it is within the invisible where a struggle for liberation can take place. While hers is a provocative and convincing argument, it breaks down when examining beauty pageants, for it is precisely the threat of the invisible, interior qualities of the black contestant that serve to position and define blackness in terms of the representational power of whiteness.

49. Ibid.

50. *Miss or Myth*, produced by Geoffrey Dunn and Mark Schwartz (Gold Mountain Productions, 1986).

51. Ibid.

52. hooks, *Black Looks*, 63.

53. For more on this kind of "managed democracy," please see Newfield, "What Was Political Correctness?"

54. For a further discussion, see Collins, *Black Feminist Thought*. Collins claims that black people, and black women in particular, have historically been constructed as the "others" of society. In her words, "As the 'Others' of society who can never really belong, strangers threaten the moral and social order. But they are simultaneously essential for its survival because those individuals who stand at the margins of society clarify its boundaries. African-American women, by not belonging, emphasize the significance of belonging" (68). Collins observes that African American women, like other women of color, are necessary for the racial (and sexual) hierarchy to function in American society. Racial and ethnic categories like

"African American," "Asian American," and "Latino" are developed in the United States in terms of their relationship to normalized and universal whiteness. As Collins remarks, "The foundations of a complex social hierarchy become grounded in the interwoven concepts of either/or dichotomous thinking, oppositional difference, and objectification. With domination based on difference forming an essential underpinning for this entire system of thought, these concepts invariably imply relationships of superiority and inferiority, hierarchical bonds that mesh with political economics of race, gender, and class oppression"(70). These concepts of either-or dichotomous thinking and objectification serve as the foundation for the construction of blackness, so that this category becomes reified in every realm of culture, from the legal system, to the mass media, to popular culture such as film and television. The dominant position that whiteness holds in this society can sustain its dominance only in relation to difference, so it is inevitable that the spaces where identity making occurs are involved in a dual process of exploiting and containing difference. To the question of whether it makes sense for black women to compete in the pageant, we need to add: given the assumption of empowerment that accompanies visibility, is it empowering for black women to participate in the pageant? Phelan provides a compelling answer to this question: "If representational visibility equals power, then almost-naked young white women should be running Western culture." Phelan, *Unmarked*, 26.

55. Carby, *Reconstructing Womanhood*; Jacquelyn Dowd Hall, "'The Mind That Burns in Each Body': Women, Rape, and Racial Violence," in *Powers of Desire: The Politics of Sexuality*, edited by Ann Snitow, Christine Stansell, and Sharon Thompson (New York: Monthly Review Press, 1983).

56. hooks, *Black Looks*, 65–66.

57. The more accurate account is that the attempt—to be both sexual and serious—was made *on* her; she even expressed the release of the photographs in terms of rape and violation.

58. R. Cohen, "Pageant of Hypocrisy."

59. Goldsby, "Queen for 307 Days," 120.

60. Interestingly, this is the same discursive process that shaped the social construction of Clarence Thomas as a particular kind of raced being during the Hill-Thomas hearings—although with very different effects. Thomas, after vigorously (and viciously) constructing himself as an individual who "made it" without the help of affirmative action or welfare (apparently the only ways other black Americans "make it"), "played the race card" to establish himself as a victim of racial discrimination, and more specifically, the victim of a "high tech lynching." See Morrison, *Race-ing Justice, En-gendering Power*.

61. Goldsby, "Queen for 307 Days," 116.

62. Dorothy Gilliam, "A Sad Lesson," *Washington Post*, 26 July 1984.

63. I emphasize "included within" these parameters here. At no time did the pageant reorganize or restructure those barriers of femininity; rather, the parameters remained

intact and black women were admitted within them, as long as they constructed themselves according to the terms and limitations of white femininity.

64. "Black Leaders Praise Choice."

65. Gilliam, "A Sad Lesson."

66. Campbell, "A New Black Freedom." Campbell has more to say:

> Unlike Thurgood Marshall, the first black Supreme Court Justice, there was no background check of Williams. So when she took on the mantle of Miss America—unlike many other Firsts—she brought to the position a damaging flaw. It was created by an error in judgment, a human error. Williams wasn't careful. And that was her downfall. Hers alone. . . . Yet, some blacks seemingly feel themselves a part of her disgrace. Is that racial solidarity or foolishness? If blacks swell with pride at the achievement, must we then feel shame at the failure? . . . Lucy Heim, of Melbourne, Fla., the white executive director of the pageant's Brevard County Contest: "I really felt like this was the time for a young black woman. . . . She [Williams] was very charming, very aware. She deserved to win, and frankly, she blew it."

67. Goldsby, "Queen For 307 Days," 121.

68. In fact, this is the most commonly asked question whenever I discuss Vanessa Williams.

69. Gilliam, "A Sad Lesson."

70. Safire, "There She Goes."

71. Campbell, "A New Black Freedom."

72. I am indebted to Michael Schudson for directing me to this point.

73. Donald Janson, "Miss America Asked to Quit over Photos Showing Her Nude," *New York Times,* 21 July 1984.

74. Elizabeth Kastor, "Miss America Asked to Resign."

75. Safire, "There She Goes."

76. Crenshaw, "Whose Story Is It, Anyway?"

77. Ibid., 411.

78. Goldsby, "Queen for 307 Days," 117.

79. Ibid., 116.

80. Crenshaw, "Whose Story Is It, Anyway?" 403.

81. Goldsby, "Queen for 307 Days," 118.

82. Kastor, "Miss America Asked to Resign."

83. Raspberry, "Missed America."

84. Kastor, "Miss America Asked to Resign."

85. Susan Sontag, *On Photography* (New York: Anchor Books, Doubleday, 1973), 5. For more on photographic evidence, see also Marita Sturken, *Tangled Memories: The Vietnam War, the AIDS Epidemic, and the Politics of Remembering* (Berkeley: University of California Press, 1997), 21.

86. Elizabeth Kastor, "Miss America Says Photos Were Private," *Washington Post,* 23 July 1984; emphasis added.

87. Elizabeth Kastor, "Miss America Resigns amid Controversy," *Washington Post,* 24 July 1984.

88. Goldsby, "Queen for 307 Days," 119–120.

89. Richard Bernstein, *Dictatorship of Virtue: Multiculturalism and the Battle for America's Future* (New York: A. A. Knopf, 1994).

90. Crenshaw, "Whose Story Is It, Anyway?" 424.

91. Joan Wallach Scott, *Gender and the Politics of History* (New York: Columbia University Press, 1988).

CHAPTER 5. THE REPRESENTATIONAL POLITICS OF WHITENESS AND THE NATIONAL BODY

1. These are concepts that are clearly part of a process of inventing traditions. A place of ordinariness, typicality, and authenticity as these are defined by the Miss America pageant has existed for only a very privileged few. This is not to say, however, that these categories do not exist in powerful ways in the national imaginary.

2. Berlant, *Queen of America*, 13.

3. Ibid.

4. S. Dworkin, *Miss America, 1945*.

5. Ibid., 105. During this time, the pageant initiated what was to become an intimate relationship with the military—not only were photographs of the contestants sent to soldiers overseas, but Miss America and her runners-up traveled on USO tours to entertain the troops. In addition, the 1945 contestants participated in a swimsuit parade for the wounded veterans at various hospitals, a practice that continues to this day, especially with the smaller, local franchises of the Miss America pageant.

6. I am not arguing that Myerson bore the burden of this kind of displacement alone. On the contrary, at this particular historical moment, as Michael Rogin has argued, many forms of entertainment and popular culture "served the Americanization plot." Michael Rogin, *Blackface, White Noise: Jewish Immigrants in the Hollywood Melting Pot* (Berkeley: University of California Press, 1996), 62. The Miss America pageant, with its dual emphasis on respectable femininity and national identity, was one of those forms, and it found a particularly effective representative of its claims in Bess Myerson.

7. See Geoff Eley and Ronald Grigor Suny, eds., *Becoming National: A Reader* (New York: Oxford University Press, 1996); Mosse, *Nationalism and Sexuality*; and Gopal Balakrishnan, ed., *Mapping the Nation* (London: Verso, 1996).

8. Berlant, *Queen of America*, 27.

9. Eley and Suny, *Becoming National*, 27.

10. Berlant describes the National Symbolic as:

the order of discursive practices whose reign within a national space produces, and also refers to, the "law" in which the accident of birth within a geographic/political boundary transforms individuals into subjects of a collectively-held history. Its traditional icons, its metaphors, its heroes, its rituals, and its narratives, provide an alphabet for a collective consciousness or national subjectivity; through the National Symbolic the historical nation aspires to achieve the inevitability of the status of natural law, a birthright.

Lauren Berlant, *Anatomy of a National Fantasy: Hawthorne, Utopia, and Everyday Life* (Chicago: University of Chicago Press, 1991), 20.

11. Ibid.

12. Eley and Suny, *Becoming National*, 28.

13. Lisa Lowe, *Immigrant Acts: On Asian American Cultural Politics* (Durham: Duke University Press, 1996), 18.

14. George Lipsitz, "The Possessive Investment in Whiteness: Racialized Social Democracy and the 'White' Problem in American Studies," *American Quarterly* 47 (September 1995).

15. See Richard Dyer, "White," *Screen* 29 (fall 1988): 44–64; Cheryl Harris, "Whiteness as Property," *Harvard Law Review* 106 (June 1993); David R. Roediger, *The Wages of Whiteness: Race and the Making of the American Working Class* (London: Verso, 1992); Vron Ware, *Beyond the Pale: White Women, Racism, and History* (London: Verso, 1992); Eric Lott, *Love and Theft*; Ruth Frankenberg *White Women, Race Matters: The Social Construction of Whiteness* (Minneapolis: University of Minnesota Press, 1993).

16. Lipsitz, "Possessive Investment in Whiteness," 383.

17. Rogin, *Blackface, White Noise*. see also Lott, *Love and Theft*; Roediger, *Wages of Whiteness*; Lipsitz, "Possessive Investment in Whiteness."

18. Rogin, *Blackface, White Noise*, 62–63.

19. Ibid., 64.

20. Berlant, *Queen of America*, 5.

21. Ibid., 5.

22. Wiegman, *American Anatomies*.

23. "The New Face of America," *Time*, special issue, fall 1993; "What Color Is Black? What Color Is White?" *Newsweek*, 13 February 1995; Donna J. Haraway, "Universal Donors in a Vampire Culture: It's All in the Family. Biological Kinship Categories in the Twentieth-Century United States," in *Uncommon Ground: Toward Reinventing Nature*, ed. William Cronon (New York: Norton, 1995); and Evelyn Hammonds, "New Technologies of Race," in *Processed Lives: Gender and Technology in Everyday Life*, eds. Jennifer Terry and Melodie Calvert (New York: Routledge, 1997).

24. Daphne Gray, *Yes, You Can, Heather!: The Story of Heather Whitestone, Miss America 1995* (Michigan: Zondervan Publishing House, 1995).

25. D. Gray, *Yes, You Can, Heather!* 159; emphasis added.

26. Here, I do not intend to conflate a minority disability culture with a minority nonwhite culture; there are clearly differences in power relations, resources, and historical contingencies. Nonetheless, there are similarities. Perhaps one of the most significant characteristics that the deaf culture and the African American, or Latino, or Asian, cultures have in common is the way in which they are situated as part

of a dominant liberal story that is told in many ways and through many different means about what it means to be American. This story insists that citizens parcel their identities into components, so that we are all persons before we are deaf or before we are gendered or before we are raced. In that sense, the construction of Heather Whitestone's deafness as an interesting but subordinate cultural component of her identity shares characteristics with the way in which racial and ethnic cultures are positioned as peripheral to and less significant than dominant "unmarked" culture.

27. D. Gray, *Yes, You Can, Heather!* 173.

28. For more on the construction of Rodney King and his relationship to the civil uprisings in Los Angeles, see Gooding-Williams, *Reading Rodney King.*

29. "New Face of America," *Time* (fall 1993).

30. Michael B. Prince, "The Eighteenth-Century Beauty Contest," *Modern Language Quarterly* 55, no. 3 (September 1994): 315.

31. "New Face of America."

32. D. Gray, *Yes, You Can, Heather!* 214–215.

33. Personal interviews with author, 1990–1994.

34. Will, "A Kind of Compulsory Chapel," 84.

35. Dyer, "White;" Lipsitz, "Possessive Investment in Whiteness;" and Harris "Whiteness as Property."

36. Miss America pageant, 1992.

37. Wiegman, *American Anatomies,* 4.

38. Ibid., 3.

39. Lowe, *Immigrant Acts,* 3.

40. Ibid., 2.

41. Lowe makes this argument about culture in general.

42. Marita Sturken, *Tangled Memories: The Vietnam War, the AIDS Epidemic, and the Politics of Remembering* (Berkeley: University of California Press, 1997), 24.

43. Wiegman, *American Anatomies,* 5.

44. D. Gray, *Yes, You Can, Heather!* 209.

45. Ibid., 210.

46. Schapker, "Shifting 'Identity.'"

47. Ibid.

48. Neil Gotanda, "A Critique of 'Our Constitution Is Color-Blind.'" *Stanford Law Review* 44, no. 1 (1991).

49. Barbara Lippert, "Cleavages and Causes," *Glamour* (December 1994): 211.

50. Berlant, *Queen of America,* 183.

51. Robyn Wiegman has suggested that Whitestone, rather than trumping identity politics, actually creates a new kind of identity politics—that of being white. In other words, in the particular U.S. cultural climate of 1998, being white, having an identity that is about whiteness as a marked category, is in fact a new (and dangerous) realization of identity politics. Although I think that this argument is

compelling, it remains the case that whiteness continues to be an unmarked, and thus "normal," category of identity. Whitestone may be creating a new identity politics of whiteness, but she is also reaffirming the normality and necessity of being "just a person."

52. D. Gray, *Yes, You Can, Heather!* 213.

53. Deford, *There She Is.*

CHAPTER 6. INTERNATIONAL SPECTACLES, NATIONAL BORDERS

1. "Beauty on Parade against Sarajevo's Agony."

2. Bohlen, "Italians Contemplate Beauty in a Caribbean Brow."

3. Ibid.

4. In fact, one man did more than threaten; he set himself on fire and committed suicide. *ABC News*, November 1996.

5. Richard Wilk, "Introduction: Beauty Queens on the Global Stage," in *Beauty Queens on the Global Stage: Gender, Contests, and Power,* edited by Colleen Ballerino Cohen, Richard Wilk, and Beverly Stoeltje (New York: Routledge, 1996), 220.

6. Ibid., 218.

7. Telephone interview by author, Miss Universe, Inc., Los Angeles, California, 22 February 1994.

8. Anthropologist Liisa Malkki directed me to the concept of the "family of nations," which I refer to in this chapter's subtitle. See Malkki, "Citizens of Humanity." For the claim about securing a place in the family of nations by using representation of the female body to resolve nationalist tensions, see Liisa Malkki, "National Geographic: The Rooting of Peoples and the Territorialization of National Identity among Scholars and Refugees," *Cultural Anthropology* 7, no. 1 (1992): 24–44.

9. Parker et al., *Nationalisms and Sexualities,* 13–14.

10. Ibid.

11. B. Anderson, *Imagined Communities.*

12. Malkki, "Citizens of Humanity," 42.

13. Ibid., 50.

14. Ibid.

15. Malkki, "Citizens of Humanity," 51.

16. Ibid.

17. John-Thor Dahlburg, "Pageant Victories Inspire Debate over Women's Roles," *Los Angeles Times,* 25 November 1994.

18. Ibid.

19. Of course, this *is* the world as defined by the Miss World pageant.

20. Mosse, *Nationalism and Sexuality.*

21. Dahlburg, "Pageant Victories."

22. Chandra Mohanty, "Under Western Eyes: Feminist Scholarship and Colonial Discourses," in *Third World Women and the Politics of Feminism*, edited by Chandra Mohanty, Mary Russo, and Lourdes Torres (Bloomington: Indiana University Press, 1991), 51–80. She continues her analysis by examining different sites targeted by Western feminists as Third World "problem areas," such as male violence, marriage, and familial systems. Particular political, economic, and cultural conditions in the Third World are identified—and through this identification, legitimated—by Western feminists as "women's issues" deserving of attention. Western feminists automatically assume that the women who live within those conditions are "victims" of those conditions. Mohanty objects to this assumption that all Third World women are victims—of marriage in a colonial context, of sexual domination, and of particular kinship systems—precisely because the assumption solidifies and naturalizes a dichotomy between Third World women and Western women as one of victims and enlightened critics.

23. Partha Chatterjee, "Whose Imagined Community," in Balakrishnan, *Mapping the Nation*, 217.

24. Carole McGranahan, "Miss Tibet, or Tibet Misrepresented? The Trope of Woman-as-Nation in the Struggle for Tibet," in Cohen, Wilk, and Stoeltje, *Beauty Queens on the Global Stage*; emphasis added.

25. Ibid., 169.

26. Dahlburg, "Pageant Victories."

27. Arjun Appadurai, "Disjuncture and Difference in the Global Cultural Economy," *Public Culture* 2 (spring 1990): 4.

28. Appadurai, "Disjuncture and Difference."

29. Laura Mulvey, "The Spectacle Is Vulnerable: Miss World 1970," in *Visual and Other Pleasures* (Bloomington: Indiana University Press, 1989), 3.

30. The root of the word *ambassador* and the use of this particular title within the context of Miss Universe and other international pageants needs to be explored further.

31. This is not to say that the femininity produced in pageants, which claims to be "typical" or "representative" of the ideal woman—a sort of authentic femininity unmarred by the money and glamour of fashion modeling or the seduction and competition of Hollywood—does not then make grandiose identity claims in the midst of all this convention and domestication. Pageants are, of course, based upon competition among women; they claim loftier ideals than the ignoble pursuit of profit, dedicated instead to "showcasing" each contestant's personality and talent. In line with this, pageant directors commonly cheer, "Remember, you're *all* winners out there!"

32. Mulvey, "The Spectacle Is Vulnerable," 5.

33. Mosse, *Nationalism and Sexuality*, 1.

34. Ibid., 9.

35. Nora Boustany, "The Beauty Queen Exiled for a Smile," *Washington Post*, 19 May 1994.

36. Ibid.

37. Although the particular conflict involving Lebanon, Israel, and Ghada Turk took place offstage, the potential for disruption and crisis is always present on the pageant stage as well. Indeed, this is precisely what makes the pageant's claim of representing "one" world so powerful; this claim is predicated on the pageant's ability to domesticate and "resolve" any international tensions or crises through the spectacular display of national femininities.

38. Boustany, "Beauty Queen Exiled for a Smile."

39. A further example of this kind of nationalist positioning emerged in an interview with a contestant who was crowned Miss Philippines South Bay and San Diego in the early 1990s. When I asked her what it meant to be a goodwill ambassador for a beauty pageant, she replied, "Pageants help to keep parts of our culture from being forgotten." Of course, her comment—and the culture she speaks of—is embedded in a U.S. context; she and other women of Asian descent participated in the Miss Asia San Diego pageant. Kay [pseud.], interview by author, San Diego, California, 17 December 1993.

40. Boustany, "Exiled for a Smile."

41. Parker et. al., *Nationalisms and Sexualities*, 13–14.

42. Bill Keller, "Apartheid's End Transforms Beauty Show," *New York Times*, 16 September 1993. As an example of the significance South Africa places on beauty pageants, the article reads: "Few countries take beauty pageants quite as seriously as South Africa, where the mundane marital troubles of the 1974 Miss World are still copiously reported on the front pages, where a cabinet member was once rumored to have tried to fix the Miss Universe contest, and where the African National Congress briefly contemplated holding a rival pageant."

43. Ibid.

44. *Miss Universe in Peru* (Grupo Chaski Production, 1982).

45. Philip Shenon, "Where Beauty Queens Preen, No Eyesores, Please," *New York Times*, 21 August 1991.

46. William Branigin, "In Manila, the Beauty Pageant That Turned Ugly," *Washington Post*, 20 May 1994.

47. Edgardo Angara and Vicente Carlos quoted in ibid.

48. Ibid.

49. Ibid.

50. Mosse, *Nationalism and Sexuality*, 9.

51. Newfield, "What Was Political Correctness?"

52. As part of this "makeover," Trump publicly chastised a recent Miss Universe for gaining weight since the time of her crowning.

53. Shohat and Stam, *Unthinking Eurocentrism*, 238.

54. Laura Martinez-Herring cited in Lawrence H. Fuchs, *The American Kaleidoscope:*

Race, Ethnicity, and the Civic Culture (Hannover: University Press of New England, 1990), 270.

55. Her expression of gratitude for the voice lessons was reprinted from a San Antonio newspaper article in the 1989 Miss California pageant program.

56. Newfield, "What Was Political Correctness?" 322; emphasis in original.

57. Examples such as the mass media coverage of Vanessa Williams—the first African American Miss America, who was decrowned after the release of pornographic photographs—make it clear that the morality of African Americans is what determines place on the racial hierarchy. See chapter 4 for a detailed discussion of Vanessa Williams.

CONCLUSION

1. Lippert, "Cleavages and Causes," 211.

2. The fact that *Glamour* magazine produces narratives about ideal femininity does not mean that men are out of the picture; in fact, *Glamour* has many male readers, and articles are designed with both men and women in mind.

3. In the 1995 pageant the "Miss America dancers," who were all white males, performed several hip-hop numbers, and Tiffany Storm, Miss Indiana, performed a song from the film *Yentl*, "Papa Can You Hear Me." As Lippert points out, Storm's costume "brought her closer to *Oklahoma!* than a Polish shtetl." Lippert, "Cleavages and Causes," 211.

4. Ibid.

5. De Lauretis, *Technologies of Gender*, 3.

6. hooks, *Black Looks*, 25.

7. Newfield, "What Was Political Correctness?"

8. *Miss or Myth.*

9. I am indebted to Vince Rafael for his clarifying remarks about agency and what it means to imagine agency in the context of the beauty pageant.

10. De Lauretis, *Technologies of Gender*, 3.

BIBLIOGRAPHY

1982. "Miss World Losers Criticize the Winner." *Washington Post,* November 20.

1983. "Black Leaders Praise Choice of First Black Miss America." *New York Times,* September 19.

1984. "Miss America Exposed: Vanessa the Undressa." *New York Daily News,* July 21.

1988. "Contestant Disrupts Beauty Pageant." *New York Times,* June 16.

1993. "Beauty on Parade against Sarajevo's Agony." *The European,* June 3–6.

1993. "The New Face of America." *Time,* special issue, fall.

1994. "Shape Up, Miss America!" *Woman's Day,* September 1.

1995. "What Color Is Black? What Color Is White?" *Newsweek,* February 13.

Abel, Elizabeth.

1993. "Black Writing, White Reading: Race and the Politics of Feminist Interpretation." *Critical Inquiry* 19 (spring).

Agar, Michael H.

1980. *The Professional Stranger: An Informal Introduction to Ethnography.* Orlando: Academic Press.

Allen, Robert C.
1991.   *Horrible Prettiness: Burlesque and American Culture.* Chapel Hill: University of North Carolina Press.
Anderson, Benedict Richard O'G.
1983.   *Imagined Communities: Reflections on the Origin and Spread of Nationalism.* London: Verso.
Anderson, Michelle.
1988.   "Beauty Queen Says End Reign of Tiara." *Ms. Magazine* (September).
Ang, Ien.
1996.   *Living Room Wars: Rethinking Media Audiences for a Postmodern World.* London: Routledge.
Anzaldua, Gloria, ed.
1990.   *Making Face, Making Soul=Haciendo Caras: Creative and Critical Perspectives by Feminists of Color.* San Francisco: Aunt Lute Books.
Appadurai, Arjun.
1990.   "Disjuncture and Difference in the Global Cultural Economy." *Public Culture* 2 (spring).
Armstrong, Nancy, and Leonard Tennenhouse, eds.
1987.   *The Ideology of Conduct: Essays on Literature and the History of Sexuality.* New York: Methuen.
Balakrishnan, Gopal, ed.
1996.   *Mapping the Nation.* London: Verso.
Banner, Lois W.
1983.   *American Beauty.* New York: Knopf.
Bartky, Sandra Lee.
1990.   *Femininity and Domination: Studies in the Phenomenology of Oppression.* New York: Routledge.
Beauvoir, Simone de.
1989.   *The Second Sex.* Translated by H. M. Parshley. New York: Vintage Books. (Orig. 1952.)
Bellah, Robert N., Richard Madsen, William M. Sullivan, Ann Swidler, and Steve M. Tipton.
1986.   *Habits of the Heart: Individualism and Commitment in American Life.* New York: Perennial Library, Harper and Row.
Berger, John.
1972.   *Ways of Seeing.* London: British Broadcasting Corporation and Penguin Books.
Berlant, Lauren.
1991.   *Anatomy of a National Fantasy: Hawthorne, Utopia, and Everyday Life.* Chicago: University of Chicago Press.
1997.   *The Queen of America Goes to Washington City: Essays on Sex and Citizenship.* Durham: Duke University Press.

Bernstein, Richard.
    1994.   *Dictatorship of Virtue: Multiculturalism and the Battle for America's Future.* New York: A. A. Knopf.

Bodnar, John.
    1992.   *Remaking America: Public Memory, Commemoration, and Patriotism in the Twentieth Century.* Princeton: Princeton University Press.

Bohlen, Celestine.
    1996.   "Italians Contemplate Beauty in a Caribbean Brow." *New York Times,* 10 September.

Bolotin, Susan.
    1982.   "Voices from a Post-Feminist Generation." *New York Times Magazine,* October 17.

Bordo, Susan.
    1990.   "Material Girl: The Effacements of Postmodern Culture." *Michigan Quarterly Review* (fall): 653–677.
    1993.   *Unbearable Weight: Feminism, Western Culture, and the Body.* Berkeley: University of California Press.

Bordo, Susan, and Alison M. Jaggar, eds.
    1989.   *Gender/Body/Knowledge: Feminist Reconstructions of Being and Knowing.* New Brunswick, N.J.: Rutgers University Press.

Bourdieu, Pierre.
    1984.   *Distinction.* New York: Routledge and Kegan Paul.

Boustany, Nora.
    1994.   "The Beauty Queen Exiled for a Smile." *Washington Post,* May 19.

Branigin, William.
    1994.   "In Manila, the Beauty Pageant That Turned Ugly." *Washington Post,* May 20.

Burke, Kenneth.
    1979.   "Literature as Equipment for Living." In *Philosophy of Literary Form.* Berkeley: University of California Press.

Burke, Peter.
    1978.   *Popular Culture in Early Modern Europe.* New York: Harper Torchbooks.

Butler, Judith.
    1990.   *Gender Trouble: Feminism and the Subversion of Identity.* New York: Routledge.
    1992.   "Contingent Foundations: Feminism and the Question of 'Postmodernism.'" In *Feminists Theorize the Political,* edited by Judith Butler and Joan W. Scott. New York: Routledge.
    1993.   *Bodies That Matter: On the Discursive Limits of "Sex."* New York: Routledge.

1993.   "Endangered/Endangering: Schematic Racism and White Para-
          noia." In *Reading Rodney King, Reading Urban Uprising*, edited by
          Robert Gooding-Williams. New York: Routledge.
Butler, Judith, and Joan W. Scott, eds.
1992.   *Feminists Theorize the Political.* New York: Routledge.
Caldwell, John Thornton.
1995.   *Televisuality: Style, Crisis, and Authority in American Television.* New
          Jersey: Rutgers University Press.
Campbell, Bebe Moore.
1984.   "A New Black Freedom: To Fail." *Los Angeles Times,* April 29.
Canby, Vincent.
1987.   "Film: 'Miss . . . or Myth?' on Beauty Pageants." *New York Times,*
          September 16.
Carby, Hazel V.
1987.   *Reconstructing Womanhood: The Emergence of the Afro-American
          Woman Novelist.* New York: Oxford University Press.
1992.   "The Multicultural Wars." In *Black Popular Culture,* edited by Gina
          Dent. Seattle: Bay Press.
1992.   "Policing the Black Woman's Body in an Urban Context." *Critical
          Inquiry* 18 (summer).
Chapkis, Wendy.
1986.   *Beauty Secrets: Women and the Politics of Appearance.* Boston: South
          End Press.
Chira, Susan.
1983.   "To First Black Miss America, Victory Is a Means to an End." *New
          York Times,* September 19.
1984.   "First Black Miss America Finds Unforeseen Issues." *New York
          Times,* April 3.
Chodorow, Nancy.
1974.   "Family Structure and Feminine Personality." In *Women, Culture,
          and Society,* edited by Michelle Z. Rosaldo and Louise Lamphere.
          Stanford: Stanford University Press.
Clark, D. A.
1983.   "What Is Beauty Anyway?" *Matrix* (July).
Cohen, Cathy J., Kathleen B. Jones, and Joan C. Tronto, eds.
1997.   *Women Transforming Politics: An Alternative Reader.* New York: New
          York University Press.
Cohen, Colleen Ballerino, Richard Wilk, and Beverly Stoeltje, eds.
1996.   *Beauty Queens on the Global Stage: Gender, Contests, and Power.* New
          York: Routledge.
Cohen, Richard.
1984.   "Pageant of Hypocrisy." *New York Times,* July 25.

Collins, Patricia Hill.
  1991.   *Black Feminist Thought: Knowledge, Consciousness, and the Politics of
           Empowerment.* New York: Routledge.
Condit, Celeste Michelle.
  1989.   "The Rhetorical Limits of Polysemy." *Critical Studies in Mass
           Communication* 6 (June).
Cowell, Alan.
  1992.   "Adorning Apartheid's Stage." *New York Times,* December 20.
Crenshaw, Kimberlé.
  1991.   "Demarginalizing the Intersection of Race and Sex: A Black
           Feminist Critique of Antidiscrimination Doctrine, Feminist Theory,
           and Antiracist Politics." In *Feminist Legal Theory: Readings in Law
           and Gender,* edited by Katherine T. Bartlett and Rosanne Kennedy.
           Boulder: Westview Press.
  1992.   "Whose Story Is It, Anyway? Feminist and Antiracist Appropria-
           tions of Anita Hill." In *Race-ing Justice, En-gendering Power: Essays
           on Anita Hill, Clarence Thomas, and the Construction of Social Reality,*
           edited by Toni Morrison. New York: Pantheon Books.
Crenshaw, Kimberlé, Neil Gotanda, Gary Peller, and Kendall Thomas, eds.
  1995.   *Critical Race Theory: The Key Writings That Formed the Movement.*
           New York: Free Press.
Crenshaw, Kimberlé, and Gary Peller.
  1993.   "Reel Time/Real Justice." In *Reading Rodney King, Reading Urban
           Uprising,* edited by Robert Gooding-Williams. New York: Routledge.
Cumba, Ana Marie.
  1975.   *The World of Miss Universe.* New York: Manyland Books.
Dahlburg, John-Thor.
  1994.   "Pageant Victories Inspire Debate over Women's Roles." *Los Angeles
           Times,* November 25.
Davis, Kathy.
  1991.   "Remaking the She-Devil: A Critical Look at Feminist Approaches
           to Beauty." *Hypatia* 6 (spring)
  1995.   *Reshaping the Female Body: The Dilemma of Cosmetic Surgery.* New
           York: Routledge.
Davis, Susan G.
  1986.   *Parades and Power: Street Theatre in Nineteenth-Century Philadelphia.*
           Berkeley: University of California Press.
  1997.   *Spectacular Nature: Corporate Culture and the Sea World Experience.*
           Berkeley: University of California Press.
Deford, Frank.
  1978.   *There She Is: The Life and Times of Miss America.* New York:
           Penguin Books. (Orig. 1971.)

Delacoste, Frederique, and Priscilla Alexander, eds.
    1987.   *Sex Work: Writings by Women in the Sex Industry.* Pittsburgh: Cleis Press.
De Lauretis, Teresa.
    1987.   *Technologies of Gender: Essays on Theory, Film, and Fiction.* Blooming-
             ton: Indiana University Press.
De Lauretis, Teresa, ed.
    1986.   *Feminist Studies/Critical Studies.* Bloomington: Indiana University
             Press.
D'Emilio, John, and Estelle B. Freedman.
    1988.   *Intimate Matters: A History of Sexuality in America.* New York: Harper
             and Row.
Dent, Gina, ed.
    1992.   *Black Popular Culture.* Seattle: Bay Press.
Diamond, Irene, and Lee Quinby, eds.
    1988.   *Feminism and Foucault: Reflections on Resistance.* Boston: Northeast-
             ern University Press.
Dorst, John D.
    1989.   *The Written Suburb: An American Site, An Ethnographic Dilemma.*
             Philadelphia: University of Pennsylvania.
Douglas, Mary.
    1966.   *Purity and Danger: An Analysis of the Concepts of Pollution and Taboo.*
             London: Ark Paperbacks.
Dubois, Ellen Carol.
    1978.   *Feminism and Suffrage: The Emergence of the Independent Women's Move-
             ment in America, 1848–1869.* Ithaca, N.Y.: Cornell University Press.
Ducille, Ann.
    1994.   "Dyes and Dolls: Multicultural Barbie and the Merchandising of
             Difference." *Differences: A Journal of Feminist Cultural Studies* 6, no. 1.
Dworkin, Andrea.
    1981.   *Pornography: Men Possessing Women.* New York: Putnam.
Dworkin, Susan.
    1987.   *Miss America, 1945: Bess Myerson's Own Story.* New York: Newmar-
             ket Press.
Dyer, Richard.
    1986.   *Heavenly Bodies: Film Stars and Society.* New York: St. Martin's.
    1988.   "White." *Screen* 29 (fall): 44–64.
    1992.   *Only Entertainment.* New York: Routledge.
Dyson, Michael Eric.
    1993.   *Reflecting Black: African-American Cultural Criticism.* Minneapolis:
             University of Minnesota Press.
Eagleton, Terry.
    1991.   *Ideology: An Introduction.* London: Verso.

Early, Gerald.
    1994.   *The Culture of Bruising: Essays on Prizefighting, Literature, and Modern American Culture.* New York: Ecco Press.

Echols, Alice.
    1997.   "Nothing Distant about It: Women's Liberation and Sixties Radicalism." In *Women Transforming Politics: An Alternative Reader,* edited by Cathy J. Cohen, Kathleen B. Jones, and Joan C. Tronto. New York: New York University Press.

Eisenstein, Zillah.
    1979.   *Capitalist Patriarchy and the Case for Socialist Feminism.* New York: Monthly Review Press.
    1981.   *The Radical Future of Liberal Feminism.* New York: Longman.

Eley, Geoff, and Ronald Grigor Suny, eds.
    1996.   *Becoming National: A Reader.* New York: Oxford University Press.

Ellis, Kate, et al., eds.
    1988.   *Caught Looking: Feminism, Pornography, and Censorship.* Seattle: Real Comet Press.

Elshtain, Jean Bethke.
    1981.   *Public Man, Private Woman: Women in Social and Political Thought.* Princeton: Princeton University Press.

Engels, Friedrich.
    1972.   *The Origin of the Family, Private Property, and the State.* London: Penguin Books. (Orig. 1884.)

Erlanger, Steven.
    1988.   "There She Is: Valley Girl Wins the Hearts of Siam." *New York Times,* October 19.

Ewen, Stuart, and Elizabeth Ewen.
    1982.   *Channels of Desire: Mass Images and the Shaping of American Consciousness.* New York: McGraw-Hill.

Faludi, Susan.
    1991.   *Backlash: The Undeclared War against American Women.* New York: Crown.

Fein, Esther B.
    1984.   "Miss America Denies Giving Consent to Run Nude Photos." *New York Times,* July 23.
    1984.   "Miss America Gives Up Her Crown." *New York Times,* July 24.
    1984.   "Support Awaits Miss America at Home." *New York Times,* July 22.

Firestone, Shulamith.
    1970.   *The Dialectic of Sex: The Case for Feminist Revolution.* New York: Morrow.

Fiske, John.
    1989.   "Television: Polysemy and Popularity." *Critical Studies in Mass Communication* (June).

Fonow, Mary Margaret, and Judith A. Cook, eds.

  1991.   *Beyond Methodology: Feminist Scholarship as Lived Research.* Bloom-
            ington: Indiana University Press.

Forbes, Jack D.

  1992.   "The Hispanic Spin: Party Politics and Governmental Manipulation
            of Ethnic Identity." *Latin American Perspectives* 19 (fall): 59–78.

Foucault, Michel.

  1972.   *Power/Knowledge: Selected Interviews and Other Writings, 1972–1977.*
            Edited by C. Gordon. New York: Pantheon Books.

  1977.   *Discipline and Punish: The Birth of the Prison.* Translated by Alan
            Sheridan. New York: Pantheon Books.

  1978.   *The History of Sexuality.* Translated by Robert Hurley. New York:
            Pantheon.

Fox, Richard Wightman.

  1990.   "The Miss America Pageant: A Scholarship Organization." *Z
            Magazine* (December).

Fox, Richard Wightman, and T. J. Jackson Lears, eds.

  1983.   *The Culture of Consumption: Critical Essays in American History,
            1880–1980.* New York: Pantheon Books.

Frankenberg, Ruth.

  1993.   *White Women, Race Matters: The Social Construction of Whiteness.*
            Minneapolis: University of Minnesota Press.

Fraser, Nancy.

  1989.   *Unruly Practices: Power, Discourse, and Gender in Contemporary Social
            Theory.* Minneapolis: University of Minnesota Press.

Freedman, Rita.

  1986.   *Beauty Bound.* Lexington, Mass.: Lexington Books.

Friedan, Betty.

  1983.   *The Feminine Mystique.* New York: Dell. (Orig. 1963.)

  1986.   *The Second Stage.* Revised edition. New York: Summit Books.

Fuchs, Lawrence H.

  1990.   *The American Kaleidoscope: Race, Ethnicity, and the Civic Culture.*
            Hannover: University Press of New England.

Gaines, Jane, and Charlotte Herzog, eds.

  1990.   *Fabrications: Costume and the Female Body.* New York: Routledge.

Gallop, Jane.

  1988.   *Thinking through the Body.* New York: Columbia University Press.

Gans, Herbert J.

  1974.   *Popular Culture and High Culture.* New York: Basic Books.

Gates, Henry Louis, Jr., ed.

  1990.   *Reading Black, Reading Feminist: A Critical Anthology.* New York:
            Meridian, Penguin Books.

Geertz, Clifford.
    1973.   *The Interpretation of Cultures.* New York: Basic Books.
Geyer, Michael.
    1993.   "Multiculturalism and the Politics of General Education." *Critical Inquiry* 19 (spring).
Giddens, Anthony.
    1971.   *Capitalism and Modern Social Theory: An Analysis of the Writings of Marx, Durkheim, and Max Weber.* Cambridge: Cambridge University Press.
Gilliam, Dorothy.
    1984.   "A Sad Lesson." *Washington Post,* July 26.
Gilligan, Carol.
    1982.   *In a Different Voice: Psychological Theory and Women's Development.* Cambridge: Harvard University Press.
Gilroy, Paul.
    1987.   *"There Ain't No Black in the Union Jack": The Cultural Politics of Race and Nation.* Chicago: University of Chicago Press.
Gimenez, Martha E.
    1992.   "U.S. Ethnic Politics: Implications for Latin-Americans." *Latin American Perspectives* 19 (fall).
Gimenez, Martha E., Fred A. Lopez III, and Carlos Munoz Jr.
    1992.   "Introduction." *Latin American Perspectives* 19 (fall).
Glassberg, David.
    1990.   *American Historical Pageantry.* Chapel Hill: University of North Carolina Press.
Goad, Kimberly.
    1992.   "Rex Holt and Richard Guy: For the Gurus behind Guy Rex, Beauty Is Their Business." *Dallas Morning News,* August 9.
Goffman, Erving.
    1986.   *Frame Analysis: An Essay on the Organization of Experience.* Boston: Northeastern University Press. (Orig. 1974.)
Goldman, Robert, and Stephen Papson.
    1996.   *Sign Wars: The Cluttered Landscape of Advertising.* New York: Guilford Press.
Goldsby, Jackie.
    1993.   "Queen for 307 Days: Looking B(l)ack at Vanessa Williams and the Sex Wars." In *Sisters, Sexperts, and Queers: Beyond the Lesbian Nation,* edited by Arlene Stein. New York: Plume Books.
Goldstein, Kenneth S.
    1964.   *A Guide for Field Workers in Folklore.* Hatboro, Pa.: Folklore Associates.
Gooding-Williams, Robert, ed.
    1993.   *Reading Rodney King, Reading Urban Uprising.* New York: Routledge.

Goodman, Ellen.
　　1983.　　"'Because She's Black?'" *Washington Post,* September 24.
Gorman, Tom.
　　1991.　　"A Battle Plan for Spiffy Looks." *Los Angeles Times,* May 7.
Gotanda, Neil.
　　1991.　　"A Critique of 'Our Constitution Is Color-Blind.'" *Stanford Law Review* 44, no. 1: 1–68.
Gray, Daphne.
　　1995.　　*Yes, You Can, Heather!: The Story of Heather Whitestone, Miss America 1995.* Michigan: Zondervan Publishing House.
Gray, Herman.
　　1989.　　"Television, Black Americans, and the American Dream." *Critical Studies in Mass Communication* 6: 376–386.
　　1995.　　*Watching Race: Television and the Struggle for "Blackness."* Minneapolis: University of Minnesota Press.
Grossberg, Lawrence, Cary Nelson, and Paula Treichler, eds.
　　1992.　　*Cultural Studies.* New York: Routledge.
Habermas, Jurgen.
　　1989.　　*The Structural Transformation of the Public Sphere: An Inquiry into a Category of Bourgeois Society.* Translated by Thomas Burger Frederick Lawrence. Cambridge: MIT Press.
Hall, Jacquelyn Dowd.
　　1983.　　"'The Mind That Burns in Each Body': Women, Rape, and Racial Violence." In *Powers of Desire: The Politics of Sexuality,* edited by Ann Snitow, Christine Stansell, and Sharon Thompson. New York: Monthly Review Press.
Hall, John A.
　　1987.　　*Liberalism: Politics, Ideology, and the Market.* Chapel Hill: University of North Carolina Press.
Hall, Stuart.
　　1973.　　"Encoding and Decoding in the Television Discourse." Paper for the Council of Europe Colloquy on "Training in the Critical Reading of Televisual Language," Leicester, England, September.
　　1979.　　"Culture, Media, and the 'Ideological' Effect." In *Mass Communication and Society,* edited by James Curran, Michael Gurevitch, and Janet Woollacott. Beverly Hills: Sage.
　　1979.　　*Policing the Crisis.* New York: Macmillan.
　　1981.　　"Notes on Deconstructing 'the Popular.'" In *People's History and Socialist Theory,* edited by Raphael Samuel. London: Routledge and Kegan Paul.
　　1988.　　"New Ethnicities." Paper for the 1988 ICA Conference "Black Film, British Cinema," February.

1988.   "The Toad in the Garden: Thatcherism among the Theorists." In
        Marxism and the Interpretation of Culture, edited by Cary Nelson
        and Lawrence Grossberg. Chicago: University of Illinois Press.
1992.   "What Is This 'Black' in Black Popular Culture." In *Black Popular
        Culture*, edited by Gina Dent. Seattle: Bay Press.
Hall, Stuart, David Held, Don Hubert, and Kenneth Thompson, eds.
    1996.   *Modernity: An Introduction to Modern Societies*. Oxford: Blackwell
            Publishers.
Hammonds, Evelyn.
    1997.   "New Technologies of Race." In *Processed Lives: Gender and Technol-
            ogy in Everyday Life*, edited by Jennifer Terry and Melodie Calvert.
            New York: Routledge.
Haraway, Donna J.
    1991.   *Simians, Cyborgs, and Women: The Reinvention of Nature*. New York:
            Routledge.
    1995.   "Universal Donors in a Vampire Culture: It's All in the Family.
            Biological Kinship Categories in the Twentieth-Century United
            States." In *Uncommon Ground: Toward Reinventing Nature*, edited
            by William Cronon. New York: Norton.
Harding, Sandra, ed.
    1987.   *Feminism and Methodology: Social Science Issues*. Bloomington:
            Indiana University Press.
Harris, Cheryl.
    1993.   "Whiteness as Property." *Harvard Law Review* 106 (June).
Hartmann, Heidi.
    1981.   "The Unhappy Marriage of Marxism and Feminism: Toward a
            More Progressive Union." In *Women and Revolution*, edited by
            Lydia Sargent. Boston: South End Press.
Hartman, S. V., and Farah Jasmine Griffin.
    1991.   "Are You as Colored as That Negro?: The Politics of Being Seen in
            Julie Dash's *Illusions*." *Black American Literature Forum* 25 (summer).
Hartouni, Valerie.
    1991.   "Containing Women: Reproductive Discourse of the 1980s." In
            TechnoCulture, edited by Constance Penley and Andrew Ross.
            Minneapolis: University of Minnesota Press.
    1994.   "Breached Births: Reflections on Race, Gender, and Reproductive
            Discourse in the 1980s." *Configurations* 1: 73–88.
    1997.   *Cultural Conceptions: On Reproductive Technologies and the Remaking
            of Life*. Minneapolis: University of Minnesota Press.
Hartsock, Nancy C. M.
    1983.   *Money, Sex, and Power: Toward a Feminist Historical Materialism*. New
            York: Longman.

Harvey, David.
    1989.   *The Condition of Postmodernity*. Oxford: Basil Blackwell.
Hatfield, Elaine, and Susan Sprecher.
    1986.   *Mirror, Mirror . . . The Importance of Looks in Everyday Life*. Albany:
             State University of New York Press.
Haynes, Karima A.
    1994.   "Miss America from Vanessa Williams to Kimberly Aiken: Is the Crown
             a Stumbling Block or Steppingstone?" *Ebony* 3 (January): 42–46.
Hebdige, Dick.
    1979.   *Subculture: The Meaning of Style*. London: Methuen.
Hennessy, Rosemary.
    1993.   *Materialist Feminism and the Politics of Discourse*. New York:
             Routledge.
Herrnstein, Richard J., and Charles Murray.
    1994.   *The Bell Curve*. New York: Free Press.
Hobsbawm, Eric J.
    1990.   *Nations and Nationalism since 1780: Programme, Myth, Reality*.
             Cambridge, England: Cambridge University Press.
Hobsbawm, Eric J., and Terence Ranger, eds.
    1983.   *The Invention of Tradition*. Cambridge, England: Cambridge Univer-
             sity Press.
Hochschild, Arlie R.
    1983.   *The Managed Heart: Commercialization of Human Feeling*. Berkeley:
             University of California Press.
Holland, Dorothy C., and Margaret A. Eisenhart.
    1990.   *Educated in Romance: Women, Achievement, and College Culture*.
             Chicago: University of Chicago Press.
hooks, bell.
    1992.   *Black Looks: Race and Representation*. Boston: South End Press.
Horkheimer, Max, and Theodor Adorno.
    1972.   *The Dialectic of Enlightenment*. Translated by John Cummings. New
             York: Seabury Press.
In These Times.
    1988.   September 7–13.
Ives, Edward D.
    1974.   *The Tape-Recorded Interview: A Manual for Field Workers in Folklore
             and Oral History*. Knoxville: University of Tennessee Press.
Jacobus, Mary, Evelyn Fox Keller, and Sally Shuttleworth, eds.
    1990.   *Body/Politics: Women and the Discourses of Science*. New York:
             Routledge.
Janson, Donald.
    1984.   "Miss America Asked to Quit over Photos Showing Her Nude."
             New York Times, July 21.

Jeffords, Susan.

    1994.   *Hard Bodies: Hollywood Masculinity in the Reagan Era*. New Jersey: Rutgers University Press.

Jewell, K. Sue.

    1993.   *From Mammy to Miss America and Beyond: Cultural Images and the Shaping of U.S. Social Policy*. London: Routledge.

Jhally, Sut, and Justin Lewis, eds.

    1992.   *Enlightened Racism:* The Cosby Show, *Audiences, and the Myth of the American Dream*. Boulder, Colo.: Westview Press.

Kammen, Michael.

    1993.   *Mystic Chords of Memory: The Transformation of Tradition in American Culture*. New York: Vintage Books.

Kastor, Elizabeth.

    1984.   "Miss America Asked to Resign: Pageant Officials Act after Learning of Nude Photos." *Washington Post*, July 21.

    1984.   "Miss America Resigns amid Controversy." *Washington Post*, July 24.

    1984.   "Miss America Says Photos Were Private." *Washington Post*, July 23.

Keller, Bill.

    1993.   "Apartheid's End Transforms Beauty Show." *New York Times*, September 16.

Kennedy, J. Michael.

    1994.   "Collapse of Pageant Takes Dreams with It." *Los Angeles Times*, April 25.

Kerber, Linda.

    1980.   *Women of the Republic: Intellect and Ideology in Revolutionary America*. Chapel Hill: University of North Carolina Press.

Kerr, Peter.

    1984.   "Penthouse Says Nude Photos Are Those of Miss America." *New York Times*, July 20.

Kron, Joan.

    1991.   "When Beauty Was a Duty: Fashion in Wartime." *New York Times*, February 8.

Lakoff, Robin T., and Raquel L. Scherr.

    1984.   *Face Value: The Politics of Beauty*. Boston: Routledge and Kegan Paul.

Laqueur, Thomas.

    1990.   *Making Sex: Body and Gender from the Greeks to Freud*. Cambridge: Harvard University Press.

Larsen, Nella.

    1929.   *Passing*. Salem: Ayer Company.

Lau, Angela.

    1990.   "North County Woman Wins Miss California Crown on Fourth Try." *San Diego Union-Tribune*, June 11.

Lazar, Carol.

    1993.   "They're All out of This World!" *Sunday Tribune,* November 14.

Limbaugh, Rush.

    1992.   *The Way Things Ought to Be.* New York: Pocket Books.

Lippert, Barbara.

    1994.   "Cleavages and Causes." *Glamour* (December).

Lipsitz, George.

    1990.   *Time Passages: Collective Memory and American Popular Culture.* Minneapolis: University of Minnesota Press.

    1994.   *Dangerous Crossroads: Popular Music, Postmodernism, and the Poetics of Place.* New York: Verso.

    1995.   "The Possessive Investment in Whiteness: Racialized Social Democracy and the 'White' Problem in American Studies." *American Quarterly* 47 (September).

Locke, John.

    1982.   *Second Treatise of Government.* Arlington Heights: Harlan Davidson.

Lord, Shirley.

    1986.   "Everybody's All American." *Vogue* (September).

Lorde, Audre.

    1984.   "The Master's Tools Will Never Dismantle the Master's House." In *Sister Outsider.* New York: Crossing Press.

Lott, Eric.

    1992.   "Love and Theft: The Racial Unconscious of Blackface Minstrelsy." *Representations* 39 (summer).

    1993.   *Love and Theft: Blackface Minstrelsy and the American Working Class.* New York: Oxford University Press.

Lowe, Lisa.

    1996.   *Immigrant Acts: On Asian American Cultural Politics.* Durham: Duke University Press.

Lowenstein, Leo.

    1961.   *Literature, Popular Culture, and Society.* New Jersey: Prentice-Hall.

Lubiano, Wahneema.

    1992.   "Black Ladies, Welfare Queens, and State Minstrels: Ideological War by Narrative Means." In *Race-ing Justice, En-gendering Power: Essays on Anita Hill, Clarence Thomas, and the Construction of Social Reality,* edited by Toni Morrison. New York: Pantheon Books.

MacAloon, John J.

    1982.   "Double Visions: Olympic Games and American Culture." *Kenyon Review* 4 (winter).

    1984.   "La Pitada Olimpica: Puerto Rico, International Sport, and the Constitution of Politics." In *Text, Play, Story: Proceedings of the American*

Ethnography Society, edited by E. Bruner. Washington, D.C.: American Ethnography Society.

MacFadden, Bernarr.

1901.   *The Power and Beauty of Superb Womanhood: How They Are Lost and How They May Be Regained and Developed to the Highest Degree of Attainable Perfection.* New York: Physical Culture Publishing.

MacKinnon, Catharine.

1983.   "Feminism, Marxism, Method, and the State: Toward a Feminist Jurisprudence." *Signs: Journal of Women in Culture and Society* 8.

1987.   *Feminism Unmodified: Discourses on Life and Law.* Cambridge: Harvard University Press.

1989.   *Toward a Feminist Theory of the State.* Cambridge: Harvard University Press.

Malkki, Liisa.

1992.   "National Geographic: The Rooting of Peoples and the Territorialization of National Identity among Scholars and Refugees." *Cultural Anthropology* 7, no. 1: 24–44.

1994.   "Citizens of Humanity: Internationalism and the Imagined Community of Nations." *Diaspora* 3, no. 1: 41–68.

Mann, Judy.

1984.   "Sleaze." *Washington Post,* July 25.

Margolick, David.

1984.   "Miss America Case: Claims Conflict." *New York Times,* July 24.

Marin, Rick.

1993.   "Ms. America: Making Over an Icon Very, Very Carefully." *New York Times,* September 13.

Martin, Emily.

1987.   *The Women in the Body: A Cultural Analysis of Reproduction.* Boston: Beacon Press.

Martin, Nancie S.

1985.   *Miss America through the Looking Glass: The Story behind the Scenes.* New York: Messner Books.

Marx, Karl.

1978.   "The Communist Manifesto." In *The Marx-Engels Reader,* edited by Robert C. Tucker. New York: Norton.

1978.   "The German Ideology." In *The Marx-Engels Reader,* edited by Robert C. Tucker. New York: Norton.

May, Elaine Tyler.

1988.   *Homeward Bound: American Families in the Cold War Era.* New York: Basic Books, Harper Collins.

McCorkle, Rob. "The Powers behind the Miss USA Throne." *El Paso Times.*

McRobbie, Angela.
    1994.   *Postmodernism and Popular Culture*. London: Routledge.
Michaels, Walter Benn.
    1992.   "Race into Culture: A Critical Genealogy of Cultural Identity."
             Critical Inquiry 18 (summer): 655–685.
Mill, John Stuart.
    1975.   *On Liberty*. New York: W. W. Norton.
Minh-ha, Trinh T.
    1989.   *Woman, Native, Other: Writing Postcoloniality and Feminism*. Bloom-
             ington: Indiana University Press.
Miss or Myth.
    1986.   Produced by Geoffrey Dunn and Mark Schwartz. Gold Mountain
             Productions.
Miss Universe in Peru.
    1982.   Grupo Chaski Production.
Modleski, Tania.
    1991.   *Feminism without Women: Culture and Criticism in a "Postfeminist"*
             Age. New York: Routledge.
Mohanty, Chandra.
    1991.   "Under Western Eyes: Feminist Scholarship and Colonial Dis-
             courses." In *Third World Women and the Politics of Feminism*, edited
             by Chandra Mohanty, Mary Russo, and Lourdes Torres. Blooming-
             ton: Indiana University Press.
Moon, Michael, and Cathy N. Davidson, eds.
    1995.   *Subjects and Citizens: Nation, Race, and Gender from* Oroonoko *to*
             Anita Hill. Durham: Duke University Press.
Moore, Sally Falk, and Barbara G. Myerhoff, eds.
    1975.   *Symbol and Politics in Communal Ideology: Cases and Questions*. Ithaca:
             Cornell University Press.
Moraga, Cherrie.
    1983.   *Loving in the War Years: lo que nunca paso por sus labios*. Boston: South
             End Press.
    1986.   "From a Long Line of Vendidas: Chicanas and Feminism." In
             Feminist Studies/Critical Studies, edited by Teresa de Lauretis.
             Bloomington: Indiana University Press.
Moraga, Cherrie, and Gloria Anzaldua, eds.
    1981.   *This Bridge Called My Back: Writings by Radical Women of Color*. New
             York: Kitchen Table, Women of Color Press.
Morgan, Kathryn Pauly.
    1991.   "Women and the Knife: Cosmetic Surgery and the Colonization
             of Women's Bodies." *Hypatia* 6 (fall): 25–53.
Morganthau, Tom.
    1995.   "What Color Is Black?" *Newsweek* (February 13): 63–69.

Morrison, Toni.

    1970.   *The Bluest Eye*. New York: Pocket Books.

    1992.   *Playing in the Dark: Whiteness and the Literary Imagination*. New York: Vintage Books.

Morrison, Toni, ed.

    1992.   *Race-ing Justice, En-gendering Power: Essays on Anita Hill, Clarence Thomas, and the Construction of Social Reality*. New York: Pantheon Books.

Morrison, Toni, and Claudia Brodsky Lacour, eds.

    1997.   *Birth of a Nation'hood: Gaze, Script, and Spectacle in the OJ Simpson Case*. New York: Pantheon Books.

Mosse, George L.

    1975.   *The Nationalization of the Masses: Political Symbolism and Mass Movements in Germany from the Napoleonic Wars through the Third Reich*. Ithaca: Cornell University Press.

    1985.   *Nationalism and Sexuality: Middle-Class Morality and Sexual Norms in Modern Europe*. Madison: University of Wisconsin Press.

Mulvey, Laura.

    1989.   *Visual and Other Pleasures*. Bloomington: Indiana University Press.

Nelson, Katherine.

    1979.   "Social Cognition in a Script Framework." In *Social Cognitive Development: Frontiers and Possible Futures*, edited by John H. Flavell and Lee Ross. Cambridge: Cambridge University Press.

Neuharth, Al.

    1989.   "Feminists Who Bash Bimbos are Bumbos." *USA Today*, September 15.

Newfield, Christopher.

    1993.   "What Was Political Correctness? Race, the Right, and Managerial Democracy in the Humanities." *Critical Inquiry* 19 (winter): 308–336.

Nicholson, Linda J., ed.

    1990.   *Feminism/Postmodernism*. New York: Routledge.

Okerblom, Jim.

    1994.   "Sexist or Sexy—It's Traditional." *San Diego Union-Tribune*, July 30.

Okerblom, Jim, and Lisa Petrillo.

    1987.   "First Black Named Miss California." *San Diego Union-Tribune*, June 16.

Olsen, Frances.

    1991.   "Statutory Rape: A Feminist Critique of Rights Analysis." In *Feminist Legal Theory: Readings in Law and Gender*. Boulder: Westview Press.

Omi, Michael, and Howard Winant.

    1994.   *Racial Formation in the United States from the 1960s to the 1990s*. Second edition. New York: Routledge.

Paglia, Camille.

    1990.   *Sexual Personae: Art and Decadence from Nefertiti to Emily Dickinson*. New Haven: Yale University Press.

Painter, Nell Irvin.
    1992.   "Hill, Thomas, and the Use of Racial Stereotype." In *Race-ing Justice, En-gendering Power: Essays on Anita Hill, Clarence Thomas, and the Construction of Social Reality*, edited by Toni Morrison. New York: Pantheon Books.

Parker, Andrew, Mary Russo, Doris Sommer, and Patricia Yaeger, eds.
    1992.   *Nationalisms and Sexualities*. New York: Routledge.

Peiss, Kathy.
    1986.   *Cheap Amusements: Working Women and Leisure in Turn-of-the-Century New York*. Philadelphia: Temple University Press.
    1990.   "Making Faces: The Cosmetics Industry and the Cultural Construction of Gender, 1890–1930." *Genders* 7 (spring): 143–169.

Phelan, Peggy.
    1993.   *Unmarked: The Politics of Performance*. London: Routledge.

Prince, Michael B.
    1994.   "The Eighteenth-Century Beauty Contest." *Modern Language Quarterly* 55, no. 3 (September): 253–279.

Probyn, Espeth.
    1993.   *Sexing the Self: Gendered Positions in Cultural Studies*. London: Routledge.

Pugh, Clifford.
    1989.   "Queen Makers." In the *Miss California Pageant* program.

Quintanilla, Michael.
    1989.   "Beauty and the Beast: Glamour Groomers Turn Women into Miss USAs." *El Paso Times Herald*.

Rabinow, Paul, ed.
    1984.   *The Foucault Reader*. New York: Pantheon Books.

Radner, Hilary.
    1995.   *Shopping Around: Feminine Culture and the Pursuit of Pleasure*. New York: Routledge.

Radway, Janice.
    1984.   *Reading the Romance: Women, Patriarchy, and Popular Literature*. Chapel Hill: University of North Carolina Press.
    1990.   "The Scandal of the Middlebrow, the Book-of-the-Month Club, Class Fracture, and Cultural Authority." *South Atlantic Quarterly* 89, no. 4 (fall).
    1994.   "On the Gender of the Middlebrow Consumer and the Threat of the Culturally Fraudulent Female." *South Atlantic Quarterly* 93, no. 4 (fall).

Rafael, Vincente.
    1993.   *Contracting Colonialism: Translation and Christian Conversion in Tagalog Society under Early Spanish Rule*. Durham: Duke University Press.
    1993.   "White Love: Surveillance and Nationalist Resistance in the U.S.

Colonization of the Philippines." In *Cultures of U.S. Imperialism*, edited by Amy Kaplan and Donald E. Pease. Durham: Duke University Press.

Rapping, Elayne.
1994.   *Media-tions: Forays into the Culture and Gender Wars.* Boston: South End Press.

Raspberry, William.
1984.   "Missed America." *Washington Post*, July 23.

Reed, Adolph, Jr.
1996.   "The Fiction of Race: Skin Deep." *Village Voice*, 24 September.

Reed, Joseph Hansen, and Evelyn Reed.
1986.   *Cosmetics, Fashions, and the Exploitation of Women.* New York: Pathfinder Press.

Rich, Cynthia.
1988.   "Ageism and the Politics of Beauty." *Sojourner: The Women's Forum* (May).

Riggs, Marlon.
1992.   "Unleash the Queen." In *Black Popular Culture*, edited by Gina Dent. Seattle: Bay Press.

Riverol, A. R.
1992.   *Live from Atlantic City: The History of the Miss America Pageant before, after, and in Spite of Television.* Bowling Green, Ohio: Bowling Green State University Popular Press.

Rodriguez, America.
1993.   "Made in the U.S.A.: The Constructions of Univision News." Ph.D. diss., University of California, San Diego.

Rodriguez, Patricia.
1993.   "An Inner Beauty Pageant—in Texas." *San Francisco Chronicle*, August 15.

Roediger, David R.
1991.   *The Wages of Whiteness: Race and the Making of the American Working Class.* London: Verso.

Rogin, Michael.
1996.   *Blackface, White Noise: Jewish Immigrants in the Hollywood Melting Pot.* Berkeley: University of California Press.

Roiphe, Katie.
1993.   *The Morning After: Sex, Fear, and Feminism on Campus.* Boston: Little, Brown, and Company.

Romo, Mary.
1986.   "'Take Your Business off Our Backs.'" *Highlander* 5 (April 23).

Rosenthal, Elisabeth.
1991.   "Ethnic Ideals: Rethinking Plastic Surgery." *New York Times*, September 25.

Ross, Andrew.
    1989.   *No Respect: Intellectuals and Popular Culture.* New York: Routledge.
Rousseau, Jean-Jacques.
    1967.   *The Social Contract and Discourse on the Origin of Inequality.* Edited
             by Lester G. Crocker. New York: Penguin Books. (Orig. 1755 and
             1762.)
Rowbotham, Sheila.
    1977.   *Woman's Consciousness, Man's World.* New York: Penguin Books.
             (Orig. 1973.)
Rubin, Gayle.
    1975.   "The Traffic in Women: Notes on the 'Political Economy' of Sex."
             In *Toward an Anthropology of Women,* edited by Rayna Reiter. New
             York: Monthly Review Press.
Rubin, Joan Shelley.
    1992.   *The Making of Middlebrow Culture.* Chapel Hill: University of North
             Carolina Press.
Russell, Kathy, Midge Wilson, and Ronald Hall.
    1992.   *The Color Complex: The Politics of Skin Color among African Americans.*
             New York: Doubleday.
Safire, William.
    1984.   "There She Goes . . ." *New York Times,* July 23.
Sargent, Lydia, ed.
    1981.   *Women and Revolution.* Boston: South End Press.
Sawicki, Jana.
    1988.   "Identity Politics and Sexual Freedom: Foucault and Feminism."
             In *Feminism and Foucault: Reflections on Resistance,* edited by Irene
             Diamond and Lee Quinby. Boston: Northeastern University
             Press.
    1991.   *Disciplining Foucault: Feminism, Power, and the Body.* New York:
             Routledge.
Saxton, Alexander.
    1990.   *The Rise and Fall of the White Republic: Class Politics and Mass Culture
             in Nineteenth-Century America.* London: Verso.
Sayles, Genie Polo.
    1990.   *How to Win Pageants.* Plano, Tex.: Wordware Publishing.
Schapker, Alison.
    1996.   "Shifting 'Identity': Paul Gilroy's *The Black Atlantic* and Questions
             of Modern Subjectivity." Unpublished paper, University of Califor-
             nia, San Diego.
Schudson, Michael.
    1986.   *Advertising, the Uneasy Persuasion: Its Dubious Impact on American
             Society.* New York: Basic Books.

Schultz, April.
    1991.   "'The Pride of the Race Had Been Touched': The 1925 Norse-American Immigration Centennial and Ethnic Identity." *The Journal of American History* (March).

Scott, Joan Wallach.
    1988.   *Gender and the Politics of History.* New York: Columbia University Press.
    1992.   "Experience." In *Feminists Theorize the Political,* edited by Judith Butler and Joan W. Scott. New York: Routledge.

Shenon, Philip.
    1991.   "Where Beauty Queens Preen, No Eyesores, Please." *New York Times,* August 21.

Shohat, Ella, and Robert Stam.
    1994.   *Unthinking Eurocentrism: Multiculturalism and the Media.* New York: Routledge.

Simonton, Ann.
    1983.   "Theatre Until We're Free." *Matrix* (May).
    1988.   "Turn These Shows Off; They Degrade Us All." *USA Today,* September 9.

Skeggs, Beverley.
    1997.   *Formations of Class and Gender.* London: Sage Publications.

Sklar, Katherine Kish.
    1973.   *Catharine Beecher: A Study in American Domesticity.* New Haven: Yale University Press.

Smith, Valerie.
    1990.   "Split Affinities: The Case of Interracial Rape." In *Conflicts in Feminism,* edited by Marianne Hirsch and Evelyn Fox Keller. New York: Routledge.

Snitow, Ann, Christine Stansell, and Sharon Thompson, eds.
    1983.   *Powers of Desire: The Politics of Sexuality.* New York: Monthly Review Press.

Sontag, Susan.
    1977.   *On Photography.* New York: Anchor Books, Doubleday.

Stannard, Claire.
    1987.   "At the Movies with Queens of Protests." *Kinesis* (October).

Stansell, Christine.
    1987.   *City of Women: Sex and Class in New York, 1789–1860.* Urbana: University of Illinois Press.

Stein, Arlene, ed.
    1993.   *Sisters, Sexperts, and Queers: Beyond the Lesbian Nation.* New York: Plume Books.

Stein, Jeannine.
    1993.   "Dreams Fit for a Queen." *Los Angeles Times,* December 15.

Steinem, Gloria.
    1992.   *The Revolution Within: A Book of Self-Esteem.* Boston: Little, Brown,
         and Company.
Sturken, Marita.
    1997.   *Tangled Memories: The Vietnam War, the AIDS Epidemic, and the
         Politics of Remembering.* Berkeley: University of California Press.
"A Symposium on Popular Culture and Political Correctness."
    1993.   *Social Text* N36 (fall).
Szekely, Eva.
    1988.   *Never Too Thin.* Toronto, Ontario: Women's Press.
Tadiar, Neferti Xina M.
    1993.   "Sexual Economies in the Asia-Pacific Community." In *What Is in
         a Rim?: Critical Perspectives on the Pacific Region Idea.* Boulder:
         Westview Press.
Time.
    1993.   Special issue, fall.
Trebbe, Ann, and Valerie Heimbreck.
    1989.   "'Ideal' Is Body Beautiful and 'Clean Cut.'" *USA Today,* Septem-
         ber 15.
Trescott, Jacqueline.
    1983.   "Her Crowning Achievement. Vanessa Williams: A New Voice for
         Miss America." *Washington Post,* September 20.
    1983.   "Miss America's Winning Ways: Vanessa Williams Breaks One
         Racial Barrier." *Washington Post,* September 19.
Turner, Bryan S.
    1984.   *The Body and Society: Explorations in Social Theory.* New York: Basil
         Blackwell.
Turner, Victor.
    1982.   *Celebration: Studies in Festivity and Ritual.* Washington, D.C.:
         Smithsonian Institution Press.
Urla, Jacqueline, and Alan C. Swedlund.
    1995.   "The Anthropometry of Barbie." In *Deviant Bodies: Critical Perspec-
         tives on Difference in Science and Popular Culture.* Bloomington:
         Indiana University Press.
Vance, Carole S., ed.
    1989.   *Pleasure and Danger: Exploring Female Sexuality.* London: Pandora Press.
Wallace, Michele.
    1990.   *Invisibility Blues: From Pop to Theory.* London: Verso.
Ware, Vron.
    1992.   *Beyond the Pale: White Women, Racism, and History.* London: Verso.
Westbrook, Robert.
    1990.   "'I Want a Girl, Just Like the Girl That Married Harry James':

American Women and the Problem of Political Obligation in
World War II." *American Quarterly* 42 (December): 587–614.

Wiegman, Robyn.

1995.   *American Anatomies: Theorizing Race and Gender*. Durham: Duke
University Press.

Wilk, Richard.

1996.   "Introduction: Beauty Queens on the Global Stage." In *Beauty
Queens on the Global Stage: Gender, Contests, and Power*, edited by
Colleen Ballerino Cohen, Richard Wilk, and Beverly Stoeltje. New
York: Routledge.

Will, George F.

1994.   "A Kind of Compulsory Chapel: Multiculturalism Is a Campaign
to Lower America's Moral Status." *Newsweek*, November 14.

Williams, Linda.

1989.   *Hardcore: Power, Pleasure, and the Frenzy of the Visible*. Berkeley:
University of California Press.

Williams, Patricia J.

1991.   *The Alchemy of Race and Rights: Diary of a Law Professor*. Cambridge:
Harvard University Press.

Williams, Raymond.

1981.   *The Sociology of Culture*. New York: Schocken Books.

Willis, Susan.

1991.   *A Primer for Everyday Life*. New York: Routledge.

Wilson, Chris.

1983.   "The Rhetoric of Consumption: Mass-Market Magazines and
the Demise of the Gentle Reader, 1880–1920." In *The Culture of
Consumption: Critical Essays in American History, 1880–1980*, edited
by Richard Wightman Fox and T. J. Jackson Lears. New York:
Pantheon Books.

Wolcott, James.

1995.   "Beyond the Values of the Supervixens." *New Yorker Magazine*,
February 13.

Wolf, Naomi.

1991.   *The Beauty Myth: How Images of Beauty Are Used against Women*.
New York: W. Morrow.

Wollstonecraft, Mary.

1985.   *Vindication of the Rights of Women*. London: Penguin Classics.
(Orig. 1792.)

INDEX

abortion, in issue platform, 124

academia, popular culture research in, 4–6, 10, 210

ADL (Anti-Defamation League), 163

Adorno, Theodor, 212n9

affirmative action: argument against, 175, 176; as context, 132–33

African Americans: assimilation, 162; constraints on, 116–19, 226n31; constructed as others, 230–31n54; double exclusion of female, 151–52; "First," 126, 128, 129, 228n19, 232n66; as Miss Americas, 28, 123–25; pageant history and, 127; respectability and, 85–86, 131–32, 138, 141–42; solidarity as, 144–45; stereotypes of, 119–20, 125–26, 129, 138; talent competition and, 115–17, 118–20; television's representation of, 225–26n15; "types" of, 135–37. *See also* race; Williams, Vanessa

African National Congress, 198, 238n42

agency: definition of, 95; disciplinary rituals of beauty as, 17, 24; power and, 11; self-construction and, 93, 208–10. *See also* independence; subjectivity

AIDS, in issue platform, 205, 225n11

Aiken, Kimberly, pl6, 124–25

alcohol, 38–39, 79–80

Allen, Robert, 38

ambassadors: concept of, 203–4, 237n30, 238n39; contestants as, 193, 196–97

Americanism: definition of, 103–6; management of, 161–64, 233n6; whiteness as, 160–61

Anderson, Benedict, 6–7, 165

Angara, Edgardo, 200

Anti-Defamation League (ADL), 163

apartheid, 197–98, 238n42

Appadurai, Arjun, 190–91

appearance: evaluation of, 75; model of romance and, 224n59. *See also* beauty; cosmetics; female body; weight

Arnold, Matthew, 108–9

Atlantic City, first pageant at, 34, 35–37

audience: for bikini contests, 83–84; for blackface minstrelsy, 115, 120, 212–13n11; for international pageants, 184; for local and regional pageants, 50, 87–88; as respectable spectator, 80; size of, 1, 40–41,

audience *(continued)*
42, 206; voting by, 59–60. *See also* middlebrow culture
authenticity: celebration of, 154; interview
competition and, 104, 106; swimsuit competition and, 81–84; talent competition
and, 116–18, 119
autobiography, role of, 25

balkanization, use of term, 19
Banks, Tyra, 20
Banner, Lois, 33–34
Barbie dolls, 42, 63, 228n13
Barnum, P. T., 34
Bartel, Jean, 41
Bartky, Sandra Lee, 11, 67, 221–22n14
bathing suits, use of term, 40. *See also*
swimsuits
beauty: vs. brain, 61; construction of, 33–34;
definitions of, 9, 54–55, 68–70, 127, 207;
disciplinary rituals of, 16–17, 64–74;
evaluation of, 31, 33; inner and outer,
68–69, 70–72, 129–30; politics and, 10–11,
195–98
beauty pageants: for children, 1–2, 32; class-
based view of, 38–40, 41–42, 81–84; coherence of national body and, 173–75,
179–80; concept of, 31–33, 237n31; critique
of, 3, 8, 32, 42, 59–61, 91, 95–96, 184, 200,
221n4; differences among, 40, 44–47, 48–49,
80–84, 90; feminist debate on, 10–13, 210;
identity and representation in, 1–3, 172,
176–77; imagined community of, 6–7;
"indigenized forces" in, 190–91; multiple
meanings of, 3–6, 8–9, 77, 207; oppositional
politics in, 85–86; ordinariness of, 192–94;
origin of, 33–35; as performance and resolution of identity crisis, 7–10, 18, 21, 150–
52, 158–60, 177–80, 205–8, 233n6; political
context of, 21–25; potential for disruption
of, 238n37; protests of, 1, 10–11, 182–84,
190, 192, 193–94, 221n4, 227–28n10; theme
of, 24; use of term, 69–70. *See also* beauty;
contestants; directors; international pageants; queens; sponsors; *specific pageants
(e.g., Miss America pageant)*
Belafonte, Shari, 135
Benetton Clothing Company, 19–20, 216n39
Berlant, Lauren: on *Forrest Gump*, 178; on
National Symbolic, 159, 233–34n10; on
public sphere, 165; on valuing of cultural
sites, 4–5, 154
Betbeze, Yolande, 44, 221n6
Bhatia, Deepa, 187
bikini contests, 80–84, 224n59
bilingualism, issue of, 203–4

biographical profile, requirements for, 28
blackface minstrelsy, audience for, 115, 120,
212–13n11
Blanchard, Nina, 83
body. *See* female body
Bordo, Susan: on body and control, 68, 76;
on disciplinary beauty rituals, 16–17; on
ideal femininity, 73, 86; on power and
agency, 11
Bosnia and Hercegovina, pageant in, 182,
183, 211n3
Bourdieu, Pierre, 108
Brotherhood Campaigns (ADL), 163
burlesque industry, 38, 223n50
Bush, Barbara, 43
Butler, Judith, 11, 89–90

Campbell, Bebe Moore, 228n19, 232n66
Carby, Hazel V., 19, 20–21
career goals: different pageants and, 83;
as evidence of middle-class status, 74;
expressed in interview, 93–97
Carlos, Vicente, 200
Cartwright, Lisa, 212–13n11
Catalina Swimsuits (company), 42, 43, 221n6
Chaipel, Tom, 149
chaperones (hostessing system), 39–40
charity work, 33, 154. *See also* issue platform
Charles, Suzette, 124, 141, 145
Chatterjee, Partha, 188, 189
Cheer (product), sponsorship by, 47
Chevalier, Maurice, 34
Chevrolet (company), 47
children, rules against contestants with, 51
Children Having Children (organization),
98–99
children's beauty pageants, 1–2, 32
Chinese Communist Party, 189
Chisholm, Shirley, 143–44
Christy, Howard Chandler, 36, 55
cigarettes, ads for, 25
cities and towns, contestants as representatives of, 79–80, 101–2, 217n16. *See also*
community; Miss Mission Beach pageant;
Miss San Diego pageant
citizens: constitution of, 174–75; definition of,
203; imagination of, 154–55
citizenship: expanded, 8–9; "management"
of, 7, 202–4; national culture's shaping
of, 174–75; national discourse and, 159–
60, 165; nationalism and respectability in,
194; in self-construction, 208, 210. *See also*
democracy
civil rights movement: argument against,
175; as context, 134, 143–44
Clairol Corporation, 47

Clinton, Hillary, 102
cognitive underclass, use of term, 138, 230n45
Cohen, Richard, 142
Collins, Patricia Hill, 230–31n54
"color-blind" society, 177. *See also* multiculturalism; race
comedy act, in talent competition, 114–15
commodity culture: concept of, 109; as context for popular culture, 5–6, 173–75; diversity in, 19–21, 78, 129–31, 135–37; ethnic identity in, 105, 175; female body in, 11, 34–35, 45, 59–62, 67–68, 74, 77, 222n59; femininity in, 186–87; gender in, 63–64; identity issues negotiated in, 2–3, 63; local pageants and, 52–53; vs. material realities, 198–200; pageant's authenticity and, 81–84; pageant's link to, 34–35, 199; sexualization of difference in, 141–45; Williams's crowning linked to, 126–31. *See also* beauty; beauty pageants; femininity
community: defined in residency requirements, 52–53; imagined, 6–7, 165, 188–89, 198, 201
condom, use of term, 205, 225n11
Coney Island: beauty pageant for, 40, 217n16; competition for, 34
contestants: age of, 36, 40; ambition of, 51–52, 95; categorization of, 85–86; class of girl desired as, 38–40, 41–42, 81–84; consolation for, 55; as consumer group, 223n38; feminist influences on, 24–25, 88, 208–10; focus of, 50–51; humiliation of, 61–62, 65–66; on ideal qualities, 68–69; liberation/disciplining of, 204; marital status of, 36, 40, 51, 83, 223n53; motives of, 17, 22–25, 209–10; number of, 35, 36; as objects, 32–33; on pageants' differences, 45–46; perspective of, 3, 14–16, 215nn21–22; as political subjects, 96; in racial and class terms, 77–78, 127; racism of, 127; as representatives, 40, 79–80, 101–2, 190, 217n16; researcher's relation to, 18, 215nn21–22, 225nn9–10; rules for, 38–40, 51–52; seminars for, 71, 222–23n37; stereotypes of, 91; on swimsuit competition, 59, 60–61; tourism's link to, 192–93; unmarked status of, 209; Williams's resignation and, 124–25. *See also* autobiography; biographical profile; career goals; desire; education; female body; femininity; independence; issue platform; Miss America; pleasure; role models; voice
Corcoran, Eddie, 37
Cornett, Leanza, 60, 61, 225n11
Cosby, Bill, 126, 229n30

The Cosby Show (television program), 225–26n15, 229n30
cosmetics, diversity and, 20
cosmetic surgery, 22–23
cover story: competitive ambition effaced by, 51–52; concept of, 228–29n25; racial identity effaced by, 130–31
crave, use of term, 135, 229n35
Crenshaw, Kimberlé, 146, 151–52
crossovers, contestants as, 46
crown-chasing, use of term, 52
cult of true womanhood, 85
culture: acquisition of, 108–12, 120–21; black female body as, 140–41; constructed in entertainment, 173–75, 179–80; heroes in, 102–3; talent competition as demonstration of, 90, 106–8, 110–12, 120–22; valuing of normal, national, 4–5, 154, 159. *See also* commodity culture; popular culture
culture industry, use of term, 212n9
current events: avoiding mention of, 99–100; knowledge of, 98–99, 225n10

dance, choices in, pl5, 113–14, 117–20, 172–73, 179. *See also* music
Davis, Kathy, 22, 24, 215n20
Davis, Susan, 212–13n11
deafness: approach to, 167–68, 173; legitimated by whiteness, 168–69; of Miss America winner, pl9, 29, 155–56, 166; nonwhite minorities compared to, 234–35n26; self-representation and, 175–79
deep acting, concept of, 225n8
Deford, Frank, 3, 36, 47, 54, 219n43
de Lauretis, Teresa, 11, 15, 207, 209
democracy: emphasis on, 110–12; "managerial," 128–29, 151–52, 201. *See also* liberal politics
desire: appeal to male, 149; appropriate communication of, 80–81; exoticism and respectability in, 192–93; experience of, 12; expressed in interview, 93; mobilization of, 126–27. *See also* sexuality
difference: constructed in frame of whiteness, 128–31, 230–31n54; domestication of, 106, 195–96, 199, 202, 238n37; effaced in self-representation, 177–78, 208; exoticized/eroticized, 104, 116, 117–18, 131–32, 135, 141–42; irrelevance of, 166–71; neutralization of, 186–87; as opportunity, 170–71, 175–79; performance and resolution of, 7–10, 18, 21, 150–52, 158–60, 179–80, 233n6; political debates on, 2; recognition of, 19–21, 128, 177–78; sexualization of, 141–45; sisterhood and, 124–26; talent competition and, 115–17; as threat to national

difference *(continued)*
  identity, 18–21, 29, 127–31, 150–52, 170;
    uncolored in Williams's reign, 131–37;
    utopian fantasies of, 166; visuality of
    television and, 171–75. *See also* deafness;
    diversity; ethnic identity; multicultural-
    ism; race
DiMaggio, Paul, 108
directors: advice from, 87–88, 114–15; on
    black contestants, 140; on Williams, 146,
    232n66. *See also* Slaughter, Lenora
disability. *See* deafness
Disneyworld, 185
diversity: bounded by whiteness, 128–31;
    in commodity culture, 19–21, 78, 129–31,
    135–37; individualism's relation to, 23–
    25, 78; in international pageants, 185–86;
    language of, 20–21, 29; performance of,
    104, 124–29, 137–41, 145, 151–52, 207–8;
    tensions of, 135; as threat to national
    identity, 18–21, 29, 127–31, 150–52, 170;
    uncolored in Williams's reign, 131–37;
    utopian fantasies of, 166. *See also* differ-
    ence; multiculturalism
Ducille, Ann, 228n13
Dworkin, Susan, 39, 217n16
Dyer, Richard, 170
Dyson, Michael Eric, 212–13n11, 228n13

Ebony (magazine), on pageant, 124–25
Echols, Alice, 10
economic development, pageants' link to,
    191–92, 200
education: assimilation through, 162–63;
    commitment to, 69–70, 99–100, 103; culture
    gained through, 108–12, 120–21; emphasis
    on, 45–46, 49, 65, 110, 193; pageant's role
    in nation's, 112–13. *See also* scholarships
Eisenhart, Margaret A., 224n59
entertainment: Americanization through,
    161–63, 233n6; cultural construction in,
    173–75, 179–80; judges from field of, 53–54;
    pageants as, 32–33, 46–47; respectability
    balanced with, 41; as venue for national
    identity, 172. *See also* talent competition;
    televised coverage of pageants
environmental issues, appropriateness of, 99
Equal Rights Amendment, 124
Esprit Corporation, 20
ethnic identity: assimilation and, 161–65;
    commodification of, 105, 175; constitution
    of, 212–13n11; domestication of, 202–3;
    effaced, 18–19, 78–79, 151, 207; exoticized/
    eroticized, 116, 117–18, 120; international
    context of, 181; national identity and, 6–7,
    9–10, 18–19, 103–4; pageant focused on, 93;

vs. race, 118–19; sexuality's link to, 28, 105–
    6; talent competition and, 116, 117–20. *See
    also* Myerson, Bess
evening gown competition: cost of gowns
    for, 48; example of, pl6; in first pageant, 36;
    judging of, 54–55, 56; role of, 43, 74, 88

family: commitment to, 103; constructing
    personhood and, 229n31; questions and
    answers on, 97
fashion models vs. contestants, 193
Federated Women's Clubs of New Jersey, 39
fees. *See* sponsors
female body: construction of, 24–25, 72–73,
    183; cultural representation of, 20–23;
    domestication of, 193–94; ideal, 63–65, 68,
    72–73, 80, 221n3; implications of nonwhite,
    9, 20–21; as intelligible and useful, 76–77,
    79–80; as national body, 157–60, 170–80,
    173–75, 197–98, 204; objectification and
    commodification of, 11, 34–35, 45, 59–62,
    67–68, 74, 77, 222n59; sexualization of,
    79–80, 141–42, 221n4; as site of pleasure,
    24; as site of trangression vs. stability,
    201–2; as spectacle, 89; as victim, 11–15;
    whiteness as framework for, 128–41, 207,
    231–32n63. *See also* difference; femininity;
    sexuality
femininity: black women included in, 143–
    45; commodification of, 186–87; construc-
    tion of, 8–9, 11, 23–25, 61, 63, 151–52, 202–
    4; contestants as models of, 101–3, 107,
    192–93, 206–7; as context for constructing
    self, 92–93; definitions of, 6–7, 9–12, 131–
    32, 166–67, 189–90, 193; disciplinary prac-
    tices of, 14–15, 57, 61, 64–74, 80, 84–86, 162–
    63, 188, 207; hybridization of, 202–4; ideal
    representatives of, 28–29, 42, 45, 51, 62–65,
    221n3; in international pageants, 186–90,
    202–4; national identity and, 6–10; non-
    Western, 188–90; physical fitness embedded
    in, 59; production of, 11–17; reassurance of
    traditional, 74–86; refined performance of,
    112–13; scoring of, 53–56; surveillance of,
    38–40; typicality and respectability as com-
    ponents of, 32, 194; Victorian conventions
    of, 33–35, 37; wartime construction of,
    157–58; white norms of, 131–37, 207, 231–
    32n63. *See also* female body; global fem-
    inine; independence; individualism
feminism: evidenced in pageant, 24–25, 88,
    208–10; femininity and sexuality defined
    by, 188, 237n22; language of, 16, 170; volun-
    tarism and, 43; Williams's resignation and,
    124, 146–47. *See also* feminist critique; inde-
    pendence; voice

feminist critique: of beauty and representation, 10–13, 210; counter-critique of, 13, 22,
24; of "gender by addition," 152; media's
gloss on, 16–17; methodological implications of, 14–15; on pageant as harmful, 3, 8,
32, 42, 59, 184, 200, 221n4; of pornography,
146–48; role of, 24–25
festivals, as precursors to beauty pageants,
33–34
Fitch Shampoo Company, 42
Flagg, James Montgomery, 36, 55
Forrest Gump (film), 178–79
Foucault, Michel: on body and power, 58, 64,
76, 79, 204; on discipline, 194, 215n23
Fox, Richard Wightman, 122
France, female symbols of, 158, 213–14n13
Frankfurt School, 5
Fuentes, Daisy, 20

gender: ambivalence about, 206–7, 209;
commodification of, 63–64; construction
of, 11–13, 15, 89–92, 205–6, 209; fragmentation and, 75–76; identity crisis and, 177–
78, 205–7; in national identity, 3, 7–10, 107,
121–22, 127–28, 159–61, 209; oppressive
norms of, 10–11; performative theory of,
11–13, 89–90; as representation and self-
representation, 22, 101–2; talent competition and, 112, 115; theoretical approach
to, 4–5, 13–18. See also ethnic identity;
femininity; masculinity; men; race; social
class; women
Germany, female symbols of, 158, 213–14n13
Gifford, Kathie Lee, 43, 173
Gilliam, Dorothy, 145
girls, use of term, 222n19
Glamour (magazine), on ambivalence about
gender, 206, 239n2
global feminine, concept of, 185–86
global order: cultural imperialism in, 190–
91, 199, 201; "family of nations" in, 185–
87, 195, 196, 198–204, 236n8; pageants
as celebrations of, 185–86, 188
Godshall, Harry, 36
Goldman, Robert, 57
Goldsby, Jackie: on race, 142; on Williams,
134, 144, 147, 148, 149–50
Gorman, Margaret, 36
Gotanda, Neil, 177
Gray, Daphne (Whitestone's mother), 166,
167–68, 176
Gray, Herman, 125, 138, 229n30
Great Depression, 217–18n21, 218n22, 219n50
Gregory, Judith, 220n58
Grupo Chaski (filmmakers' union), 198–99
Guccione, Robert, 141–42, 145, 148

Hall, Stuart, 15, 212–13n11
Harris, Cheryl, 170
Harvel Watches, 42
Haughey, Lex Ann, 66–67
Heim, Lucy, 232n66
Hemingway, Ernest, 102–3
Herrnstein, Richard, 230n45
heterosexuality: commitment to, 103, 192–93;
disruption of, 28, 149–50; in swimsuit com-
petition, 74; white norms of, 154; woman
as representative of, 158–59; women
objectified in, 67–68
Hill, Anita, 146, 147, 231n60
Hobsbawm, Eric, 214n14
Hochschild, Arlie, 222n22, 225n8
Holiday Inn (Lhasa), Miss Tibet pageant
at, 189
Holland, Dorothy C., 224n59
Holland, Tara Dawn, pl10
homophobia, as context, 147–50
hooks, bell, 140, 141, 208
Hooks, Benjamin, 124
Hope, Bob, 193–94
Horkheimer, Max, 212n9
hostessing system, development of, 39–40
Hotelmen's Association (Atlantic City), 35
Houston, Whitney, 116–20, 226n31
Huffington, Arianna, 23

icons, race-transcending, 126, 228n13
identity. See ethnic identity; national identity;
race; individual identity
identity politics: concept of, 19–21; as context,
133–34; crisis of, 7–10, 18, 21, 150–52, 158–
60, 177–80, 205–8, 233n6; denial of, 155–56;
influence of, 176; labels and, 170–71; whiteness as category in, 235–36n51
ideology: of assimilation, 161–65; in legal
system, 224n61; on natural ability vs.
talent, 119–21, 227n37; popular culture
and, 4–7; public/private and, 165–66; of
visible/invisible, 139, 230n48; whiteness
as, 160–61. See also identity politics; liberal
politics
Indecent Exposure (film), 224n59
independence: contestants as models of,
101–3; emphasis on, 88; evidenced in
interview, 74, 94; increased for women,
35. See also voice
India: country pageant in, 29; international
pageant winners from, 186–90; threat to,
183. See also Miss World pageant
individual identity: construction and performance of, 89–93, 96, 105–6, 208; gender's role in, 101–2; issue of choice in,
135, 229n35; political debates and, 2–3;

individual *(continued)*
    racism located in, 171. *See also* self-
    representation
individualism: approach to, 23; commitment
    to, 103, 106, 166–67, 169–70; diversity's
    relation to, 23–24, 78; emphasis on, 25, 88,
    111–12, 136–37, 151–52, 209; vs. homoge-
    nization, 78–79; possibility in, 175–79; vs.
    representation, 143–45; used to deny itself,
    210; white norms of, 132–34, 160–61. *See
    also* democracy
inner beauty, use of term, 68–69, 70–72,
    129–30
international pageants: containment via,
    201–2; context of, 181–86; cultural impe-
    rialism and, 188, 190–91; as cultural pro-
    ductions, 204; femininity constructed in,
    186–90, 202–4; nationalist/political ten-
    sions in, 195–202; respectability and, 192–
    94; sites for, 198–202; tourism's link to, 191–
    93, 198–200. *See also* Miss Universe pageant;
    Miss World pageant
interview competition: communication skills
    in, 93–95; description of, 27; establishment
    of, 91; judging of, 54–55, 56; political frame-
    work of, 92, 95–97, 99–101; presentation
    goals in, 223n53; questions and answers in,
    95–106, 225n7, 225n9; rehearsals for, 87–89,
    96–99, 225n9; rehearsed spontaneity in, 90,
    92, 94–98, 121; role of, 43, 74, 88–90, 106;
    self and identity constructed in, 89–93, 96,
    105–6; tips on, 87, 98–99, 121. *See also* inde-
    pendence; issue platform; subjectivity
Irish heritage, pageant focused on, 93
Israel, contestants from, 195–97, 200–201
issue platform: avoiding mention of sex
    in, 98–99, 205, 225n11; concept of, 43;
    examples of, pl3, 124; mocking of, 115;
    politics in, 43, 98–100, 218–19n42; role
    models in, 102–3; role of, 27, 154
Italy, pageant in, 182, 183, 211n3

Jackson, Jesse, 20
Jaycees (Junior Chambers of Commerce), 42,
    50, 54, 219n52
Jennings, Peter, 1, 182–83
Jewish Americans, 162–64. *See also* Myerson,
    Bess
Jhally, Sut, 225–26n15
Johnson, Deborah, 139–40
Jones, Grace, 135
Jordan, Michael, 228n13
Joseph Bancroft and Sons Company, 42
judges: certification of, 55; construction of
    body hidden from, 71–74; expectations
    of, 75, 115; of first pageant, 36; motivations

of, 178; on national identity, 182; occupa-
    tions of, 36, 53–54, 182; process for, 54–56,
    58, 60, 77–79; surveillance by, 67–68; on
    Williams's winning, 134
Junior Chambers of Commerce (Jaycees), 42,
    50, 54, 219n52
Junior Miss pageants, 60, 84

Kauffman, Erika, pl2
King, Rodney, 168

Lacour, Claudia Brodsky, 228n13
ladies, use of term, 222n19
Lahoud, Nasri, 196
Latinas, as Miss USA, 203
law: ideology in, 224n61; national identity
    and, 160
Lebanon, contestant from, 195–98
Lebowitz, Fran, 1
Left, pageants critiqued by, 22
lesbianism: fear of, 147–50; race's relation
    to, 28, 142, 147
Levine, Lawrence, 108
Lewis, Justin, 225–26n15
liberal politics: diversity in, 138–39, 208;
    equal opportunity in, 166–67, 169–71;
    heroes in, 102–3; interview competition
    and, 92, 95–97, 103; minorities in, 234–
    35n26; multicul-turalism and, 104–5, 145,
    150–52; pageant's construction of, 186, 207;
    in STARS program, 176; talent competi-
    tion and, 173–75; whiteness in, 160–61.
    See also individualism; personhood
Limbaugh, Rush, 21
Lippert, Barbara, 178, 206, 239n3
Lipsitz, George, 116, 118, 160, 170
localism, international context of, 181
Lott, Eric, 115, 119, 120, 212–13n11
Lowe, Lisa, 159, 174, 235n41
Lowenstein, Leo, 212n9
Lubiano, Wahneema, 130

MacFadden, Bernarr, 75
Machado, Alicia, 66, 222n23
Madison Square Gardens, Inc., 46, 202,
    219n50
Makibaka (feminist group), 200
Malkki, Liisa, 185, 186, 236n8
Marcos, Imelda, 199–200
Marks, Albert, 134, 147
Marshall, Thurgood, 232n66
Martin, Nancie, 64
Martinez-Herring, Laura, 203
masculinity, construction of, 6
mass media: culture's redefinitions and, 108;
    diversity and, 20–21; feminism in, 16–17;

idealized femininity in, 8; identity and, 89–90; on Indian women, 186–87; masculinity in, 6; pageants critiqued in, 32–33; on Whitestone, 178; on Williams, 123–24, 131–37, 145, 148–49. *See also* televised coverage of pageants

maternity: eliminated as talent, 120–21; woman's and nation's link to, 158–59

Mattel Toy Corporation, 42

May Day celebrations, 33–34

McGranahan, Carole, 189

men: assets of, 65; Jaycees as ideal, 42; as judges, 54; magazine's inclusion of, 239n2; masculinity and, 6; national identity's link to, 158–59; panoptical surveillance by, 67–68; performance of nation's functions by, 112; regulations against contact with, 39, 40; stereotypes of, 83

Mendez, Denny, 182

Mercer, Jacque, 219n43

Mercer, Kobena, 212–13n11

Meseke, Marilyn, 40–41

methodology (research): dilemma of, 13–18; implications of, 29–30; interviews in, 215nn21–22; participant-observer status in, 225nn9–10

middlebrow culture: adherence to, 119–20; challenges to, 114–15; concept of, 108–9, 120; construction of space in, 109–10; embodiment of, 112–13; pageants as, 107–11

military, pageant's link to, 157–58, 160, 163, 195–96, 233n5

Minnelli, Liza, 116–17, 120

minorities, approach to, 234–35n26. *See also* African Americans; deafness; multiculturalism; race; women of color

Miss Alabama. *See* Whitestone, Heather

Miss America: as collective national body, 179–80; as national representative, 7–10, 21, 31, 56, 126–27, 142–45, 152, 156, 158–60, 163–66, 183–90, 194, 195–99, 202, 233n6; as "new Eve," 169; as public figure during reign, pl3, 43, 163; shifting expectations of, 25. *See also* contestants; role models; scholarships; *specific winners*

Miss American Co-Ed pageant, 48, 82

Miss America pageant: ambivalence about gender and, 206–7; critique of, 32–33, 37–38, 42, 59, 110, 122; current status of, 42–43; description of, 25–26, 56–57; history of, 33–35, 37, 127, 217–18n21, 218n22; hosts of, 43; legal status of, 41, 47–49; male dancers in, 239n3; as middlebrow culture, 107–11; multiple meanings of, 3, 5, 32–33, 85–86, 122; name of, 2, 6, 8, 36, 41, 222n32;

political economic context of, 46–47, 126–31; politics of whiteness in, 153–56, 164–66; respectability sought by, 35–42, 57, 80–81, 107, 221n6; rhetorical strategies of, 155–56, 170–71; rules for, 38–39; as utopian fantasy, 154–55, 166. *See also* audience; contestants; evening gown competition; interview competition; judges; scholarships; sponsors; swimsuit competition; talent competition; televised coverage of pageants

Miss America pageant (local or regional): description of, 50; disciplinary practices and, 64; judges for, 54; number of, 49; production of, 50–51; rehearsals for, 98–99; rules for, 51–53, 80–81; sponsors of, 50, 52–53, 219n52; swimsuit competition in, 61–62, 67–68, 73–74. *See also* Miss San Diego pageant

Miss America pageant (state): description of, 50; number of, 49; regional identities and, 160; rules for, 51–52; scholarships for, 219n49. *See also* Miss California pageant

Miss America pageant (1921): description of, 35–37; location of, 34, 35

Miss America pageant (1923), judges for, 55–56

Miss America pageant (1935): class of girl in, 38; talent competition in, 218n30

Miss America pageant (1938): popularity of, 40–41; talent competition in, 40

Miss America pageant, for 1940, incorporation and, 41

Miss America pageant, for 1943, tour following, 41

Miss America pageant, for 1945: changes in, 156–57; contestants' bodies in, 157–58, 160. *See also* Myerson, Bess

Miss America pageant, for 1951, swimsuits and, 44

Miss America pageant, for 1954, as first televised, 172

Miss America pageant, in 1968, feminist protest of, 10–11, 221n4

Miss America pageant, for 1984. *See* Charles, Suzette; Williams, Vanessa

Miss America pageant, for 1990, winner of, 124

Miss America pageant, for 1991, interview question in, 104, 106

Miss America pageant, for 1992, contestants in, 170–71

Miss America pageant, for 1993, winner of, 60, 61, 225n11

Miss America pageant, for 1994, winner of, pl6, 124–25

Miss America pageant, for 1995, television's

Miss America pageant *(continued)*
impact on, 171–75. *See also* Whitestone,
Heather
Miss America pageant, for 1996, winner
of, pl3
Miss America pageant, for 1998: contestants
in, pl1; issue platform in, 205, 225n11;
talent competition in, 113; winner of, pl10
Miss America pageant, for 1999, talent com-
petition in, 239n3
Miss America Program, Inc. *See* Miss America
pageant
Miss America Scholarship Program. *See* Miss
America pageant; scholarships
Miss Asia San Diego pageant, 238n39
Miss Black America, 139
Miss Budweiser, 31
Miss California pageant: contestants in,
139–41; eligibility for, 50; judges from,
54; protests of, 221n4, 227–28n10
Miss Colleen pageant, ethnic focus of, 93
Miss Coney Island, 40, 217n16
Miss Deaf Alabama, 167
Miss Florida, pl5
Miss Hawaii, pl2
Miss India pageant, femininity constructed
in, 29
Miss Italy pageant, national identity and,
182, 183, 211n3
Miss Mission Beach pageant, as bikini
contest, 83–84
Miss New York (1991), authenticity of, 104,
106
Miss North Carolina, pl4
Miss Philippines South Bay and San Diego,
238n39
Miss San Diego County Teen (1993), 67
Miss San Diego pageant: judges for, 54;
"pageant family" and, 219n46; production
of, 50–51; rules for, 51–52
Miss Sarajevo under Siege Competition,
significance of, 182, 183, 211n3
Miss South Africa, 197–98
Miss South Carolina, pl6
Miss Texas pageant, weight regulations of,
66–67
Miss Tibet pageant: femininity constructed
in, 29; nationalist claims in, 189
Miss Tulip, 31
Miss Universe in Peru (film), 198–99
Miss Universe pageant: Americanization of,
191; contestants in, 192–93, 204; context
of, 184–86; establishment of, 44; femininity
constructed in, 29, 186–90, 202–4; franchises
of, 191; material realities juxtaposed to, 198–
200; owner of, 46, 191, 202, 222n23; polit-

ical tensions in, 200–202; respectability
in, 192–94; sites for, 198–202; sponsor of,
221n6; tourism's link to, 191–92; weight
gain and, 66, 222n23. *See also specific country's pageants (e.g., Miss USA pageant)*
Miss USA pageant: as beauty contest, 44,
221n6; cash and prizes in, 45, 81, 223–
24n57; franchises of, 31; interview segments of, 46, 102–3; judging of, 56, 220n68;
organization of, 219n54; political economic
context of, 46–47; winner of, 203
Miss World pageant: Americanization of,
191; contestants in, 182, 192–93; context of,
184–86, 236n19; femininity constructed in,
29, 186–90; franchises of, 182–83; political
tensions in, 195–98; protests of, 1, 182–84,
190, 192, 193–94
Mofokeng, Palesa Jacqui, 197–98
Mohanty, Chandra, 237n22
morality: racial coding of, 85–86, 138, 141–
42; in (re)producing pageant, 38; swimsuit
competition linked to, 79; women as guardians of, 34
morals: crisis of, 19; emphasis on particular,
51–52, 57, 83–84; evidence of restraint in,
68–69, 70–71, 74, 75–76, 79–80; pageant's
role in building, 81–82
Morrison, Toni, 228n13
Mosse, George, 187, 194, 195, 201, 213–14n13
Movietone News, on Miss America pageant, 40
Moyers, Bill, 229n30
multiculturalism: computer-morphed
representations of, 168–69; dilution of,
103–6; liberal politics and, 104–5, 145,
150–52; marketing of, 127–28, 228n13;
pageant's claim of, 78–79, 118–19, 208;
political debates on, 18–21, 29, 175; as
threat to national identity, 18–21, 29, 127–
31, 150–52, 170; whiteness normalized in,
154; women of color as evidence of, 104,
124–29, 137–41, 145, 151–52, 207–8. *See also*
difference; diversity; ethnic identity; race
Mulvey, Laura, 192, 193–94
Murray, Charles, 230n45
music, choices in, pl3, 113–20, 172, 226n31,
239n3. *See also* dance
Myerson, Bess: assimilation and, 161–65;
crowning of, pl8; as ideal of femininity,
28–29, 165–66; as Jewish American, 29,
155–58; on rules, 40

NAACP (National Association for the Ad-
vancement of Colored People), 124, 143
nation: approach to, 188, 214n14; construction of, 185; domestication of, 203; as

imagined, 213–14n13; "legitimation ad" for ideal, 57; non-Western construction of, 188–90; pageant's role in educating, 112–13; political space of, 159, 184; uncoloring of, 131–37; utopian fantasies of, 154–55, 166; woman as representative of, 7–10, 21, 31, 56, 126–27, 142–45, 152, 156, 158–60, 163–66, 183–90, 194, 195–99, 202, 233n6. *See also* global order

national identity: beauty pageants as performance and resolution of crisis in, 7–10, 18, 21, 150–52, 158–60, 179–80, 205–8, 233n6; construction of, 103–8; construction of women's, 63–64, 89–90, 121–22, 189–90; femininity and, 6–10; festivals' role in, 34; international context of, 182–86; management of, 185; masculine terms for, 6; multiculturalism as threat in, 18–21, 29, 127–31, 150–52, 170; redefinitions of, 125–26; stabilization of, 22; venues for production of, 158–59, 233–34n10; visual regimes for, 164–66, 172–73. *See also* difference; ethnic identity; gender; international pageants; race; social class; whiteness

nationalism: definitions of, 184–85, 195, 214n14; discourses on, 198–202; identity constructions in, 7–9; international context of, 181, 185–86; respectability and, 194, 201; sexuality's relation to, 187–90, 194, 195, 201–2, 213–14n13. *See also* national identity

National Symbolic, concept of, 159, 233–34n10

Neuman, Christy, pl5

Newfield, Christopher, 18, 128, 201, 203

New Jersey State Senate, Miss America's address to, pl3

Nogic, Imela, 182

Noonan, Peggy, 23

nudity: class-based construction of, 83; rules banning, 51, 81; Williams's photos and, 124, 148–49

objectivity, pageant structured in, 77–78. *See also* judges

Olympic Games, 185

ordinariness, construction of, 192–94

Oscar Awards, 178

"pageant family," use of term, 45, 219n46

Paglia, Camille, 13, 24

Papson, Stephen, 57

parades, pageants and, 57, 233n5

Paris, myth of, 33

Parker, Andrew, 184

Parks, Bert, 43

Pauley, Jane, 100

Penthouse (magazine): feminist critique of, 146; mass media on, 145; Williams's photos in, 28, 124, 131, 141–45, 147–50

people, use of term, 170

personality, evaluation of, 31, 75

personhood: affirmation of, 235–36n51; concept of, 133–34, 177; construction of, 135–36, 229n31; rhetoric of, 170–71, 208; used to deny itself, 210. *See also* individualism; self; subjectivity

Peru: Miss Universe pageant in, 198–99; pageant franchise in, 191

Phelan, Peggy, 138–39, 230n48, 230–31n54

Philbin, Regis, 43, 173

Philippine Commission on Human Rights, 200

Philippine House of Representatives, 200–201

Philippines: Miss Universe pageant in, 199–201; pageant franchise in, 191; pageant winner from, 238n39

Phillips, Adrian, 39

photographic contests, of beauty, 34

physical fitness: competition for, 25; definition of, 59

pinups, research on, 6

pleasure: body as site for, 24; of power, 22; in production of femininity, 12

pluralism. *See* difference; diversity; multiculturalism

poise, evaluation of, 31, 75

politeness, as code of femininity, 80

politics: of beauty, 10–11, 195–98; heroes defined in, 102–3; of interview competition, 92, 95–97, 99–101; of issue platform, 43, 98–100, 218–19n42; in pageants' context, 21–25; of race, 125–31, 139–41. *See also* identity politics; Left; liberal politics; multiculturalism; Right

popular culture: Americanization through, 161–63, 233n6; assimilation and difference in, 150–52; attitudes toward research on, 4–6, 10, 210; in commodity culture, 5–6, 173–75; multiculturalism as threat in, 19–21; respectability and, 107; talent competition's link to, 107, 110–11; whiteness as marker in, 128–31, 160–61. *See also* beauty pageants; entertainment; mass media; middlebrow culture

Porat, Tamara, 195–97

pornography: patriarchal framework of, 149–50; women's organization against, 146–48. *See also Penthouse* (magazine)

postfeminism, 12–13, 24–25, 30

power: agency and, 11; dissociated from body, 76; exclusion through integra-

power *(continued)*
tionism, 203; feminine exercise of, 23–
25, 210; pleasure of, 22; theoretical approach to, 13–18; visibility and, 230–
31n54. *See also* femininity, disciplinary
practices of
Pretty Woman (film), 224n59
Prince, Michael, 169
prostitution, 39, 83–84
public speaking skills, 93–95
purity, reclaimed, 178–79

Queen Latifah, 20
queens: crowning of, 31; duties of, 94,
219n56; implications of, 216n4; Miss
America differentiated from, 43; as role
models, 101–3; selection of, 33–34, 69;
weight gain by, 66–67, 222n23, 238n52.
See also specific women

race: blackface minstrelsy and, 212–13n11;
definitions of, 139; discourse on, 150–52;
effaced by pageant, 18–19, 128–31, 138–
40, 151–52, 177, 209; vs. ethnicity, 118–19;
homogenized by pageant, 74–75, 78–79,
85–86, 207; multiculturalism as code word
for, 19; in national identity, 8–10, 63, 103–
4, 107, 121–22, 127–28, 151–52, 206, 211n3;
natural ability and, 119–21, 227n37; pageant focused on, 139; politics of, 125–31,
139–41; representation and, 18–21, 28–29,
142–45; respectability and, 85–86, 131–32,
138, 141–42; sexuality's link to, 28, 105–6,
131–32, 138, 140–52; talent competition
and, 27–28, 115–20; uncolored in Williams's
reign, 131–37. *See also* African Americans;
apartheid; ethnic identity; gender; social
class; whiteness
racism: of contestants, 127; denial of, 145–46;
institutionalization of, 139–41, 143; integrationism and, 203; interview question on,
104, 171; targets of, 162, 163–64
Radway, Janice, 108, 109, 212–13n11
Rafael, Vince, 239n9
Rainbow Coalition, 20
Ramsey, Jon-Benet, 1–2, 32
reading, as social event, 212–13n11
Reaganism, racial politics of, 125–27
Reed, Adolph, Jr., 118
representation: appearance of, 149–50; complexity on national scale, 101–2; experience
and, 15–16; of female body, 20–23; feminist
critique of, 10–13; vs. individualism, 143–
45; race and, 18–21, 28–29, 142–45; rule on
state, 40, 217n16; sexual surveillance and,

79–80. *See also* self-representation; televised
coverage of pageants
respectability: challenge to pageant's, 147–
48; disruption of, 195–98; entertainment
balanced with, 41; institutionalization of,
194, 195; nationalism and sexuality linked
to, 187–90, 194, 195, 201–2, 213–14n13;
nonprofit status and, 47; pageant's desire
for, 35–42, 57, 80–81, 107, 221n6; performance of, 190, 192–94; race and, 85–86,
131–32, 138, 141–42; talent performances
constrained by, 114–15. *See also* sexuality
rhetoric: of "free choice," 16–17; of pageant,
155–56, 170–71; of personhood, 170–71, 208
Riggs, Marlon, 212–13n11
Right: on multiculturalism, 19–20; pageants
critiqued by, 22; racial politics of, 125–27
Riverol, A. R., 37
Robinson, Jackie, 124
Rockwell, Norman, 36, 55
Rogin, Michael, 161, 162, 233n6
Roiphe, Katie, 13, 24
role models: African Americans as, 123–24;
function of, 101–3, 193; Jewish American
as, 163
romance, model of, 224n59
Rose, Tricia, 212–13n11
Rosie the Riveter, 157
Ross, Andrew, 111–12, 113
Rubin, Gayle, 77, 223n56
Rubin, Joan, 108
Russo, Mary, 184

Safire, William, 145
San Diego (Calif.). *See* Miss San Diego
pageant
Sandy Valley Grocery Company, 42
Sarajevo, pageant in, 182, 183, 211n3
Sayles, Genie Polo: on swimsuit competition,
64–65, 73; on talent competition, 111, 113–
14, 119
scholarships: vs. beauty, 61; emphasis on, 33,
45–46, 49, 65, 81, 110; establishment of, 41–
42, 156–57; as legitimate money, 81–85, 223–
24n57; program for, 31
Schudson, Michael, 232n72
Scott, Joan Wallach, 15–16, 17–18
self: agency and, 93, 208–10; body linked to,
222n16; components allowed in, 143, 146;
construction and performance of, 89–93,
96, 105–6; control of, 68–69; desirable type
of, 103–4; emphasis on, 88. *See also* individualism; self-image; self-representation;
subjectivity
self-care, use of term, 65, 222n16

self-image, dissatisfaction with, 16–17
self-representation: difference effaced in,
    177–78, 208; feminism in, 24–25; gender
    and, 22, 101–2; identity formulated in,
    176–77. *See also* representation; self
self-respect, use of term, 65, 222n16
Sen, Sushmita, 189–90
sexual exploitation, as trope in narratives
    on Williams, 146–47, 149
sexuality: avoiding mention of, 98–99, 205,
    225n11; constructed in whiteness, 143,
    147–48; contradictions in, 142; definitions
    of, 184–85, 188, 189–90, 195, 237n22; narra-
    tives of black women's, 28, 131–32, 138,
    140–52; nationalism's relation to, 187–90,
    194, 195, 201–2, 213–14n13; pageant's use
    of, 75; race and ethnicity filtered through,
    28, 105–6; restraint of, 68–69, 70–71, 74,
    75–76, 79–86, 142; rules related to, 39, 40,
    51. *See also* heterosexuality; lesbianism;
    nudity
Shinde, Katherine, pl10
Shohat, Ella, 202
sign language, pl9, 167. *See also* deafness
Simonton, Ann, 208, 221n4, 227–28n10
Simpson, O. J., 228n13
Skeggs, Beverley, 41
Slater, Kelly, 70
Slaton, Karen, 67
Slaughter, Lenora: directorship of, 37–38, 56,
    57; respectability emphasized by, 38–40,
    44, 47; on scholarships, 41–42
Smith, Shawntel, pl3
social class: acquisition of culture removed
    from, 110–12; career goals as evidence of,
    74; display of body constructed in, 81–84;
    in judging process, 77–78; in national iden-
    tity, 107–8, 121–22; pageant's preferences
    in, 38–40, 41–42, 81–84; racist representa-
    tions and, 125–26; rearrangement of, 108–
    9; respectability as signifier of, 41. *See also*
    ethnic identity; gender; middlebrow cul-
    ture; morality; morals; race
Sommer, Doris, 184
Sontag, Susan, 149
South Africa, pageants in, 197–98, 238n42
speech. *See* public speaking skills; voice
Spivak, Gayatri Chakravorti, 18
sponsors: disputes with, 44; of local, regional,
    and state pageants, 47–49, 50, 219n52; re-
    liance on, 36–37; respectable vs. unre-
    spectable, 42, 47; solicitation of, 219n53
sporting events: African Americans in, 119,
    124; pageants as, 57
Stam, Robert, 202

STARS program, 175–79
state-hopping, use of term, 52
states, contestants as representatives of, 40,
    217n16
statistics, used in interview answers, 103
Stewart, E. B., 44, 219n43
Storm, Tiffany, 239n3
Sturken, Marita, 174, 212–13n11
subjectivity: construction of, 23–25, 135–37;
    disciplinary practices in, 215n23; diversity
    and, 21; political context of, 189; produc-
    tion of, 14–18, 175, 207; swimsuit compe-
    tition as contradiction to, 61–62, 80. *See
    also* ethnic identity; individual identity;
    national identity; self
surveillance: of femininity, 38–40; ideal
    needed for, 194; by judges, 67–68; repre-
    sentation and, 79–80; of weight, 66–67,
    222n23, 238n52
Swedlund, Alan C., 63–64
swimsuit competition: ambivalence of, 62–
    64, 65; bikini contests compared to, 80–84;
    body enabled/disabled in, 77; choreogra-
    phy of, 58–59; critique of, 59–61, 77–78, 148;
    description of, 26–27, 61–62; disciplinary
    practices in, 64–74; example of, pl2; in first
    pageant, 36, 37; high heels in, 25; judging
    of, 54–55, 56, 58; name of, 25; reassurance
    of traditional femininity in, 74–86; role of,
    43, 63–64; tips on, 68, 71–73; visuality of,
    79; vulnerability of, 68–69, 222n32. *See also*
    female body; physical fitness
swimsuits: cost of, 48, 220–21n2; market for,
    223n38; types of, pl2, 58–59; use of term, 40

talent: coded as whiteness, 27–28; definition
    of, 113, 120–21; evaluation of, 31, 33; vs.
    natural ability, 119–21, 227n37
talent competition: choices and constraints
    in, pl4, 113–20, 226n31; context of, 109–12;
    as demonstration of culture, 90, 106–8, 110–
    12, 120–22; description of, 27–28, 61; estab-
    lishment of, 40, 106–7; examples of, pl4–5;
    identity constituted in, 89–90, 107–8, 172–
    73; judging of, 54–55; nation educated
    through, 112–13; presentation goals in,
    223n53; rehearsals for, 87–89; role of, 43,
    56–57, 74, 88–90; tips on, 111, 113–14, 119.
    See also individualism; subjectivity
T & A Swimwear (company), 71, 73
televised coverage of pageants: difference
    obscured in, 177–78, 201–2; effects of, 29,
    89; judging explained on, 56, 220n68;
    national identity constructed in, 171–75;
    politics of whiteness and, 164–66; public

televised coverage of pageants *(continued)*
voting in, 59–60; tourism promoted
through, 191–92
television: black characters on, 225–26n15;
news as dominant/oppositional,
212–13n11
Thailand: Miss Universe pageant in, 199–200;
pageant franchise in, 191
Thomas, Clarence, 126, 146, 231n60
Tibet, pageant in, 29, 189
Time (magazine), on multiculturalism,
168–69
tourism, pageant's link to, 36–37, 184, 191–
93, 198–200
Trump, Donald, 46, 191, 202, 222n23
Truth, Sojourner, 131
Turk, Ghada, 195–96
typicality: as component of femininity, 32;
white norms of, 154–56

United States: cultural imperialism of, 190–
91, 199, 201; division of labor in, 135–36;
female symbols of, 158; international pageants produced by, 183–84; pageantry
in early, 216n3; pageants debated in, 1–2;
"queen" crowned in, 216n4; representation
of race in, 18–21. *See also* global order
Universal-International Corporation, 44, 46
universalism, shortcomings of, 188
universal sex opposition, concept of, 16,
215n27
Urla, Jacqueline, 63–64

veterans' hospitals, swimsuit parades at,
233n5
Virginia Slims (cigarettes), ads for, 25
virtue, crisis of, 19
Vogue (magazine), on diversity, 20
voice: accent in, 203; in interview competition, 93–95; in self-construction, 208, 209;
separated from body, 77, 80; silenced in
swimsuit competition, 75–76. *See also*
public speaking skills
volunteers, role of, 39–40, 47–49

Wallace, Michelle, 212–13n11
Walters, Suzanne, 89
Warren, Michelle, pl4
wartime: femininity in, 157–58; masculinity
in, 6. *See also* World War II
weight: restrictions on flight attendants',
222n22; surveillance of, 66–67, 222n23,
238n52
welfare, politics of, 138
White Men Can't Jump (film), 119
whiteness: access to, 161–62; as category in

identity politics, 235–36n51; celebration
of, 9, 21, 138–41, 151; construction of, 115–
17, 131–32; contingent membership in, 118–
20; difference legitimated by, 168–69; diversity bounded by, 128–31; femininity
constructed in, 128–41, 207, 231–32n63;
healing injury of, 178–79; individualism's
norms constructed in, 132–34, 160–61; as
neutral starting point, 225n7; other constructed in frame of, 230–31n54; personhood constructed in, 133–34; politics of,
in pageant, 153–56, 164–66; primacy of,
125–26, 135–36, 160–64, 169–71, 178, 203,
207; sexuality constructed in, 143, 147–48;
in swimsuit competition, 74–75, 78–79,
85–86; talent coded as, 27–28
Whitestone, Heather: crowned as Miss
America, pl9; dance choice of, 172–73, 179;
disability of, 29, 155–56, 166; family and
childhood of, 167–68; as ideal of femininity, 28–29; individualism of, 169–71; self-
representation of, 177–79; STARS program
of, 175–79; television and, 172–73
Whiting, Pam, 67
Wiegman, Robyn, 85, 172, 175, 178, 235–36n51
Wilk, Richard, 183
Will, George, 19, 170
Williams, Vanessa: crowned as Miss America,
pl7, 123–24, 125; diversity's definition and,
128–31; as example, 28, 239n57; as national
representative, 126–27, 142–45, 152; *Penthouse* photos of, 28, 124, 131–32, 141–45,
147–50; as pop-star, 150–52; reign and commodification of, 131–37; resignation of, 124,
141–42, 145–46; sexuality and race of, 138,
141–42, 146–50
Willis, Susan, 78
Winfrey, Oprah, 170
Wolcott, James, 216n45
Wolf, Naomi, 13, 25
women: assets of, 65, 75, 81; as "civilizers,"
112; as consumers, 34; defining issues for,
237n22; experience of and theory on, 13–
18, 209; independence of, 35; rights of, 198;
"talents" of, 120–21; trafficking in, 77–78,
223n53; "types" of, 83–84; use of term, 188.
See also female body; femininity; gender;
maternity; women of color
Women Against Pornography, 146, 148
women of color: as evidence of diversity,
104, 124–29, 137–41, 145, 151–52, 207–8;
exoticized/eroticized, 104, 116; pageant's
homogenization of, 78–79; skin tone of, 135–
36; talent competition and, 115–16; as threat,
139–41. *See also* African Americans; race
women's groups: hostessing system and,

39; pageant criticized by, 37–38; against pornography, 146–48; Williams's resignation and, 124

World War II: contestants' bodies and, 157–58, 160; Jewish American assimilation and, 162–63; selling war bonds in, 41

Yaeger, Patricia, 184

Yarkoni, Ravit, 200–201

Yentl (film), 239n3

Young, Iris, 24

Young, Kara, 135

Young Woman of the Year pageant, 84. *See also* Junior Miss pageants

zip codes, community defined by, 52–53

Indexer: Margie Towery
Designer: Margery Cantor
Compositor: Integrated Composition Systems
Text: 10/14 Palatino
Display: Water Titling
Printer: Bookcrafters